D0149583

NEW REGIONAL
DEVELOPMENT PARADIGMS

VOLUME 3

NEW REGIONAL DEVELOPMENT PARADIGMS

VOLUME 3

Decentralization, Governance, and the New Planning for Local-Level Development

Edited by Walter B. Stöhr, Josefa S. Edralin, and Devyani Mani

FOREWORD BY YO KIMURA

Published in cooperation with the United Nations
and the United Nations Centre for Regional Development

Contributions in Economics and Economic History, Number 225

GREENWOOD PRESS
Westport, Connecticut • London

Library of Congress Cataloging-in-Publication Data

New Regional development paradigms / edited by Asfaw Kumssa and Terry G. McGee.
    p. cm.—(Contributions in economics and economic history, ISSN 0084–9235 ; no. 225)
    Includes bibliographical references and index.
    Contents: v. 1. Globalization and the new regional development / edited by Asfaw Kumssa and Terry G. McGee—v. 2. New regions—concepts, issues, and practices / edited by David W. Edgington, Antonio L. Fernandez, and Claudia Hoshino—v. 3. Decentralization, governance, and the new planning for local-level development / edited by Walter B. Stöhr, Josefa S. Edralin, and Devyani Mani—v. 4. Environmental management, poverty reduction, and sustainable regional development / edited by James E. Nickum and Kenji Oya.
    ISBN 0–313–31917–0 (set : alk. paper)—ISBN 0–313–31765–8 (v. 1 : alk. paper)—
ISBN 0–313–31766–6 (v. 2 : alk. paper)—ISBN 0–313–31767–4 (v. 3 : alk. paper)—
ISBN 0–313–31768–2 (v. 4 : alk. paper)
    1. Regional planning—Developing countries. 2. Globalization. 3. Sustainable development. I. Kumssa, Asfaw. II. McGee, T. G. III. Series.
HT395.D44N48   2001
338.9—dc21   00–049088

British Library Cataloguing in Publication Data is available.

Copyright © 2001 by United Nations Centre for Regional Development

All rights reserved. No portion of this book may be
reproduced, by any process or technique, without the
express written consent of the publisher.

Library of Congress Catalog Card Number: 00–049088
ISBN: 0–313–31917–0 (set)
      0–313–31765–8 (vol. 1)
      0–313–31766–6 (vol. 2)
      0–313–31767–4 (vol. 3)
      0–313–31768–2 (vol. 4)
ISSN: 0084–9235

First published in 2001

Greenwood Press, 88 Post Road West, Westport, CT 06881
An imprint of Greenwood Publishing Group, Inc.
www.greenwood.com

Printed in the United States of America

The paper used in this book complies with the
Permanent Paper Standard issued by the National
Information Standards Organization (Z39.48–1984).

10 9 8 7 6 5 4 3 2 1

Contents

List of Illustrations

TABLES

Foreword

The United Nations Centre for Regional Development (UNCRD) organized three forums on regional development in 1997–98. The participants in the forums reviewed the regional development theory and practice, problems and issues, and policy responses in Asia, Latin America, and Africa. The reports on the forums were well received, providing an update and overview as well as offering conclusions and policy recommendations arising from the discussions.

The success of the forums inspired UNCRD to convene a Global Forum on Regional Development Policy in December 1998 in Nagoya, Japan. The forum was designed to consolidate and summarize the results and lessons learned from the three forums as well as take a forward look at the regional development issues in the new century. A series of theme contributions were requested from leading scholars, policymakers, and practitioners in regional development. Regional development issues were high on the global forum agenda, from the question of the significance of globalization in regional development, the role of decentralization and governance in local development, the planning of regions in an environmentally sustainable way, and new thinking on regional development. These issues are likely to condition the form and content of future regional policy in developing countries.

The New Regional Development Paradigms represent the results of the global forum. Most of the papers selected for publication in volumes 1–4 have been revised for publication. Additional papers have been included which offer a necessary international and national perspective on the regional development issues. The titles of volumes 1–4 are listed as follows:

Volume 1: *Globalization and the New Regional Development*, edited by Asfaw Kumssa and T. G. McGee.

Volume 2: *New Regions—Concepts, Issues, and Practices*, edited by David W. Edgington, Antonio L. Fernandez, and Claudia Hoshino.

Volume 3: *Decentralization, Governance, and the New Planning for Local-Level Development*, edited by Walter B. Stöhr, Josefa S. Edralin, and Devyani Mani.

Volume 4: *Environmental Management, Poverty Reduction, and Sustainable Regional Development*, edited by James E. Nickum and Kenji Oya.

It is the hope of the editors and the authors that these volumes will further stimulate discussion on the issues highlighted as well as provide an overview of the challenges and opportunities facing regional development in the twenty-first century.

Yo Kimura
Director, UNCRD

1

Introduction

Walter B. Stöhr

This book is concerned with three basic developmental concepts, which are presently being increasingly practiced worldwide as a response to the growing trend toward economic, political, and cultural globalization:

1. There is a growing trend and political pressure toward decentralization of administrative processes and political decision-making, to which individual countries react in different ways.

2. In this connection, new ways of governance and cooperation between the public sector, the private sector, and civil society are being developed at national, regional, and local levels for building a stronger economy and a better society.

3. Consequently, new concepts and procedures for planning at different levels have emerged, whereby this book focuses primarily on new ways of planning for local-level development. Most chapters, however, also show the important roles that national government and general frame conditions play for successful action at the local level.

This book presents experiences of how such new practices are being promoted by worldwide networking between different countries and continents, especially in Asia, Africa, Europe, and the Americas. In some countries analyzed in this volume, this is done by the external promotion of local self-help activities in sectors such as service provision. In other cases, decentralization is used as an instrument to foster true local self-empowerment. In some cases, the strengthening of rural-urban linkages is seen as a method to reach "integration" for more equal spatial development; and individual case studies describe efforts to make public agencies in metropolitan areas more responsive, accountable, and oriented toward sustainability regarding natural and financial resources.

Many authors who have contributed to the book are directly involved in practical efforts to design or implement related projects, in either multilateral agencies, nongovernmental organizations (NGOs), research centers, and/or universities.

Although with increasing globalization remarkable advances in economic, technological, and democratic terms have taken place in many countries, at the same time poverty, hunger, health hazards, and exclusion from the benefits of technological progress and consequent disparities in human welfare have increased.[1] Developmental efforts, therefore, have to be directed mainly toward those population strata and areas that have increasingly been left behind in the progress of general development. Important action for this purpose has to be taken at the local level, close to and involving, as much as possible, the respective population groups. This essentially requires decentralization of administrative and decision-making processes.

DIVERSITY OF APPROACHES

The main issues dealt with in this book, decentralization, new forms of governance, and local-level development, are all characterized by one common denominator, diversity. Uniform solutions and simple standardized recipes of the past have failed to bring positive results and must be overcome. Decentralization means that different solutions may be relevant for different areas depending on their respective historical conditions, resources, and problems. Therefore, uniform models and central decisions cannot sensibly solve their problems. Governance structures similarly have to be differentiated and, as Work puts it in his chapter, have to begin in communities, villages, and towns.[2] In general, new governance structures will have to be more complex than the straightforward central-government-run ones of the past, and they will have to involve—apart from government—more than in the past, civil society and the private sector. Consequently, local and regional planning and development will have to pursue new patterns of cooperation and new procedures of operation.

DECENTRALIZATION

The United Nations Development Programme (UNDP) distinguishes between four major forms of decentralization (devolution, delegation, deconcentration, and divestment) as different forms of transferring responsibility to central government field units, to subnational units of government, to semiautonomous public corporations, to areawide regional authorities, or to NGOs or private organizations. Good decentralized governance is defined as "the forms and procedures that allow a society to achieve at the subnational and local levels the goals of poverty reduction, sustainable livelihood, environmental regeneration, and gender equity."[3] Beyond this, however, decentralization plays an important broader societal function—it facilitates "more venues in which civil society organizations can develop and find sustenance and influence" and at the same time provides opportunities for political opposition parties to play an important role within democratic governance systems, facilitates the accommodation of different preferences for the delivery of public services and the participation of individuals in local initiatives, the emergence of civil society institutions, and the strengthening of local cultural identity.[4]

Of these different forms of decentralization, most chapters in this book deal with either of the following two forms: (1) deconcentration, as the spatial delegation of administrative and planning authority to lower levels but within central government ministries or agencies; and (2) devolution, as the transfer of responsibility for governing and decision-making on planning and budgetary issues to local and regional levels, substantially outside the direct control of central government. Both are variations of the top-down administrative and political processes of decentralization described above. Mani in her chapter compares these two forms of decentralization in two case studies of urban service delivery regarding service coverage, transparency of budgeting and expenditure, and mobilization of financial and human resources in two emerging Indian metropolises.[5] She finds that in the "devolution" case, there is a lack of coordination between the different local dependencies of central agencies, but they are more innovative in forming partnerships with the private sector and NGOs in the generation of local finances for infrastructure; in the "deconcentration" case, on the other hand, the existence of a single responsible entity made resource allocation between different tasks easier and cost recovery by the imposition of user charges based on service consumption more efficient. More comparative analyses of alternative models of decentralization would—irrespective of the politics involved—provide guidelines for the selection of optimum forms of decentralization for specific developmental purposes. In many cases, however, the rhetoric of a devolution policy, as described in Antipolo's chapter,[6] obscures the fact that decentralization in reality is hardly taking place or is undertaken only to increase the effectiveness of central government policies, as described by Mequanent and Taylor.[7]

But some chapters also deal with efforts that Friedmann has called "local empowerment" as a real "bottom-up" process of development, in which decision-making is structured from the neighborhood or local level upward.[8] Stöhr in his chapter deals with it in conceptual terms of "subsidiarity."[9]

There are, however, practical restrictions to the implementation of theoretical concepts such as decentralization, devolution, and local empowerment. These are dealt with in various chapters, particularly those by Work, Mequanent and Taylor, and Stremplat-Platte.[10] These restrictions are mainly related to a lack of know-how, and human and financial resources at subnational levels, as well as a lack of civil society and the capacity for self-organization. One of the most important practical lessons learned in these experiences is that decentralization is not a panacea for all ills and should not be pursued as a predefined theoretical concept. It should rather be handled strategically, taking advantage of "windows of opportunity"[11] in a flexible process, allowing central/local dynamics to evolve.

Sabatini, Valenzuela, and Reyes in their chapter touch upon a more general dilemma of decentralization and increased local autonomy—without the application of general standards at a larger scale. These two concepts can become counterproductive with the present trend toward globalization, as negative phenomena may just be externalized to other areas.[12] The authors find that such common standards must cover social and environmental standards but also the application of human rights and democratic principles within local areas. The main dilemma in their view is that the increasingly fierce competition between cities and localities that has emerged as a consequence of globalization may deprive them of their theoretical "autonomy" to apply such standards; instead, they often see their only chance to effectively compete as a location for economic activity by relaxing social and environmental standards and fair standards of local governance.

Mequanent and Taylor raise another important issue when they ask under which conditions decentralization, particularly in a multiethnic country such as Ethiopia, can lead to disintegration of the country by centrifugal forces.[13] This is an important question for many developing countries, particularly those with a colonial history that disregarded ethnic boundaries and are multiethnic in their composition.

GOVERNANCE

Governance is the second main issue dealt with in this volume. It is considered as the way in which the public sector, private sector, and civil society work together as partners in building a stronger economy and a better society. Governance has been defined in different ways: some authors argue that a vibrant, vocal, and engaged civil society is the key factor; others stress that the private sector is the engine of economic growth and prosperity and, therefore, needs to take the lead and be liberated from government regulation; and still others argue that government must maintain ultimate power for public policy even if this means checking the power of civil society and the marketplace, for example as emphasized by Lauder and Gonzalez.[14] Work in his chapter defines governance in a broader way as comprising the mechanisms, processes, and institutions through which citizen groups and communities pursue their visions, articulate their interests, exercise their legal rights, meet their obligations, and mediate their differences.[15] He argues that good governance for sustainable development requires decentralization in a system of subsidiarity, a concept dealt with extensively in the chapter by Stöhr, who considers subsidiarity as an interactive multilevel planning and decision-making process.[16] New governance processes between government, business, and civil society can more readily be developed in response to common issues, which are a priority in a specific community, such as waste management, job creation, and cultural vibrancy. Various chapters in this book report on how such concrete community tasks served to introduce new governance schemes at the local level. These issues are very similar to those pursued in Stöhr, where particularly the characteristics of leaders of local initiatives and the problem areas that these initiatives address are analyzed in a systematic survey.[17]

In this book, a great number of programs are described that help to improve governance and planning structures at local levels. Of UNDP's country programs, more than 60 percent include activities to support decentralized governance activities in different countries.[18] UNDP's Local Initiative Facility for Urban Environment (LIFE) Programme promotes "local-local" dialogue to improve the living conditions of the urban poor in over sixty cities in twelve pilot countries, one experience of which is described in Baqir's chapter.[19] Other international development agencies such as the Canadian International Development Agency (CIDA) sponsor pilot projects to improve local governance processes in different countries.[20] The Deutsche Gesellschaft für Technische Zusammenarbeit (GTZ) today promotes decentralized, multilevel, participatory, and process-oriented approaches in its programs for local and regional development in different countries instead of the earlier practiced centralized, technical, master-plan-type conception of regional planning.[21] The experiences of one of these concrete programs are described in the chapter by Boguslawski.[22]

SUBSIDIARITY

Subsidiarity is defined by Stöhr as a societal system in which those processes and decisions that can best be performed at local or regional levels should be executed there and only those that cannot be satisfactorily performed at these levels should be "delegated" to higher levels.[23] Like Mequanent and Taylor,[24] he concludes that neither pure bottom-up nor pure top-down policies are operational in practice but only a combination of the two embedded in the principle of subsidiarity. He then defines criteria and proposes, on the basis of former empirical work, which activities would have a comparative advantage to be performed at specific spatial levels. Mequanent and Taylor propose a similar division of functions but differentiated by policies, programs, and projects.[25] Baqir in his chapter allocates the mobilization of "soft" factors (human and social capital) to local communities, while central government should supply the "hard" factors such as physical capital and costly infrastructure.[26]

EQUITY

This is another recurring issue in many chapters of this volume, which has always been an important objective of local and regional planning and development. Globalization, as indicated in the UNDP *Human Development Report 1999* and in Work's paper,[27] is accompanied by increasing inequalities between regions and population strata that are able to take advantage of global systems, as against those that for various reasons are not able to do so. Support systems and redistributive mechanisms to aid these disadvantaged areas and societal sectors are therefore often considered essential. Mequanent and Taylor in their chapter fear that, particularly in a developing country like Ethiopia, decentralization may mainly lead to the disempowerment of the already disadvantaged areas and groups.[28] Antipolo deals with the question whether equity is promoted or hindered by devolution and local self-empowerment in an interesting empirical analysis in his chapter on the Philippines.[29] He found that the policy of deconcentration and regionalization in the Philippines and the consequent higher allocation of national taxes to local government units, at least in statistical terms, have not led to an increase in interregional income disparities. These findings cannot be generalized however. Stöhr in his chapter maintains that even in a governance system guided by the principle of subsidiarity, national and supranational actors and agencies, apart from redistributive action, have to play an important role in promoting equity by facilitating disadvantaged areas' and groups' access to worldwide information networks, sources of innovation, and training and financing, to mobilize their endogenous development potential and take advantage of the opportunities offered by globalization.[30]

SUSTAINABILITY

Sustainability is another important issue in this book. Equity, with a long-term perspective, is also related to sustainability, which, in Work's words, needs to give "highest priority to poverty reduction, promoting sustainable livelihoods, supporting environmental regeneration."[31] This means that sustainability must safeguard the long-term ability to regenerate in a self-supporting way not only for environmental systems but also for human and social systems. In concrete terms, Baqir describes a key principle of the UNDP program—sustainability of local action—in terms of long-term economic inputs (in-kind inputs by beneficiaries, application of low-cost technology, and cost recovery from beneficiaries), in social terms (community involvement and institution building at the local level), and also in environmental terms (composting of kitchen wastes to replace chemical fertilizer).[32]

THE IMPORTANCE OF CIVIL SOCIETY

Civil society since the mid-1970s has increasingly emerged—and been called for—as an agent for development, particularly at the local level. Friedmann considers it the new challenge for planners to make their "work congruent with . . . the hallmark of the new political economy, the reemergence of civil society as a collective actor in the construction of our cities and regions, in search of the good life."[33] He attributes this increased role of civil society to the consequences of globalization and the ensuing restructuring process, accompanied by a retreat of the state. He defines civil society as "those social organizations, associations and institutions that exist beyond the sphere of direct supervision and control by the state."[34] Douglass and Friedmann maintain that "alongside a corporate economy seeking global hegemony, struggles for collective empowerment . . . will usher in the next millennium."[35] They are local manifestations of a worldwide social movement, a rising of civil society in all its forms.

Friedmann distinguishes two major conceptions of civil society: one of an institutional type mediating between the individual and the state following the early thinking of de Tocqueville, and the other, more radical conception of a (leftist) movement for political mobilization and active resistance (against the state) of the type of social movements, self-management, and the practice of direct democracy.[36] In this sense, the conception of civil society has much in common with that of subsidiarity, which is concerned with a division of functions between the individual and small groups (the family, neighborhood, and local community), and the state. Regarding subsidiarity there is also one strand of thinking that "the lower social levels should fend for themselves, and the State and higher levels should exercise only a minimum of functions" and another strand that considers the lower levels "as a social order, oriented against the totalitarian and centralist state,"[37] to which Friedmann adds opposition to the corporate economy.[38] However, a common characteristic of both civil society and subsidiarity in their opposition to the state and the corporate economy, and also between different societal levels, is solidarity (in line with the individual person's social nature) so that the individual and the small group can rely on help from others and from above if they cannot cope with a problem.

GLOBALIZATION, DECENTRALIZATION, AND THE DANGER OF DISINTEGRATION OF CIVIL SOCIETY AND OF LOCAL POWER

Globalization is related to decentralization in an ambiguous way: on the one hand, decentralization has in many countries been introduced due to the need for more flexible and adaptable decision-making.[39] On the other hand, the competitive pressure it has produced has led to individualization, atomization, and a loss of solidarity.

Dahrendorf states that "globalization means centralization. It individualizes and centralizes at the same time . . . competitiveness in world markets helps destroy communities. But. . . . It is possible to counteract the simultaneous pressures towards individualization and centralization by a new emphasis on local power. . . . Local communities . . . can provide a practical basis . . . for personal involvement and participation, for strengthening the public domain—in short, for civil society."[40] The strengthening of local power is one way of integrating important stakeholders of economic processes such as the workforce, the local community, local training facilities and service providers, the representatives of local business, etc. into the decision-making process. In his view, this is an important prerequisite for "squaring the circle" of wealth creation, social co-hesion, and political freedom.

Dahrendorf feels that globalization is seriously threatening the very bases of civil society by creating new kinds of economic, social, and political inequality and exclusion.[41] These new inequalities—which he prefers to call "inequaliza-tion"—are "building paths to the top for some and digging holes for others, creating cleavages, splitting" and leading to an increasing number of persons who "have lost touch with the official world, with the labour market, the political community, the wider society."[42] This splitting leads to "discrimination, xeno-phobia, often violence" and to growing sectors of population who are "simply not needed" either as workforce or as (poverty-stricken) consumers or voters (as many of them have become uprooted, without sense of belonging or com-mitment). This is the ideal breeding ground for the increasing temptation of authoritarianism not only in Western but also in developing countries "which embrace modern economic ways before their societies have become civil and their politics democratic."[43]

Dahrendorf therefore feels that the combination of the three main objectives of a liberal society—wealth creation, social cohesion, and political freedom—has become increasingly difficult to realize.[44] Civil society and local power would play a key role in this context.

CHANGING PUBLIC ATTITUDES

Changing public attitudes is a key prerequisite for the promotion of civil society: from one of dependency (nurtured often during centuries of colonialism, feudalism, military, or other authoritarian sociopolitical systems), to one of broad participation, initiatives, and self-empowerment. It is, therefore, one of the key issues dealt with in most of the contributions to this book.

Some authors are rather pessimistic about the possibility of real progress in this respect in the near future[45]; other authors elsewhere feel that this is not an imminent issue and that at least in the near future development can as well, if not better, be reached by making central government policy more rational and more efficient.[46]

But a number of the case studies presented in this book show that encouraging results can indeed be reached if adequate strategies are chosen for training and institution building at the local level. Boguslawski stresses the role of commu-nity organizers in the context of participatory Village Development Planning, and at the same time, however, the need for administrators and educated staff to learn "giving the stick away."[47] Baqir speaks of four types of barriers that have to be overcome in this context: psychological barriers, or the widespread belief that development work is the exclusive responsibility of government; eco-nomic barriers caused by the opinion that formal service delivery systems are expensive and therefore unaffordable to poor communities; social barriers due to the fact that people do not cooperate but rather pursue individual solutions

(Hirschman's "exit" rather than "voice" option[48]); and finally technical barriers due to lack of know-how in local communities.[49] He feels that while material results of decentralization within a few years were generally satisfactory, changes in attitude and community mobilization could hardly be reached in such a short period. It is necessary to initiate these changes in attitude with caution and patience as they involve behavioral and structural changes of the entire sociopolitical structure involving all major social actors and societal levels from the local through to the national level, and the interaction between them.[50]

Mequanent and Taylor[51] see regional planning as a useful frame within which to develop a flexible and adaptive strategy of learning and experience accumulation in which different levels of planning functions and areas of responsibility are defined corresponding to the capacity of each agency at different scales of activity (also refer to the concept of subsidiarity in Stöhr's chapter[52]). They then propose criteria for activities that different administrative levels could fulfill best, differentiated by policies, programs, and projects. Cooperation between different administrative levels and agencies will be a main requirement, but here the main problem is to overcome the desire of each entity to gain/maintain as much power as possible. They propose the formation of district advisory and technical teams to promote this cooperation.

CHANCES OF SUCCESS

These are of course evaluated differently for various cases and by different authors, depending largely on the historical and political background of the respective country and region. Most case studies, therefore, contain a detailed analysis of the past evolution of the political and administrative system in order to explain the problems to be overcome in future policies. Oyugi feels that, in continuation of the colonial history and the subsequent centralized and mostly dictatorial governments, not a single African country has deliberately attempted to strengthen local authorities as instruments of either political participation or socioeconomic development.[53] The scarce cases of more autonomy at subnational levels have been the result of assistance by foreign donor institutions.

Baqir shows that institution building and attitudinal changes cannot be achieved in just a few years.[54] He stresses the importance of medium- to long-term (at least ten to fifteen years) involvement of sponsors, which facilitates the change from community-based organizations (CBOs) to NGOs, from volunteerism to professionalism, from projects to programs, and from implementation activities to the establishment of training resource centers. The main objective in his view is the creation of a large network of NGOs communicating with one another and successively becoming integrated with formal governmental and entrepreneurial systems. Among the recommendations drawn from his evaluation are, therefore, an exchange of experiences between ongoing projects, the extension of project duration, and continuing monitoring, consultancy, and financial support from outside until self-sustenance can be reached.[55]

As in most structural reform policies, be they economic, social, or political, propositions vary between two extremes: at the one end, a one-shot "shock" reform, and at the other end, a series of gradual and cautious changes. The shock therapists, as in recently attempted economic reforms in formerly centrally planned economies, distrust a gradual change, as they fear that reform may be watered down and become ineffective, while they trust the shock to lead to an integral change of the system. On the other hand, the shocks of an integral change may disintegrate the social fabric and create chaotic conditions. The gradual therapies again may be very time-consuming and frustrate the expectations of those sectors that are to benefit from them. In any case, reform should essentially come from within and not from outside, as Solzhenitsyn criticizes for his own country, Russia. With regard to decentralization, a recurring question is whether it should take place only once the required human and organizational capacity at subnational levels exists, or whether this capacity will have to be acquired in a process of learning-by-doing once the basic transfers of decision-making power and financing to lower levels have been made. In this case, cost-effectiveness cannot be expected in the short run but at best in the medium or long term. The experiences of both UNDP[56] and of GTZ[57] recommend the latter procedure. In essence, one is here confronted with a very complex issue, namely, the (re)formation of civil society.

The issues at stake in this book: decentralization, governance, and the new planning for local-level development, in a similar way appear as an effort to square the circle, as does the triad Dahrendorf dealt with: wealth creation, social cohesion, and political freedom.[58] Maybe this is why most of these issues have been postulated and discussed at least during the past half-century—possibly with different terminology—but in most countries still appear unsolved. Essentially, the problem in both cases is that the market mechanism "favours groups and production systems which are most competitive, leaving aside the weakest groups,"[59] which at the same time increases disparities in living levels. Work therefore considers it an important role of government—and in a decentralized system particularly of local government—to regulate the "market mechanisms in order to better rationalize the allocation of resources towards communities with fewer advantages." The question is whether decentralization and the newly emerging models of local governance can achieve this.

A SYNOPSIS OF INDIVIDUAL CHAPTERS

Work in his chapter "Decentralization, Governance, and Sustainable Regional Development" describes the experience of UNDP in this field, which has created the "increasing conviction that governance begins in communities, villages, and towns." The majority of UNDP's country programs now include activities to support decentralized governance, some of which are analyzed in detail in other contributions to this book.[60] The chapter then goes on to outline the major lessons learned from these programs: that decentralization needs to be combined with centralized activities, that it is a cross-cutting (intersectoral) issue to be dealt with in a systems approach, and that it requires both political commitment by the leadership and a consensus of the population to participate. The appendix to this chapter then offers a conceptual overview of decentralization as developed by UNDP.

Stöhr in his chapter "Subsidiarity: A Key Concept for Regional Development Policy" applies to the field of regional policy the concept of subsidiarity defined as a "social order, oriented against the totalitarian and centralist state, in which the larger community acknowledges the potentials of the subordinate ones and exercises only those tasks that the latter cannot fulfill." Under these conditions, important prerequisites for dynamic local development such as clusters, networks, local initiatives, and innovative milieus can operate best. In this concept, higher societal levels, however, also have important functions for local development, and subsidiarity is a combination of approaches of development from below and from above. The author then defines actions that in his view have a comparative advantage at the local/regional, national, and supranational levels. At the local level, these are mainly problem perception, intensity of interaction and synergy, local initiatives, local strategy formulation, and collective learning; important functions at the national and supranational levels are to facilitate local/ regional decision-making powers combined with access to wider information, training, innovation, cooperation, and risk-financing networks, and to create framework conditions that help to reduce interregional disparities and overcome regional restructuring problems. Important global requirements include the creation of international standards that define not only the rights but—in contrast to the presently negotiated Multilateral Agreement on Investment (MAI)—also the obligations of multinational enterprises vis-à-vis territorial communities and at the same time confirm the rights of the State to implement policies of equitable and sustainable development.

Three chapters deal with the international cooperation networks for local development, decentralization, and the reduction of spatial inequalities: the first by Stremplat-Platte of GTZ; the second by Lauder and Gonzalez reporting on a cooperation network between CIDA and pilot projects in Asia; and the third by Evans describing the experiences of a concept for regional development via rural-urban linkages applied in different countries.

The chapter by Stremplat-Platte on "From Sophisticated Plans to Daily Business in Regional Development Planning: Experiences of GTZ" describes the change from an earlier centralized, technical, master-plan-type conception of regional planning, now considered "obsolete," to decentralized, multilevel, participatory, and process-oriented programs now supported by GTZ in different countries. Communicative planning, human resource development, and capacity building at subnational levels are important tools in these projects. The role of GTZ, the external agency, has also changed from a foreign team taking over planning functions to an advisory function accompanying agencies at different societal levels.

The chapter by Lauder and Gonzalez on "Governance and Sustainable Regional Development" covers another international network project. It starts from a pragmatic definition of the concept of governance as "the way in which power is exercised, decisions are made, and citizens have their say," a process that is in a permanent state of transition. By a process of participatory action research, funded by CIDA and managed by the Institute on Governance (IOG), Kuala Lumpur, Malaysia, six pilot projects in four Association of Southeast Asian Nations (ASEAN) of Malaysia, Philippines, Thailand, and Vietnam are analyzed to shed light on new ways of sharing power, on how important decisions are made, and on engaging more stakeholders in decision-making at the local level. Questions surveyed include changes in individual attitudes toward participation in the governance process, how groups of people organize in networks around specific issues, how change agents develop and are nurtured and what their characteristics are, and what the impact of the specific governance mechanism on some practical aspects of development is.

The chapter by Evans on "Regional Development through Rural-Urban Linkages: The PARUL Program in Indonesia" deals with a spatial integration approach to the reduction of geographic inequalities and regional development. He starts with Tiebout's export base theory from which he follows that transactions and linkages between potential producers and markets are a precondition for the growth of less developed (particularly rural) areas. These linkages require on the one hand an efficient infrastructure network connecting the area with the outside and on the other hand, linkages between economic activities within the respective region in the form of interactive clusters grouped around what Hirschman would have called a leading activity. To mobilize such linkages, the Poverty Alleviation through Urban-Rural Linkages (PARUL) Program proposes to promote an institutional framework that facilitates the participation of the numerous actors—public and private—needed for the planning and execution of the strategy, as well as investment in the required infrastructure network. The main emphasis of this project is to empower public-private coalitions at local and regional levels to prepare action plans and to facilitate the implementation of these plans. "Central to this strategy are provincial and district coalitions whose function is to facilitate collaboration between government, private firms, small businesses, and others in designing and implementing action plans to strengthen linkages and promote production and trade."

The program is presently tested in three pilot provinces of Eastern Indonesia, later to be extended to other districts, and to be incorporated into the next five-year national development plan. It would seem that in Indonesia decentralization must be a very ambiguous issue: on the one hand, there exists great political pressure for it in view of the multiethnic composition of this greatly dispersed country and on the other hand—not to mention the East Timor problem—the transmigration policy of former President Suharto has created great tensions particularly in the immigration areas so that peaceful governance there may be extremely difficult.

Two chapters deal with Africa. The chapter by Oyugi on "Decentralization in Africa: Trends and Prospects for the Twenty-First Century" compares, in a multinational perspective, different forms of decentralization in various formerly British colonized African countries especially since independence. Of the many forms that decentralization can take, mainly political (devolution) and administrative (deconcentration) forms of decentralization are being considered. The roots are traced back to the respective colonial regimes. In contrast to the highly centralized French colonies, in British colonies, there existed semi-independent local authorities, but mainly for the white-settled areas, while the native areas were either subjected to direct central rule or relegated to chieftainships. Oyugi describes how, after independence, different forms of one-party or military rule, which invented different forms of penetration and control of local affairs, followed colonial rule. "Functional congestion" at the center however, in many countries led to administrative deconcentration to make developmental policy more efficient; in others, however, verbal claims for decentralization remained mainly symbolic. Based on postwar British planning philosophy, district development committees were established in many of the countries studied. The author then analyzes the political and administrative support given to them and the sociocultural influences that determined the degree to which decentralization was actually granted in individual countries, given the respective financial and staffing resources available. Finally, the author contrasts the theoretical postulates of decentralization with the pragmatic ways of organizing government operations in Africa. A key question, according to the author, is the degree of qualification and maturity available at local/district levels, and the confidence in them on the part of central authorities.

The chapter by Mequanent and Taylor on "Decentralization and Local Autonomy: Regional Planning in Ethiopia" deals in more concrete terms with one African country. It starts from the assertion, made also by Oyugi, that decentralization of power and organizational resources have been gradually introduced in many African countries since the 1980s due to the need for more flexible and adaptable decision-making required by the increasing integration into the global economy and the pressure of international financial institutions and bilateral aid agencies to reform centralized political systems and economic planning. A key question, however, is whether decentralization is undertaken mainly to increase the effectiveness of planning, budgeting, and implementation of programs or projects, or whether a major objective is the real transfer of resources and decision-making powers to local-level agencies and increased local autonomy.

Neither pure top-down nor pure bottom-up planning strategies are operational in their view, but only a combination of the two embedded in the principle of subsidiarity. The degree to which local or regional levels will be able to mobilize the necessary resources and organizational capacity to meet their task requirements is a key question.

The new constitution of the Federal Democratic Republic of Ethiopia inaugurated in 1995 in theory gives ample opportunities to promote regional autonomy and local self-government. Actual practice is then analyzed for one case area, the Gondar region. A major problem is posed by the conflicting criteria and objectives of local councils versus zonal offices of the central government's line agencies, the latter of which traditionally used to exercise sole power. Cooperation between different administrative levels and agencies, in the authors' view, will be a main requirement, but here the main problem is to overcome the desire of each of these entities to gain/maintain as much power as possible. They propose the formation of district advisory and technical teams to promote this cooperation.

Two chapters focusing on the Philippines relate to the question about whether and under what conditions decentralization, in practice, can lead to local empowerment and also the real developmental effects of decentralization. One chapter by an external project advisor, Boguslawski, analyzes the institution-building and behavioral problems of decentralization to be overcome in the transition from feudalism to democracy; and the other chapter by Antipolo concentrates on the quantitative (including budgetary) consequences of decentralization and on the actual impact of devolution on regional development and equity. Both investigate their questions in specific, though different test regions of the Philippines.

The chapter by Boguslawski on "Regional Development under Participation: Some Experiences from the Philippines" describes the evolution of the institutional process of administrative decentralization after independence from Spanish, American, Japanese, and once again American colonialism in 1946, and of devolution since the passing of the Local Government Code in 1991. It discusses the practical problems associated with this intended transition from feudalism to democracy, particularly in the "forgotten barangays (villages)" of the rural areas. The experiences of one case-study area are then analyzed in detail, showing the difficulties encountered in efforts to transform deeply entrenched dominance and dependency structures to participatory and self-empowered social patterns. Main emphasis was put on the introduction of community organizers in the context of participatory Village Development Planning initiated in 1997. Finally, the preliminary experiences are evaluated, particularly the role of local leaders and external resource persons in local institution-building and planning efforts to mobilize endogenous resources, and the change from an attitude of waiting for support from above to one of actively supporting ones own productive projects. One important basis for effective planning at the local level was the establishment of an exact mapping procedure through a geographic information system (GIS), to be used primarily for local planning from below (in contrast to the use from above as described by Pasaribu).[61] A key prerequisite, according to the author, is for administrators and educated staff to learn to give the stick away and develop new top-down coordination mechanisms without destroying the young but growing flower of people's empowerment.[62]

The chapter by Antipolo on "Rhetoric and Reality: Decentralization, Planning, and Development in the Southern Mindanao Region, Philippines" starts from the frequently posed question whether official announcements of decentralization by intention have remained only rhetoric without effective devolution being implemented in practice. Questions raised include: what powers are actually decentralized and which regions benefit from it, and to what extent does decentralization include control over finances? Even if decentralization was implemented, what has been its actual impact, particularly upon the spatial equity between rich and poor municipalities? Field investigation on these questions has been carried out in a test region in Southern Mindanao. A number of hypotheses were tested and showed the following results: for the period during which a deconcentration and regionalization policy was applied, it was not accompanied by a significant change in interregional disparities; and in contrast to regional allocation of social infrastructure, the allocation of economic infrastructure did have a significant impact on regional growth and development. Regarding the rhetoric and reality of decentralization, the study showed a significant gap between the investment requirements defined by the rhetoric of the regional development plan and the actual budget appropriations. Regarding the significance of devolution, Antipolo finds that it has not put poorer regions at a disadvantage.

The last three chapters deal with urban governance systems. The chapters by Baqir and by Mani are concerned with urban service delivery in intermediate cities, and the chapter by Sabatini, Valenzuela, and Reyes is concerned with a novel integral governance system in a metropolitan area.

The chapter by Baqir on "Development of Grass-Roots Institutions: Experience of LIFE in Pakistan (1993–98)" analyzes the experience of a UNDP-sponsored program for helping to build grass-roots institutions for the delivery of urban basic services for low-income communities in pilot projects in Pakistan. Given the rapid urbanization in most developing countries, the program aims at initiating sustainable low-cost service delivery systems by improving participation in, and governance of, these services. This involves the mobilization of soft factors such as human and social capital[63] by local communities, while central government is expected to supply hard factors such as physical capital and costly infrastructure. This local internal-external development model has been applied to service delivery in sanitation, solid waste management, health, education, and income generation.

The chapter by Mani on "Comparing Parastatal and Local Government Service Delivery in Emerging Indian Metropolises" compares service delivery by two types of public agencies, namely, by state government administrative line agencies and by municipal government agencies in two emerging Indian metropolises, Ahmedabad and Bangalore, with regard to their responsiveness to local needs, accountability to the consumer, and sustainability in terms of local affordability. The institutional, financial, and political environments and the incentives facing the various stakeholders are analyzed in detail and policy recommendations are made on this basis. In these cases, an improvement in the structure and performance of public agencies is sought regarding service coverage, transparency of budgeting and expenditure, and mobilization of financial and human resources. Public participation, however, is found to be only a marginal requirement to increase public satisfaction with service delivery and to create more environmental awareness.

The chapter by Sabatini, Valenzuela, and Reyes on "Public-Private Partnership for the Renewal of Santiago City Center" analyzes the results of a new urban governance system for the central areas of the capital city of Santiago de Chile, initiated in 1992 by the Corporation for the Development of Santiago (CDS), a private nonprofit entity created to foster urban renovation with the active participation of civil society and private business. The objective of this program was to reverse the depopulation and environmental deterioration of the core of Santiago, which—similar to other metropolitan cores worldwide—had taken place in the past half-century. CDS, run as a private enterprise, with participation of municipal government, public utility companies, local universities, the private sector, and trade unions, has the advantage of being able to manage public and private resources with great flexibility and, through its City Participation Program also involves neighbors and users of the commune. It offers real estate and specialized consulting services, accompanied by an Urban Renewal Subsidy granted by the national Ministry for Housing and Urban Development and programs initiated by the city to improve the image of the city core. CDS has been able to complement spontaneous private urban renewal projects and helped to strengthen and expand them toward formerly depressed city areas. With the establishment of CDS, Santiago has moved away from the traditional physical zoning planning method to a management approach of urban strategic planning focusing mainly on creating conditions that attract private real estate investment.

The key issue addressed in this chapter, and related to the topic of decentralization and governance, is the following: with the present Chilean neoliberal economic policy combined with administrative decentralization, the thirty-four municipalities constituting the metropolitan area have been given the legal, institutional, and financial tools to attract private investment—mainly by relaxing zoning regulations. Important questions in this context are: How can the eviction of poor residents and their replacement by wealthier ones be avoided? (If the poor ones are evicted, they will congregate in other areas and, thereby, aggravate social problems including delinquency in the metropolitan area as a whole.) To what extent does this new regime curtail municipal autonomy to pursue its own objectives, for example, promote environmental and social recovery, and the conservation of architectural and environmental heritage?

Here the more general dilemma is that decentralization and increased local autonomy without the application of general standards can become counterproductive as local communities may just try to maximize their benefits and externalize negative phenomena to neighboring or other areas.

The proposal of the authors is to combine increased public participation at the local level with the adoption of nationwide standards for urban renewal that include social, cultural, and environmental concerns. They reason that many of these problems (e.g., environmental ones) are related to processes originating on a larger scale. They also expect that democratically organized public participation may counterbalance private interests in an effective way and lead to the inclusion of environmental, amenity, social, and cultural requirements in real estate investment. This, in the authors' view, should be implemented by a systematic negotiation between the city and the real estate developers to exchange building permits for the consideration of (and even financial contributions to) public spaces and environmental and social programs.

In conclusion, the chapters drawn together in this volume represent a wealth of novel concepts and practical experiences with them. It is hoped that they may inspire new ideas and improvements in the practice of local/regional development planning and policy worldwide.

NOTES

1. Robertson Work, "Decentralization, Governance, and Sustainable Regional Development," in this volume.

2. Ibid.

3. Ibid, see appendix.

4. Ibid.

5. Devyani Mani, "Comparing Parastatal and Local Government Service Delivery in Emerging Indian Metropolises," in this volume.

6. Sophremiano B. Antipolo, "Rhetoric and Reality: Decentralization, Planning, and Development in the Southern Mindanao Region, Philippines," in this volume.

7. Getachew Mequanent and D. R. Fraser Taylor, "Decentralization and Local Autonomy: Regional Planning in Ethiopia," in this volume.

8. John Friedmann, *Empowerment: The Politics of Alternative Development* (Cambridge, MA: Blackwell, 1992).

9. Walter B. Stöhr, "Subsidiarity: A Key Concept for Regional Development Policy," in this volume.

10. See Work, "Decentralization, Governance, and Sustainable Regional Development"; Mequanent and Taylor, "Decentralization and Local Autonomy"; and Petra Stremplat-Platte, "From Sophisticated Plans to Daily Business in Regional Development Planning: Experiences of GTZ," in this volume.

11. Work, "Decentralization, Governance, and Sustainable Regional Development."

12. Francisco Sabatini, Jaime Valenzuela, and Marcelo Reyes, "Public-Private Partnership for the Renewal of Santiago City Center," in this volume.

13. Mequanent and Taylor, "Decentralization and Local Autonomy."

14. Kathleen Lauder and Joaquin L. Gonzalez III, "Governance and Sustainable Regional Development," in this volume.

15. Work, "Decentralization, Governance, and Sustainable Regional Development."

16. Stöhr, "Subsidiarity."

17. Walter B. Stöhr, "Local Initiatives in Peripheral Areas: An Intercultural Comparison between Two Case Studies in Brazil and Austria" in Harvey Lithwick and Yehuda Gradus, eds., *Developing Frontier Cities: Global Perspectives—Regional Contexts* (Dordrecht: Kluwer Academic Publications, 2000), pp. 233–254.

18. Work, "Decentralization, Governance, and Sustainable Regional Development."

19. Fayyaz Baqir, "Development of Grass-Roots Institutions: Experience of LIFE in Pakistan (1993–98)," in this volume.

20. See Lauder and Gonzalez, "Governance and Sustainable Regional Development."

21. See Stremplat-Platte, "From Sophisticated Plans."

22. Michael von Boguslawski, "Regional Development under Participation: Some Experiences from the Philippines," in this volume.

23. Stöhr, "Subsidiarity."

24. Mequanent and Taylor, "Decentralization and Local Autonomy."

25. Ibid.

26. Baqir, "Development of Grass-Roots Institutions."

27. Work, "Decentralization, Governance, and Sustainable Regional Development."

28. Mequanent and Taylor, "Decentralization and Local Autonomy."

29. Antipolo, "Rhetoric and Reality."

30. Stöhr, "Subsidiarity."

31. Work, "Decentralization, Governance, and Sustainable Regional Development."

32. Baqir, "Development of Grass-Roots Institutions."

33. John Friedmann, "The New Political Economy of Planning: The Rise of Civil Society," p. 20, in M. Douglass and J. Friedmann, eds., *Cities for Citizens: Planning and the Rise of Civil Society in a Global Age* (Chichester: Wiley, 1998), pp. 19–35.

34. Ibid, p. 21.

35. Ibid, p. 20.

36. Friedmann, "The New Political Economy of Planning."

37. Stöhr, "Subsidiarity."

38. Friedmann, "The New Political Economy of Planning," p. 22.

39. See Mequanent and Taylor, "Decentralization and Local Autonomy."

40. Ralf Dahrendorf, "Economic Opportunity, Civil Society, and Political Liberty" (Discussion Paper 58) (Geneva: United Nations Research Institute for Social Development [UNRISD], 1995).

41. Ibid.

42. Ibid, p. 9.

43. Ibid, p. 13

44. Ibid.

45. Walter O. Oyugi, "Decentralization in Africa: Trends and Prospects for the Twenty-First Century," in this volume.

46. Maurits Pasaribu, "Innovative Regional Infrastructure Information System to Support Regional Development Planning in Indonesia" (Paper presented at the Global Forum, Nagoya, 1–4 December 1998).

47. Boguslawski, "Regional Development under Participation."

48. Stöhr, "Local Initiatives in Peripheral Areas."

49. Baqir, "Development of Grass-Roots Institutions."

50. See Stremplat-Platte, "From Sophisticated Plans."

51. Mequanent and Taylor, "Decentralization and Local Autonomy."

52. Stöhr, "Subsidiarity."

53. Oyugi, "Decentralization in Africa."

54. Baqir, "Development of Grass-Roots Institutions."

55. Ibid.

56. Work, "Decentralization, Governance, and Sustainable Regional Development"; and Baqir, "Development of Grass-Roots Institutions."

57. Stremplat-Platte, "From Sophisticated Plans."

58. Dahrendorf, "Economic Opportunity, Civil Society, and Political Liberty."

59. Work, "Decentralization, Governance, and Sustainable Regional Development."

60. Baqir, "Development of Grass-Roots Institutions"; and Hugh E. Evans, "Regional Development through Rural-Urban Linkages: The PARUL Program in Indonesia," in this volume.

61. Pasaribu, "Innovative Regional Infrastructure Information System."

62. See Stöhr, "Subsidiarity."

63. See Sergio Boisier, "Regional Development and Synergetic Capital" (paper presented at the Global Forum on Regional Development Policy, Nagoya, 1–4 December 1998).

2

Decentralization, Governance, and Sustainable Regional Development

Robertson Work

THE CONTEXT: A WORLD OF CONTRASTS

If one looks closely at the world today, what emerges is an arresting picture of unprecedented human progress and unspeakable human misery; of humanity's advance on several fronts mixed with humanity's retreat on several others; and of a breathtaking globalization of prosperity side by side with a depressing globalization of poverty. The record of human development over the past fifty years is unprecedented, with the developing countries setting a pace three times faster than the industrialized countries did a century ago. The wealth of nations has multiplied in these fifty years with global gross domestic product (GDP) increasing sevenfold, from about US$3 trillion to US$22 trillion.[1] Human ingenuity has led to several technological innovations and startling breakthroughs ranging from exciting space explorations to a revolution in information and communication technologies, and from ever-new medical frontiers to ever-greater additions to knowledge in every field. Many nations have taken significant steps toward introducing democratic principles and freedoms. In 1993 alone, elections were held in forty-five countries for the first time.[2]

One must, however, speak of success with a note of caution as it contrasts starkly with present realities. The world is one of disturbing contrasts. Despite all of humanity's technological breakthroughs, a fifth of the developing world's population still goes hungry every night, a quarter still lacks access to even basic necessities such as safe drinking water, and a third still lives in a state of abject poverty.[3] Global military spending, despite some decline, still equals the combined income of one-half of humanity each year.⁴ And the richest billion people command sixty times the income of the poorest billion.⁵

KEY ISSUES IN DEVELOPMENT, GOVERNANCE, AND DECENTRALIZATION

Sustainable Human Development

Against this background of human achievement and human distress, development practitioners have sought a new paradigm of sustainable human development that seeks to bring humanity together through a more equitable sharing of economic opportunities and responsibilities. This paradigm of development is, above all, people-centered. It gives the highest priority to poverty reduction, promoting sustainable livelihoods, supporting environmental regeneration, and enabling women's participation in all phases of the development process. The goal of sustainable human development is to create an enabling environment where all people can act to improve the quality of their lives, generation after generation.

Governance

It has become increasingly clear in recent years that the ability of nations to achieve their human development goals hinges largely on the quality of governance. There is a growing international consensus that good governance and sustainable human development are indivisible and that developing the capacity for good governance can and should be the primary means to eliminate poverty and inequality. The challenge for all societies, therefore, is to create a system of governance that promotes, supports, and sustains human development in order to realize the highest potential of everyone and the well-being of all, thus eliminating poverty and all other forms of exclusion.

Good Governance. Governance can be seen as the exercise of authority to manage all aspects of a country's affairs at all levels and in all spheres (public, private, and civic). While the definitions used by different development practitioners vary, the fundamental principles of good governance are universal. They include respect for human rights, particularly the rights of women and children; respect for the rule of law; political openness, participation, and tolerance; accountability and transparency; and administrative and bureaucratic capacity and efficiency. These principles of good governance are clearly interrelated, mutually reinforcing, and cannot stand alone.

While the economic, political, and administrative aspects of governance have often been the main focus of international summits and conferences over the last decade, they also reflect a growing recognition of the need for a more holistic concept of governance. For example, the United Nations Development Programme (UNDP) defines governance holistically as comprising the mechanisms, processes, and institutions through which citizens, groups, and communities pursue their visions, articulate their interests, exercise their legal rights, meet their obligations, and mediate their differences.[6] It is also generally accepted that good governance ensures that the political, social, and economic priorities are based on broad consensus in society and that the voices of the poorest and most vulnerable are heard in decision-making over the allocation of development resources. In this view, good governance also entails the creation of effective partnerships. For development to be sustainable, alliances between different actors are necessary, drawing on the comparative advantages of the public sector, private sector, and civil society.

Role of Government. The debate and increasing advocacy of good governance has forced an urgency into the debate on the need for more effective and efficient government in terms of development performance, streamlining public finances, ensuring transparency and accountability of actions, and redressing deficit-ridden systems. Technological advances and greater global integration of markets have also changed the size of government needed to manage economic systems. Political changes during the past decade have spurred people's interest in democratic ideals of freedom and human rights, placing increasing pressure on governments to relinquish some element of decision-making power to bodies that can more closely represent the needs and wants of citizens.

Decentralization

These issues have brought to the fore the principle of subsidiarity as a means of guiding government administration, development planning, and implementation. This entails the decentralization of decision-making powers, development responsibilities, and control over resources to the lowest possible level. Decentralization, combined with democratic local governance, is a key mechanism that can be and is being used by nation-states to broaden public sector legitimacy, transparency, and accountability, and so contribute to effective governance and service delivery. While the local dimension has in most countries been only partially present in national political life, decentralization is beginning to alter this landscape, creating local institutions that can encourage traditional central authorities to change their organization and practices.

Decentralization refers to a restructuring or reorganization of political, fiscal, and administrative authority. Decentralized governance entails a system of co-responsibility between governance institutions at the central, regional, and local levels according to the principle of subsidiarity. It increases the authority and capabilities of governance institutions at the subnational level, while increasing the overall quality and effectiveness of governance in a nation as a whole.

Benefits of Decentralization. During the past three decades, governments in developing countries have attempted to implement a range of decentralization policies, from those that are more comprehensive and designed to devolve development planning and management responsibilities to local government units

(LGUs) to those that are more narrowly conceived, deconcentrating or reallo-
cating administrative tasks among the units of central government. Despite these
differences, however, it is clear that central governments are today allocating,
on an unprecedented scale, large portions of the national budget to LGUs, along
with more administrative authority, economic responsibility, and political autonomy. Over sixty countries around the world with populations of more than
five million are now in some stage of decentralization.[7]

In light of the challenges facing nation-states today, there are a number of
fundamental reasons for, and benefits deriving from, organizing government
structures in a decentralized fashion.

- First, decentralized governance systems represent one (and perhaps the single most
  important) means for exercising checks and balances on a government structure and
  for responding to increasing demands for accountability and transparency in government operations. The establishment of multiple levels, jurisdictions, and units of government, each of which has some measure of independence and autonomy, ensures that
  power, authority, and accountability are not concentrated in only one body. Decentralization of responsibility brings with it local accountability.

- Second, decentralization can facilitate the participation of new social actors. Nongovernmental organizations (NGOs), grass-roots organizations, business associations, labor
  unions, and indigenous groups are now joining the ranks of those actors who have
  traditionally dominated local governance contexts. By generating more centers of
  power, there are inevitably more venues in which civil society organizations can develop and find sustenance and influence. This is extremely important in terms of the
  promotion of democracy in that it contributes significantly to the creation of nongovernmental centers of authority and power within a society. Such centers of power,
  particularly when they operate independently of governmental control, can also serve
  to hold governments accountable.

- Third, decentralized governance helps to create opportunities for the emergence of
  opposition political groups, and in particular creates resources for opposition political
  parties. This can be seen in a number of Latin American countries that have recently
  established elected local governments. The second most important elected political
  office in the country, the mayoralty of the capital city, is often in the hands of the
  opposition party. Decentralized governance provides opportunities for political opposition parties to play an important role within democratic governance systems, allowing
  them to participate in elections and, if successful, exercise political power at the local
  or regional levels.

- Fourth, decentralized governance provides more options for individual citizens seeking
  a positive response from government. Local governments can usually accommodate
  different preferences better than a one-size-fits-all, centrally supplied basket of goods
  and services. This introduces choice in public services. In principle, people can move
  to a jurisdiction that provides more of what they want for the taxes they are willing to
  pay. Decentralization opens the way to local experimentation in meeting public needs.
  Local officials often have a greater stake in good government performance since they
  can be clearly identified by the voters and taxpayers as the architects of success or
  failure. In addition, having alternative levels of governance provides options for indi-

vidual citizens seeking the provision of a particular kind of governmental service or the redress of a particular problem. If individuals are unable to receive desired assistance at one level, they then have the option of pursuing, over the short or long run, strategies designed to elicit a more positive response from another level or unit of government.

• Fifth, decentralized governance provides the opportunity for local economic initiative, and thereby, a means of allowing individuals to participate in increasingly competitive market environments. Highly centralized governance systems tend to concentrate both political and economic power in the capital city of the nation. Centralization of this kind often leads to a neglect of the interests and concerns of other cities and communities in a country. When power is highly centralized, communities some distance from the capital city often have great difficulty in creating an environment that can facilitate community and economic development. They typically lack revenue to invest in the kind of infrastructure necessary to make it feasible for private economic development to take place. Decentralized authority and resources serve to provide much greater opportunities for meaningful and responsive economic development.

• It is worth mentioning that market mechanisms tend to favor groups and production systems that are most competitive, leaving aside the weakest groups, and those systems of local production that are most traditional, thereby affecting those communities with fewer comparative advantages. The growing role played by market mechanisms today makes it necessary to redefine the structure and role of the state. This is particularly true with regard to local, municipal, or provincial government institutions. Local government must assume greater responsibility as an agent operating for the common welfare. This implies that decentralization should be geared toward: (a) achieving better regulation of market mechanisms in order to better rationalize the allocation of resources toward communities with fewer advantages; and (b) developing mechanisms for management and social integration that reinforce the capacity to govern and increase participation at the local level.

• Finally, decentralized governance can be a very important element in the facilitation of an active and lively civil society. The more decentralized government is and the stronger local capacity is, the more opportunities are provided for the emergence of civil society institutions. In fact, it is often the existence of local governance, combined with the emergence of local civil society institutions, that truly creates the pluralism that is fundamental to democratic institutional development. Decentralization at the local level also takes place within a context in which diverse political and administrative structures, social organizations, productive systems, families, and communities coexist. At the local level, the social and cultural identity of individuals, families, and communities is expressed more clearly. Decentralization therefore offers an opportunity to strengthen local cultural identity.

EXPERIENCE OF THE UNITED NATIONS DEVELOPMENT PROGRAMME

As mentioned earlier, there has been a growing consensus among the international community that effective and good governance is crucial for human development. The UNDP has been at the forefront of this consensus. Approximately one-half of UNDP's current resources are devoted to activities that support good governance.[8] This shift in UNDP's work has been accompanied by an increasing conviction that governance begins in communities, villages, and towns, and that local governance provides the basis for the concept and the structure of governance. Decentralizing governance is one of the priorities identified in the UNDP policy document on governance. From 1992 to 1997, UNDP's support to decentralization programs totaled over US$414 million.[9] More than 60 percent of UNDP's country programs now include activities to support decentralized governance activities including Moldova, Nepal, Uganda, Venezuela, and Yemen.[10] In Nepal, UNDP has been supporting decentralization for almost ten years through a program known as the Participatory District Development Programme (PDDP).

In addition, UNDP has several major regional and global programs promoting decentralization including the Local Initiative Facility for Urban Environment (LIFE) Programme, the Urban Management Programme (UMP), and the Decentralized Governance Programme. LIFE promotes "local-local" dialog to improve the living conditions of the urban poor in over sixty cities in twelve pilot countries. The UMP is a twelve-year-old, multidonor effort aimed at improving urban governance, environment, and equity. The Decentralized Governance Programme is UNDP's new global effort to better understand and improve the mechanisms of design and implementation of decentralized governance policies and programs at the country level.

Lessons Learned

UNDP's ongoing support to governments in many developing countries throughout the world in the area of decentralization is providing many valuable lessons. A first lesson is that decentralization is not an alternative to centralization. Both are needed. The complementary roles of national and subnational actors should be determined by analyzing the most effective ways and means of achieving a desired objective. To take several examples: a national road system should be designed with both local input and national coordination; foreign policy should be a national function based on the views of the citizenry; and solid waste management should primarily be dealt with through local mechanisms. In designing a decentralization strategy, it is imperative that such an analysis be done.

A second lesson learned through UNDP's experience in this field is that the multidimensional aspect of decentralization suggests three important implications that heavily influence the context for thinking about decentralization. First, decentralization reform can change the mobilization and allocation of public resources. Because of this, it can affect a wide range of issues from service delivery to poverty reduction to macroeconomic stability. It is in this sense a cross-cutting issue. Second, decentralization encompasses a very diverse set of country-specific activities that can only be understood, analyzed, and guided on the basis of in-depth local institutional knowledge. A third challenge is that there still exists only limited empirical evidence about what works and what does not work in specific contexts, posing a challenge for those responsible for designing and managing decentralization.

A third lesson is that decentralization requires two critical prerequisites: (a) political commitment by the leadership; and (b) consensus of the population. The national authorities must acknowledge a degree of local accountability. The population must articulate a demand for participation and power in a way that conforms to the prevailing societal values. Decentralization cannot be imposed from the outside, nor can popular demand always be assumed.

Additional Lessons

Looking at UNDP experience and that gained by other development practitioners, some further lessons are revealed. These include the following key points:

- Political commitment needs to be supported by a local basis of human and economic resources to sustain a diffusion of power. Adequate capacity and sufficient financial resources are essential elements to either have in place or build up in any decentralization development effort.
- Decentralization is a complex phenomenon involving many geographic entities, societal actors, and social sectors. The geographic entities include the international, national, subnational, and local. The societal actors include government, the private sector, and civil society. The social sectors include all development themes—political, social, cultural, and environmental. In designing decentralization policies and programs, it is essential to use a systems approach that encompasses these overlapping entities, actors, and sectors and the different requirements that each makes.
- Clarity is essential in establishing decentralization goals, and in building up a sense of direction and purpose. Clarity of the process—a plan to reach the goals and identifying who is responsible for doing what—is also important, keeping sight of the long term so as not to be distracted by short-term interests. Design and implementation of decentralization policies and programs must build in clear strategies and mechanisms that ensure greater participation of and service to the poor, especially girls and women.
- The plan for decentralization should be strategic, rather than a predefined and overly structured one, so as to take advantage of "windows of opportunity." It should follow a flexible process, allowing the central/local dynamics to evolve.
- Success depends on having qualified and highly capable leaders and managers to implement the decentralization strategy chosen. These individuals must demonstrate integrity, patience, caution, consistency, and transparency.

CONCLUSION

The main conclusion of this chapter is perhaps the most important lesson of all: decentralization is not a panacea for all ills. Furthermore, there is still much to be learned with regard to the impact that the different arrangements subsumed under decentralization have on the poor. However, there are clear indications that it is only through decentralization that the opportunities can arise for people to participate more directly in, take responsibility for, and benefit from, the decisions that affect their lives and promote sustainable regional development.

NOTES

1. United Nations Development Programme (UNDP), *Human Development Report 1994* (New York, 1994).
2. UNDP, *Human Development Report 1998* (New York, 1998).
3. Ibid.
4. Ibid.
5. Ibid.
6. Governance is defined by UNDP as the exercise of economic, political, and administrative authority to manage a country's affairs at all levels, comprising the mechanisms, processes, and institutions through which that authority is directed. Good governance is, among other things, participatory, transparent, accountable, and efficient. It promotes the rule of law and equal justice under the law. It also recognizes that governance is exercised by the private sector and civil society, as well as the state, all of which have important roles to play in promoting sustainable human development.
7. UNDP, *Governance for Sustainable Human Development* (UNDP Policy Paper Series) (New York, 1997).
8. UNDP, "Decentralized Governance Programme Document" (New York, 1997) (http://magnet.undp.org/Docs/dec/DECEN923/DECENPRO.HTM).
9. Ibid.
10. Ibid.

APPENDIX: DECENTRALIZATION: A CONCEPTUAL OVERVIEW

Management Development and Governance Division, UNDP

Decentralizing key functions of government from the center to regions, districts, municipalities, and local communities is an effective mechanism for enabling people to participate in governance and is therefore, a major determinant of whether a nation is able to create and sustain equitable opportunities for all of its people.

Decentralization can be defined as the transfer of responsibility for planning, management, and resource raising and allocation from the central government and its agencies to: (a) field units of central government ministries or agencies; (b) subordinate units or levels of government; (c) semiautonomous public authorities or corporations; (d) area-wide, regional, or functional authorities; or (e) nongovernmental, private, or voluntary organizations.[1]

Forms of Decentralization

There are a variety of different arrangements, which are often included in the discussions on decentralization. Cheema and Rondinelli[2] have identified four major forms of decentralization: (a) devolution; (b) delegation; (c) deconcentration; and (d) divestment.

Devolution. Transfer of responsibility for governing, understood more broadly as the creation or strengthening, financially or legally, of subnational units of government, whose activities are substantially outside the direct control of central government.

Delegation. Assignment of specific decision-making authority, or the transfer of managerial responsibility for specifically defined functions to public organizations (e.g., local governments or parastatals) outside the normal bureaucratic structure of central government.

Deconcentration. Spatial relocation of decision-making, or the transfer of some administrative responsibility or authority to lower levels within central government ministries or agencies.

Divestment. Best treated as decentralization and it occurs when planning and administrative responsibility or other public functions are transferred from government to voluntary, private, or nongovernmental institutions with clear benefits to and involvement of the public.

What Decentralization Is

A counterpoint to globalization. Decentralization is a counterpoint to globalization. Globalization often removes decisions from the local and national stage to the global sphere of multinational or nonnational interests. Decentralization, on the other hand, brings decision-making back to the subnational and local levels.

An integral part of democratization. Decentralization is an integral part of the logic of democratization—the power of people to determine their own government, representation, policies, and services.

A phenomenon involving multiple dimensions, actors, and sectors. Decentralization is a complex phenomenon involving many geographic entities, social actors, and social sectors. The geographic entities include the international, national, subnational, and local. The social actors include government, the private sector, and civil society. The social sector includes development themes—political, legal, social, cultural, and environmental.

A logical application of core characteristics of good governance. Decentralization is the logical application of the core characteristics of good governance at the subnational and local levels. These characteristics include accountability, transparency, rule of law, and responsiveness.

A mix of types of functions and relationships. Decentralization is a mixture of administrative, fiscal, and political functions and relationships.

A mix of four dimensions. Decentralization involves four dimensions—the collective/exterior, the collective/interior, the individual/exterior, and the individual/interior. The collective/exterior has to do with the institutional and legal forms and procedures. The collective/interior deals with the social culture—the set of values and assumptions that are often unspoken or unacknowledged but nevertheless play a powerful role in human relationships. The individual/exterior dimension has to do with observable behavior of individuals within the various social institutions, whether government, private sector, or civil society. The dimension of the individual/interior deals with mindset, worldview, mental models, emotions, and intuitions of individuals within institutions.

A new form of communication. Decentralization involves new communication and information flows between each geographic area, societal actor, and social sector.

What Decentralization Is Not

An alternative to centralization. Decentralization is not an alternative to centralization. Both are needed. The complementary roles of national and subnational actors should be determined by analyzing the most effective ways and means of achieving a desired objective. For example, a national road system should be designed with both local input and national coordination. Foreign policy should be a national function based on the views of the citizenry. Solid waste management should primarily be dealt with through local mechanisms.

Exclusive public sector reform. Decentralization is much more than public sector, civil service, and administrative reform. It involves the roles and relationships of all societal actors, whether governmental, private sector, or civil society.

Why Decentralize?

To achieve the goals of sustainable and people-centered development. Decentralization is a form and process of governance. Just as there can be good governance at the national level, there can be good decentralized governance. Good governance includes the mechanisms and processes that enable a society to achieve more sustainable and people-centered development. Good decentralized governance includes the forms and procedures that allow a society to achieve at the subnational and local levels the goals of poverty reduction, sustainable livelihoods, environmental regeneration, and gender equity.

How to Decentralize

Consider the existing cultural elements. Decentralization is affected by the cultural elements of a society—the images, assumptions, and internal psychic of the population regarding the issues of authority, role of the government, role of the citizen, conflict, consensus, power, role of elites, role of the poor, the role of women, and a host of other issues.

Consider changing relationships. Decentralization always involves changes of relationship between and among different societal actors, social sectors, and geographic areas. These changes can be threatening or can be seen as enabling for all parties—a win-win situation.

Consider timing and sequence. Decentralization is a long-term effort in which timing and phasing are crucial.

Consider enhancing mechanisms of participation and partnership. Decentralization is increased in effectiveness through mechanisms of full participation and partnership. Participation must involve all the societal actors playing their optimal and legitimate roles in policy formulation, resource management, and service provision. Popular participation is crucial in each phase of decentralization, from situational analysis, design, implementation, monitoring, evaluation, and feedback. Partnership must be based on mutual trust and understanding of the various actors, acknowledging that each has both strengths and weaknesses. Each actor must both enable the other actors in their legitimate roles and hold them accountable if they step outside their legitimate mandates.

Consider the mental model that is being used. Decentralization as a term comes from a mental model containing a center and a periphery. This is only a model just as a pyramidic social structure is only a mental model. When we view a society as a whole system we see not vertical layers (as in a pyramid) or concentric layers (as in the centric model), but rather a horizontal environment with autonomous yet interrelated actors, sectors, and geographic area. In designing decentralization policies and programs, it is necessary to be self-conscious of the mental model one is using and, if necessary, to adapt or completely change the model to better fit reality.

What Is a Donor's Role in Decentralization?

Decentralization is a sensitive national issue. Donors should not attempt to control this process but rather play a facilitative role. Donors should see decentralization as a learning process and should allow for mistakes to be made and learning to take place. Donors should use a process consultation approach in the design of programs involving the local and national actors in each phase of the program cycle.

What Are Some of the Major Issues in Decentralization?

In analyzing the concept of decentralization and local governance, several major issues continuously appear. These issues often form the bedrock of comprehensive and systematic strategies to promote and facilitate decentralization practices. Some of the most prevalent issues emerging from the analysis of the concept and its various dimensions are as follows:

- Issue 1: *Decentralization is a political issue* that often arises from political commitment and pressure outside of any given sector. When decentralization is initiated first in a specific sector (e.g., education), it often meets resistance by officials who do not want to transfer their power.

- Issue 2: *Often guiding principles are the mission components of decentralization.* Decentralization principles should include the purpose of decentralization, rationale, objectives, and implementation design, and include a clear definition of roles for the various management levels and the linkages between them.

- Issue 3: *Not all government functions should be decentralized.* A function should not be transferred to a lower level if it is critical to the achievement of central-level goals and its sustainability at the local level cannot be guaranteed, the capacity to perform the function does not exist at the lower level, or undertaking this function at the peripheral level is not cost-effective.

- Issue 4: *National leaders and donor organizations should fully appreciate the complexity of decentralization.* The complexity of decentralization often is reflected in three key areas: transfer of finances; procurement systems; and management of human resources. For the decentralization process to be effective, details of these priority areas should be identified and crystallized well in advance of the implementation of the decentralization process.

- Issue 5: *Decentralization requires improved legal, regulatory, and financial framework* to ensure clear division of responsibilities, accountability, and transparency.

- Issue 6: *Regional and local capacities for decentralization should be fully assessed* prior to implementation of a countrywide decentralization process.

- Issue 7: *Creating, coordinating, and assisting linkages are essential for effective implementation of decentralization.* If decentralization is to be effective, means must be found of reorienting central administrators' perceptions of their roles from control and direction to support and facilitation. This requires strengthening capacity at the central level to perform their new functions effectively.

- Issue 8: *Standards and norms are essential for equity and quality.* The transfer of extensive power to more peripheral management levels should be based on a system that balances central and local priorities without which there would be negative impact on national equity. Clear national standards and service norms and an ongoing system of monitoring are essential for safeguarding equity and quality.

- Issue 9: *Support for decentralization policies must be deliberately and carefully mobilized among all critical players.* This includes: leaders in central ministries and departments; state, provincial, municipal, district, and local units of administration; autonomous and regional agencies; political parties; and interest groups that will be affected by the decentralization process. The mass media, training and public information programs, and political bargaining must be used to forge a base of support for decentralization policies if they are to be implemented successfully. In most countries, changes must be made in civil service systems to provide incentives and rewards for those officials who promote development at the local level.

- Issue 10: *Stages and procedures for the implementation of decentralization should be identified.* Experiences indicate that decentralization can be implemented most successfully if the process is incremental and iterative. Those aspects or programs that are least likely to be opposed and for which there is adequate administrative capacity should be expanded as political support and administration competence increase. Greater attention should be given to building administrative capacity from the "bottom up" as well as from the "top down" and to finding ways of using and strengthening existing organizations and traditional decision-making procedures in the rural areas. Policy and demonstration projects may be needed to gauge the ability of the local government to assume greater responsibility.

- Issue 11: *Financial and human resources should be proportionate with decentralization responsibilities.* For effective implementation of decentralization policy, the central-level government must be prepared to allocate appropriate resources in terms of financial and human capital, and technical assistance to the localities. In most cases, the localities cannot undertake decentralization responsibilities unless supported by the central administration.

- Issue 12: *The private sector can be a critical partner in the design and implementation of decentralization.* Public-private partnership in the design and implementation of decentralization is essential for mobilization of resources and delivery of services at the local level.

- Issue 13: *Broad participation is needed for a successful decentralization process.* For decentralization to be effective, it should be built on the needs, priorities, and views of the people who are most affected by it. Appropriate mechanisms should be developed to promote and encourage popular participation and involvement in the identification of local needs to finding most suitable approaches and strategies to respond to such needs.

- Issue 14: *Decentralization can facilitate empowerment.* Local participation in identifying community strengths and weaknesses, and their involvement in mobilizing resources needed to enhance development at the local level, facilitates and promotes empowerment.

- Issue 15: *Creative local solutions should be encouraged and disseminated.* Decentralization is expected to enhance creative problem-solving at the local level.

- Issue 16: *Monitoring and evaluation procedures for decentralization should be specified.* To assess the impact of decentralization policies on improving the quality of life at the localities, the concept of decentralization should be further narrowed to specific and tangible measures that can be used as reliable indicators to monitor and evaluate the progress of decentralization policies and programs. To plan, adjust, and adapt decentralization policies to meet local priorities and realities requires a comprehensive monitoring and evaluation tool capable of detecting their effects on improving the quality of life of the population.

NOTES

1. G. Shabbir Cheema and D. A. Rondinelli, eds., *Decentralization and Development: Policy Implementation in Developing Countries* (Beverly Hills: Sage, 1983); and J. R. Nellis, "Decentralization in North Africa: Problems of Policy Implementation" in the above book.

2. Ibid.

3

Subsidiarity: A Key Concept for Regional Development Policy

Walter B. Stöhr

INTRODUCTION

Regional development has typically moved between two extreme prototypes, namely, as a central government responsibility (mainly in the 1960s and 1970s) and as a local/regional self-help agenda (mainly since the 1980s). The first usually manifested itself in the form of rigid central planning for regions (predominantly in countries that at that time were called the Second and Third World), while the latter prototype tended to manifest itself as community bootstrap operations, often called by names such as community action or local/regional initiatives. For simplicity's sake let us call the first prototype "central regional policy," or CRP (or "development from above"), and the second, "local development action," or LDA (or "development from below").[1]

CRP, in the earlier postwar period, was characterized not only by the dominant role of central government but also by a high degree of confidence in the previsibility of future development trends, "rational" action, the ultimate capacity of government to solve economic and social problems, and the availability of relatively abundant public funds (usually stemming from nationally owned natural resources or manufacturing industries). These policies were predominantly applied in periods of relatively high postwar growth rates, with reasonably predictable markets, modest technological change, and within essentially "closed" national economies characterized by relatively high tariff barriers and a predominance of import substitution policies (particularly in the Second and Third World countries). Decision-making processes were to a high degree centralized and were therefore rather inflexible and little able to adapt to local requirements or external change. Local or regional communities were subjected to being "history-takers" in this process, partly because of the lack of power and funds.

LDA has in most respects the opposite characteristics, and has recently emerged not only because of the lack of central government funds but also due to its inability to solve local problems during periods of rapid change. With the opening up of national economies and increasing "globalization," local economies continuously have to reposition themselves in national and global markets. They have to participate as—and compete with—a swarm of "history-makers" such as "world cities," core regions, and world financial centers. Technological change has accelerated and future market trends have become much less predictable. To cope with these rapidly changing external conditions, highly adaptable and flexible action is required to mobilize local and external resources in an optimum way in order to compete on the world market. This requires a much higher degree of decentralized decision-making and local/regional initiatives and action. "No organizational strategy from the top can fully appreciate the differences between and among regions and no central government department has the long-term capacity to deal with anything beyond sectoral perspectives. . . . Hence, it is only through the empowerment of regions that their long-term interests will be served."[2]

In practice, however, neither of these two prototypes between which regional development policy has been oscillating can operate satisfactorily under present and foreseeable conditions. CRP has insufficient resources and flexibility to cope with ongoing global change and LDA has insufficient knowledge of global trends and often lacks the access to external resources and information.

In the past, central authorities tended to retain as many functions and decisions as possible and delegate to lower levels only those that they were unable to perform adequately or were of minor political interest to them. With increasing awareness that this procedure was unable to solve local/regional problems in a sustained way, central governments started to encourage local development initiatives. In many cases, however, this took the form of central authorities ridding themselves of responsibilities and leaving localities and regions to fend for themselves without giving them the required support and resources to do so successfully.

For future requirements, a more effective regional development policy will therefore have to be conceived of as a multilevel process characterized by the principle of "subsidiarity." This means that, contrary to past dominant practice, those processes and decisions that can best be performed at local or regional levels should be executed there. Only those that cannot be performed satisfactorily at lower levels should be "delegated" to higher levels. Similarly, for the mobilization of resources (including taxes) and decision-making on them, priority should be given to the local and regional levels, which would then "contract out" certain functions or services to higher levels of government, the private sector, or nongovernmental organizations (NGOs).

The purpose of this chapter is to specify criteria and define, on the basis of previous empirical work, which activities have a comparative advantage at the local or regional level and which, in a complementary way, have to be performed at higher levels or by external public or private actors. While this author has worked extensively in developing countries, the present chapter is written from a mainly European perspective.

RECENT TRENDS IN LOCAL/REGIONAL DEVELOPMENT THEORY AND PRACTICE

In the past decade, a number of new concepts for territorial development have emerged, such as "clusters," "networks," "innovative milieus," and "regional innovation complexes." These have been used and applied in practice in an often rather fuzzy way. Are these concepts really new or are they just old wine in new casks? Although they have new names, these concepts are based on and further developed from previously used concepts such as spatially determined "growth centers,"[3] intersectoral "growth poles,"[4] and "industrial districts"—although these are often not explicitly stated. In theoretical terms, all these concepts are concerned with varying combinations of specific types of externalities such as agglomeration economies[5] and external scale economies (including those associated with learning, innovation, knowledge spillovers, and increased specialization), as Feser has aptly shown.[6]

According to Bergman, clusters consist of firms linked actively together and in close spatial proximity.[7] They are, therefore, explicitly spatially determined. The concept was initially developed by Porter[8] to indicate the significance of interindustry linkages in the competitiveness of national (and regional) economies. He specified three critical conditions for competitiveness through cluster formation:

First, what makes nations, states, and cities prosperous and companies competitive is a relentless focus on innovation and upgrading. Second, competitiveness depends on creating and sustaining specialized and unique local advantages. Third, the public and private sectors must work separately and in tandem to encourage clusters to form, grow, and diversify.[9] Elsewhere, clusters were considered as local networks that consistently cross organizational and intersectoral boundaries, including both firms as well as, sometimes, government agencies and community associations, thereby, influencing new forms of regional governance. Clusters have been associated with new thinking on innovation[10] as well as network-oriented approaches to economic and spatial development.[11] Clusters—although this concept is hardly ever explicitly stated—in essence are a further development of the growth-centre concept[12] enriched by institutional, cultural, and historical factors. Clusters are therefore, burdened with similar problems for regional development as are growth centres, i.e., "as industrial and locational advantage begets advantage through increasing returns, economic activity is further concentrated in selected places."[13] This would mean that, although cluster areas may accelerate their own growth and innovation rate, they may at the same time—like the old growth centres—

contribute to a widening of intranational and intraregional disparities and to increased "backwash effects"[14] from peripheral areas.

Networks, in contrast, are not necessarily spatially determined. They have been defined as forms of organization typified by reciprocal patterns of communication and exchange and contrasted with market and hierarchical governance structures.[15] They are characterized "by a long-term relation of different partners who cooperate on the same hierarchical level in an environment of mutual understanding and trust."[16] The emergence of networks is explained not primarily by cost aspects, but by strategic interests, the wish for appropriability and realizing synergetic effects resulting from technological and other complementarities.[17] They are institutional arrangements aimed at acquiring and sharing resources by "relatively loose, informal, implicit, decomposable, and recombinable systems of inter-relationships."[18] While networks are not necessarily spatially determined, case studies indicate that "firms in central regions show a higher probability for interregional interactions, while in rural areas, intraregional contacts dominate" and "that innovation-intensive firms exhibit indeed a stronger emphasis on interregional networking. Access to external knowledge sources seems to be more important for service than for manufacturing firms."[19] The spatial extension of networks therefore appears to be differentiated between area types and sectors.

Elsewhere, the network paradigm is considered a new trend in corporate and regional development, which refers to the practice of cooperation between agencies as an aspect of economic restructuring in specific regions. Regional networks reflect changes that are taking place in our society including the ways communities participate in their development.[20] Some authors describe networks as "the twenty-first century organization."[21]

Innovative milieu is a concept originally developed by the French-based Groupe de Recherche Européen sur les Milieux Innovateurs (GREMI).[22] GREMI defines a successful milieu as "a set of territorial relationships encompassing in a coherent way a production system, different economic and social actors, a specific culture, and a representation system and generating a dynamic collective learning process."[23] This regional collective learning process is concerned with regional mechanisms that reduce the uncertainty faced by firms in a rapidly changing technological environment such as that associated with a "competence gap" arising from a firm's limited ability to process and understand available information. Reducing or eliminating this competence gap demands the development by the firm of effective "transcoding functions," which "translate external information into a language that the firm may understand," functions that can merge both codified and tacit information into firm-specific knowledge, including research and development (R&D) knowledge.[24] "Regional collective learning thus focuses on links and networking between firms and via the regional labour market."[25] For Camagni, the milieu relationship links the firm to its contiguous environment, while wider networks link it explicitly to selected partners in its (wider) operational environment.[26] Such wider networks are important "in three strategic areas of local firm activity, namely, external innovation inputs, inter-firm research collaboration, and scientific and professional labour markets."[27]

The "regional milieu" concept is a further development of Marshall's industrial district[28] and is the only one of the three "new" concepts mentioned so far, where this is explicitly acknowledged in the related literature.

These concepts have been preceded by that of "regional innovation complexes,"[29] where "regional networks of synergetic interaction . . . (between) educational and training institutions, R&D, technological and management consulting, risk financing, production, and locally-rooted decision-making functions . . . either within or between specialized regional institutions or . . . by informal cooperation between . . . firms"[30] have, on the basis of empirical case studies, been determined as main factors of regional innovation and development.

All these concepts relate to competitiveness and comparative advantage by cooperation and interaction at the scale of regions or localities in national and global contexts. A major question, however, is to what extent are they determined by actors at the local/regional, national, or supranational/global scale? At this stage, we want to introduce the concept of subsidiarity.

THE CONCEPT OF SUBSIDIARITY

Subsidiarity relates to a social system "which is structured from below, starting with the family and the primary groups which are characterized by personal contact between its members and transparent structures, through local or functional secondary groups, to the state as a comprehensive political community." It can be defined as "a social order, oriented against the totalitarian and centralist state, in which the larger community acknowledges the potentials of the subordinate ones and exercises only those tasks which the latter cannot fulfill."[31] In practice, there are at least two interpretations of this concept: one maintains that each social level should take care of what it can do best, but at the same time, in a spirit of solidarity, it can rely on help "from above" if it cannot solve a problem (e.g., in catholic social philosophy, refer to next paragraph); and the other is more related to neoliberal thinking, and maintains that each individual and the lower social levels should fend for themselves, and the state and higher levels should exercise only a minimum of functions.

The concept as well as the term of subsidiarity has been little used until quite recently and even less applied. In the European context, it has been derived from catholic social philosophy, which since the end of the last century has used this concept in its claim for federalism and the independence of the individual and the family from the state. A very broad political discussion of the concept of subsidiarity and almost unanimous demands for its general implementation have arisen recently in the European Community (EC) as a reaction to the 1992

Maastricht Treaty, which has widely been criticized as being too centralist, bureaucratic, and distant from the citizen. The European Union (EU) and all its member countries have made at least verbal commitments to remedy this in the forthcoming EU reform process. In EC law, however, it has so far been incorporated explicitly only in connection with environmental protection policies (where it tends to avoid uniform standards).

Let us now apply this concept to regional planning and development in general.

Subsidiarity in the Realm of Development Policy

Although many of its determinants may stem from higher levels, concrete development cannot validly be evaluated by national or international aggregate variables, but always manifests itself in specific localities or regions where people do (or do not) find employment, housing, and basic services, to cover their elementary personal and social needs. The size of the area within which individuals and social groups must have access to these activities or outputs of development varies according to geographic factors (relief and physical obstacles to movement) and to available infrastructure and technology (transport and communications). In some cases, these basic areas of development may be single municipalities, and in others, rather large, internally well-connected regions. In an earlier context, we have defined the size of such a basic development unit as the area within which intensive common interaction for development takes place, within which the benefits of this action should also have their major impact, and where major control over related decision-making processes should therefore be exercised.[32]

While in earlier periods the intensity of interaction tended to be highest within small areas, modern transport and communications technology have tended to increase the scale of intense interactions. This has, however, not led to the dissolution of regional networks as "clusters of competence,"[33] which require a preexisting knowledge base for the adoption of innovations. For one of the few countries established by voluntary aggregation of formerly independent small units, Switzerland, for example, Rossi[34] pleads for the creation of "macroregions for regional planning" out of the present twenty-six cantons. He argues that this would create economies of scale in "marketing" the regions in the exterior, "cooperation synergies" in dealing with the federal government and possibly later vis-à-vis the EU (whose Nomenclature of Territorial Units for Statistics [NUTS] Regions are five to ten times larger than the present Swiss planning and policy regions), and a reduction of transaction costs for access to market and institutional information.

Common local action for development or "local initiatives" have gained increasing importance since the 1980s, as it turned out that central government was less and less able to cope with the problems and challenges created by globalization and subsequent global restructuring for specific localities and regions.[35] Although it may seem like a contradiction in itself, the increasing trend toward multinational integration and globalization has at the same time led to an increasing importance of action at the local/regional level.[36] Sabel even states that globalization gives a new rise to regional economies around the world.[37]

Globalization and the creation of macroregional economic blocks (e.g., EU, North American Free Trade Association [NAFTA], and MERCOSUR) have in fact shifted functions and decision-making powers between different scales of the spatial hierarchy. National states have ceded powers to their respective macroregional economic blocks, "a new layer of decision-making at least one more step removed from the national systems of governments that represent their people."[38] At the same time, national governments have "devolved" certain functions to regional/local authorities, NGOs, or the private sector. This is in line with the recent trend toward "lean" government in the frame of neoliberal economic thinking as well as a response to a newly emerging wave of regionalism.

The concerns of the central state are therefore shifting in two directions—upwards to the supranational level and to international priorities, and downwards to the sub-national level and to local domestic issues. This "dual orientation" . . . redirects the resources of the state and reduces its capacity to exercise effective control and influence at the national level. . . . Consequences include the formation of "intermediate associations, social networks, and a whole range of looser social, economic, and political pressure groups . . . (which) increasingly challenge the role and function of the central state."[39]

COMPARATIVE ADVANTAGES OF ACTION AT THE LOCAL/REGIONAL LEVEL

Let us now see what the comparative advantages of action at the local/regional level can be.

Direct Problem Perception

Actual needs as well as adequate strategies[40] to deal with problems are usually best perceived at the local/regional level, although for their objective evaluation, access to information on comparative interregional standards and methods may often have to be facilitated at higher levels.

Intensivity of Interaction

Cooperation, networking, and informal exchange of information for new developmental initiatives can best be achieved at the local/regional level, provided that the necessary degree of solidarity and identification of actors within the region exists. If this is not the case, very often *animateurs*[41] or "local development agents"[42] can be helpful in promoting this interaction. These actors must not necessarily be endogenous but can also be of external origin (e.g., managers

of branch plants with external headquarters who have come to identify themselves with the region) or local "return migrants" who have spent time and
gained expertise abroad.

Local and Regional Synergy

Intensive interaction between different agents for development is likely to
increase the sum of their effects in a synergetic way.[43] This would refer to the
regional interaction of research and training institutions, consulting and other
entrepreneurial service facilities, financing institutions, and legal services.[44] In
spite of the opportunities that the new telecommunications media offer for such
interaction, face-to-face contacts still maintain an important role.

Potential for Local Economic and Social Initiatives

Local/regional initiatives will often be the result of intensive local interaction.
Economic initiatives will need to be paralleled by social initiatives. Local economic initiatives will frequently require what Johannisson[45] called the "social
entrepreneur," i.e., an entrepreneur who also pursues local stakeholder interests
instead of mere shareholder interests. Local social initiatives, in contrast, according to a recent transnational study of local initiatives in a developed and a
threshold country,[46] are also likely to be triggered by specific types of persons,
i.e., not so much by persons with ample disposable time or those most inflicted
by or subjectively aware of major local problems, but rather by persons already
holding (often various) jobs, frequently in the public sector, which gives them
good access to information, sources of financing, and political decision-makers.
Founders of local economic or social initiatives usually will be members of both
horizontal (local) and vertical (national or global) networks. They would also
likely be the catalysts for what Friedmann[47] calls local "empowerment."

Local Strategy Formulation

Actors or agencies at the local/regional level are "better placed to develop
strategies tailored to the specific problems of the individual region"[48] than those
at higher levels. These may be mainstream local authorities, if they have innovative staff and are flexible enough to deal with modern developmental challenges,[49] independent regional development agencies established especially for
this purpose,[50] or informal business or community action groups. Such strategies
may substantively range from an intensification of existing structures (rationalization, specialization) through product innovation in existing dominant sectors,[51] the creation of intersectoral clusters, the complete abandonment of the
past economic base and creating a completely new one,[52] or the establishment
of high-technology-oriented technology parks[53] and technopolises.[54]

Collective Learning within Regional Clusters and Networks

Geographic, institutional, and social proximity facilitates "continuity over time of local technological and scientific know-how . . . stable inter-SME linkages and a stable local labour market . . . these relationships become qualitatively greater, since they are based on trust and social interactions, which set in motion an informal and tacit transfer of information and know-how, and of non-codified immaterial assets among local firms which help in determining . . . an industrial atmosphere and reduction of transaction costs."[55]

In an empirical analysis, Capello found that radical innovation is primarily related to small and medium enterprises (SMEs) based on collective learning through "socialized mechanisms of spatial transfer of knowledge" within the local milieu, where it represents an externality, while process innovation "seems to require mostly internal knowledge cumulated by the firm, and some technological proximity with suppliers and customers."[56] "Local creative know-how thus cumulates outside the firm and is in this sense, the result of a process of socialization facilitated by the common cultural and organizational rules and codes."[57]

Need of Extraregional Innovation Linkages

However, as mentioned earlier, the majority of firms in innovative local milieus also need external innovation impulses,[58] which must be "translated . . . into a language which the firm may understand."[59] Empirical analyses in different countries have shown that this applies to 85 percent of sampled firms both in the Italian case-study regions[60] and in the Cambridge region of Great Britain,[61] while the percentage of firms relying for their innovative impulses only on the local "milieu" is only 2 percent and 14 percent, respectively. External information access and cooperative linkages are therefore vital for innovation to become a self-sustaining regional process.

Individual regions or countries will therefore have a differentiated capacity for endogenous development, and consequently, a differentiated need for central or external developmental inputs.

IMPORTANT FUNCTIONS OF NATIONAL OR SUPRANATIONAL ACTORS

Strategies of endogenous or "bottom-up" development[62] have often been misused by central authorities as an excuse to withdraw from their own responsibilities for regional development and let problem localities/regions fend for themselves. However, they do have important functions in a system of subsidiary regional development, which many regions cannot fulfill themselves but need to undertake in order to be able to mobilize their endogenous development potential.

The important functions of national or supranational agencies are to:[63]

- Facilitate access to information on: marketing opportunities (national and worldwide); cofinancing of regional training and R&D centers; and cofinancing of local and regional development organizations.

- Promote innovative persons, groups, and entrepreneurship at the local/regional level.

- Promote the establishment of risk-financing institutions.

- Promote the flexibility of institutional structures at all levels for purposes of development.

- Provide substantial scope for decision-making, action, and financial autonomy at the regional/local level. This is, at the same time, a means to counteract excessive functional and geographic concentration of capital, economic activities, and population. A system based on subsidiarity in economic, political, and geographic terms tends to have a higher potential for overall efficiency than one ruled by top-down policies.

- Promote framework conditions that facilitate the reduction of interregional disparities in levels of development. This includes the extension of conditions that permit the formation of clusters and networks, also in less developed areas, by network brokering, technology transfer, and information provision. An important prerequisite is that knowledge accumulation (learning) as a form of investment that generates social externalities[64] is also facilitated in peripheral areas.

- Grant permission to promote linkage to transregional cooperative networks. In almost all the cases studied,[65] endogenous development was possible only if the respective central government agencies were willing to either promote or tolerate such linkages in ways that were not primarily guided by central-agency interests. Furthermore, it proved essential that endogenous development was supported by (frequently, informal) cooperative networks or "committed link cadres," not politically dominated by established central institutions. These link cadres frequently fulfilled important functions in strengthening the bargaining position of regional groups vis-à-vis central authorities or external (multiregional) economic enterprises, in training and consulting as well as in increasing the local consciousness of the reasons underlying existing problems and of the required self-organization for overcoming them. This, therefore, was an important factor for promoting the emergence of local development initiatives.

- Include external economic actors, if sufficient facilities or capabilities are not available within the region. Often these may be branch-plants of multinational enterprises (MNEs) or branches of universities or research centers. In order to reach a self-sustained development of the region, i.e., without unilateral dependence on external inputs, these functions should be internalized as far as possible. MNEs interested in investing within a region should be given incentives (or in the case of subsidies being granted, contractually obliged) to also locate some of their key functions (R&D, decision making, or headquarters) within the region. Once established, branches of universities or research centers should be upgraded as soon as possible to full-fledged autonomous institutions.[66]

• Allow central authorities to give special assistance in localities/regions with special restructuring problems (old manufacturing or mining industries, special disadvantages for agricultural production, and special urban improvement problems). Examples are the structural funds that the EU has established for specific problem areas and sectors. Some of these programs retain certain aspects of the "old redistributive" central development policies, which are, however, to be successively phased out. Essentially these are multinational programs, although based explicitly on cost-sharing with national and subnational authorities.

MULTINATIONAL AND GLOBAL REQUIREMENTS

In Europe, the Organisation for Economic Co-operation and Development (OECD) has been promoting local initiatives for the past fifteen years through its Territorial Development Service (TDS) and its Local Economic and Employment Development Programme (LEED), as well as its predecessors. Similarly, the EC through its Structural Funds Programmes and, especially, the European Social Funds for Local Development is promoting local initiatives in the battle against unemployment. But it is only since 1993 "that the question of local development began to seriously attract the attention of European decision-makers. For many years, these ideas were considered peripheral as compared to macro-economic and other strategies," and it was only in 1995 that "the Commission in this field allowed for the production of an outline for a European Incentive Strategy for local initiatives for development and employment (Commission Communication COM (95) 273 of 13 June 1995)." By now it is realized that "competitiveness today is not only that of companies but also, and increasingly, that of regions and local areas."[67]

But there are also more informal local development initiatives on a multinational scale in Europe such as the European Business Network for Social Cohesion (EBNSC) supported by some seventy large MNEs (Philips, Daimler-Benz, Shell, British Telecom, Olivetti, and Volkswagen), which in cooperation with local NGOs assist other firms "which are willing to face their social responsibilities" in developing training and personnel upgrading programs, in the creation of new jobs, in projects for the reintegration of unemployed, and in the creation of new firms.[68] Other initiatives for interlocal communication are those of MUNICIPIA, which offers an interactive platform on the World Wide Web (http://www.municipia.at) for the interchange of over 250 "good practice" models of urban and regional planning experiences. A similar effort is supported by the European Alliance for Community Networks (EACN), which offers a dialog-oriented telematic platform for local communities (http://www.communities.org.uk) in promoting the exchange of local development experiences.[69]

Multinational programs like the above examples exist also in other emerging multinational unions such as the Americas, in Central and Eastern Europe, and in other parts of the world. Their reinforcement and expansion is important and should be aimed for.

On the global scale, the Multilateral Agreement on Investment (MAI), currently under discussion, may become of great importance to local and regional development. The objective of this agreement is to fully secure the rights of MNEs regarding their investments in any country or region of the world. For the stability of local, regional, and national development, however, it would be important to also define the responsibility of MNEs toward the regions/countries in which they invest or disinvest.

The United Nations Conference on Trade and Development (UNCTAD)[70] and the United Nations Industrial Development Organization (UNIDO) officials fear that MAI "is an agreement that has been designed for the interests of some OECD-based multinationals" and is characterized by "the absence of a genuine representative role for civil society in drawing up the MAI."[71] The World Development Movement[72] expresses concern that "currently the MAI removes the powers of governments and creates sweeping new rights for foreign investors, but includes no enforceable responsibilities for foreign investors." In more concrete terms, it foresees "an increasing 'democratic deficit' associated with replacement of rights of citizens in a democracy with enhanced corporate rights ... (and) ... reduced responsiveness and effectiveness of local-level institutions, through constraints on their ability to enact local-level solutions."[73]

If the current negotiation process on MAI does not eliminate such deficits, it would certainly run counter to the principle of subsidiarity in development policy and practically lead to a loss of sovereign rights over policymaking and legislation at the local, regional, and even national levels. This would even "contrast with the conclusions of the World Bank's *1997 World Development Report* on the role of the State ... (which) highlighted the importance of measures to build the capacity of the State to intervene capably to promote equitable and sustainable development."[74]

In both developing and developed countries, local, regional, and national governments need to be able to formulate their own development policies (e.g., strengthen and diversify their domestic industries), screen inward investment proposals (encourage those that will create development benefits and refuse those likely to harm local communities or destroy their environment, stipulate accompanying technology transfer or the use of local inputs), and define their own financial policy (e.g., control the flow of speculative capital that may lead to financial instability).

MNEs should also be obliged to participate in the cost of their disinvestment in specific regions in terms of unemployment, social standards, and remaining environmental damage. This is an issue in which uniform international standards for MNEs would need to be introduced in order to avoid MNEs "hopping" with their investments from country to country trying to maximize their short-term share-holders' profits, and neglecting longer-term stakeholders' interests including those of the respective local and regional communities.

CONCLUSION

In summary, practical experience shows that local/regional development—in spite of and partly even because of the recent trend toward globalization and deregulation—is in a phase of increasing importance, both politically and from an overall developmental point of view. Distinct from traditional redistributive practice "from above" (based mainly on experiences dating back to the third quarter of this century), local/regional development in the future will have to be related much more to empowerment at the local/regional level. This will have to be embedded in a system of subsidiarity in which the lower societal levels should be given the opportunity to define their own priorities and determine and implement their own development strategies. This requires adequate decision-making powers at these levels in order to allocate accordingly the resources they are capable of mobilizing. Functions that local communities cannot fulfill should be contracted out to higher societal levels (regional, national, or supranational) or with NGOs. These levels and organizations should, in the spirit of solidarity, be open to calls from local/regional levels and concentrate their activities on facilitating access to external mutual information, promoting flexibility and innovation at the local/regional level, and facilitating processes of "collective learning" through the formation of functional regional clusters, innovative milieu, and innovative complexes. At the same time, their integration into large-scale networks should be facilitated, which can offer external innovative and developmental impulses to local/regional communities. In such networks, multinational enterprises and inward investment are able to, in the words of the World Bank's *World Development Report 1997*, "build (their) capacity . . . to intervene capably to promote equitable and sustainable development." The proposed MAI would therefore be parallel to securing the rights of international investors, defining their responsibilities toward local, regional, and national communities, and securing for the latter a democratic role in determining their own developmental process and to participating in the formulation of the MAI. The latter agreement would have to contain also a "code of fair conduct" for multinational investors toward territorial communities concerning both their investments and their disinvestments.

NOTES

1. W. Stöhr and D. R. Fraser Taylor, *Development from Above or Below? The Dialectics of Regional Planning in Developing Countries* (Chichester: Wiley, 1981). See also the summary in A. L. Mabogunje and R. P. Misra, eds., *Regional Development Alternatives: International Perspectives* (Regional Development Series; volume 2) (Singapore: Maruzen Asia for UNCRD, 1981).

2. K. E. Haynes et al., "Regional Governance and Economic Development: Lessons from Federal States" (paper presented at the European Regional Science Conference, Zürich, 1996).

3. J. Boudeville, *Problems of Regional Economic Planning* (Edinburgh: University Press, 1966).

4. F. Perroux, *"Note sur la nation pole de croassance,"* *Economic Appliqué* 7 (1955): 307–20.

5. E. M. Hoover, *Location Theory and the Shoe and Leather Industries* (Cambridge, MA: Harvard University Press, 1937); and A. Weber, *Theory of the Location of Industries* (English translation) (Chicago, IL: University of Chicago Press, 1929).

6. E. J. Feser, "Old and New Theories of Industry Clusters" in Michael Steiner, ed., *Clusters and Regional Specialization: On Geography, Technology and Networks* (European Research in Regional Science, 8) (London: Pion, 1998).

7. E. M. Bergman, "Industrial Trade Clusters in Action: Seeing Regional Economies Whole" in Steiner, ed., *Clusters and Regional Specialization.*

8. M. E. Porter, *The Competitive Advantage of Nations* (London: Macmillan, 1990).

9. Ibid., p. 26.

10. D. Jacobs, "Knowledge-Intensive Innovation: The Potential of the Cluster Approach," *IPTS Report* 16 (1997): 22–28. Cited in Arnoud Lagendijk, "New Forms of Regional Industrial Policy in Europe: How Do Policy Makers Understand 'Competitiveness' and 'Clusters'?" (paper presented at the 38th European Regional Science Association Congress, Vienna, 1998).

11. C. Lawson et al., "Inter-Firm Links between Regionally Clustered High-Technology SMEs: A Comparison of Cambridge and Oxford Innovation Networks (ESRC Centre for Business Research, Working Paper 65), pp. 1–38. Cited in Lagendijk, "New Forms of Regional Industrial Policy in Europe."

12. Boudeville, *Problems of Regional Economic Planning*; and D. Darwent, "Growth Poles and Growth Centres in Regional Planning: A Review," *Environment and Planning* 1 (1969): 5–31.

13. Feser, "Old and New Theories of Industry Clusters," p. 349.

14. G. Myrdal, *Economic Theory and Underdeveloped Regions* (New York: Harper & Row, 1957).

15. W. Powell, "Neither Market nor Hierarchy: Network Forms of Organization," *Research in Organizational Behaviour* 12 (1990): 295.

16. C. Karlsson and L. Westin, "Patterns of a Network Economy: An Introduction" in B. Johannson, C. Karlsson, and L. Westin, eds., *Patterns of a Network Economy* (Berlin: Springer, 1994), p. 3. Cited in Knut Koschatzky, "Innovation Networks of Industry and Business-Related Services: The Impact of Innovation Intensity of Firms on Regional Inter-Firm Cooperation" (paper presented at the 38th Congress of the European Regional Science Association, Vienna, 1998).

17. C. Freeman, "Networks of Innovators: A Synthesis of Research Issues," *Research Policy* 20 (1991): 512. Cited in Koschatzky, "Innovation Networks of Industry and Business-Related Services."

18. C. DeBresson and F. Amesse, "Networks of Innovators: A Review and Introduction to the Issue," *Research Policy* 20 (1991): 364. Cited in Koschatzky, ibid.

19. Koschatzky, ibid.

20. Manuel Castells, *The Rise of the Network Society* (Oxford: Blackwell, 1996).

21. R. Chisholm, "On the Meaning of Networks," *Group and Organization Management* 21 (2:1996): 216–35; and C. Snow, R. Miles, and N. Coleman, "Managing 21st Century Network Organisations," *Organizational Dynamics* (Winter 1992): 5–19.

22. P. Aydalot, ed., *Milieux innovateurs en Europe* (Paris: GREMI, 1986); P. Aydalot

and D. Keeble, eds., *High Technology Industry and Innovative Environments: The European Experience* (London: Routledge, 1988); and Roberto Camagni, ed., *Innovation Networks: Spatial Perspectives* (London: Belhaven Press, 1991).

23. Camagni, *Innovation Networks*, p. 130.

24. Ibid., p. 127.

25. David Keeble et al., "Collective Learning Processes, Networking and 'Institutional Thickness' in the Cambridge Region" (paper presented at the 38th European Regional Science Association Congress, Vienna, 1998).

26. Camagni, *Innovation Networks*.

27. Keeble et al., "Collective Learning Processes."

28. Marshall et al., *Economics of Industry*.

29. W. Stöhr, "Regional Innovation Complexes," *Papers of the Regional Science Association* 59 (1986): 29–44.

30. Ibid., p. 42.

31. *Brockhaus Encyclopedia*; translation by this author.

32. W. Stöhr, ed., *Global Challenge and Local Response: Initiatives for Economic Regeneration in Contemporary Europe* (London: Mansell for United Nations University, 1990), p. 31 ff.

33. Gerhard Rosegger, "Globalization, Networks, and Regions" (paper presented at the 38th European Regional Science Association Congress, Vienna, 1998).

34. Angelo Rossi, "Micro-Regional and Macro-Regions: The Issue of the Adequate Institutional Setting in the Recent Debate on Swiss Regional Policy" (paper presented at the 38th European Regional Science Association Congress, Vienna, 1998).

35. H. Muegge and W. Stöhr, eds., *International Economic Restructuring and the Regional Community* (Aldershot: Gower, 1987).

36. G. Marks, I. Hooghe, and K. Blank, "European Integration from the 1980s: State-Centric versus Multi-Level Governance," *Journal of Common Market Studies* 3 (34: 1996): 341–78. Cited in H. Halkier, M. Danson, and C. Damborg, eds., *Regional Development Agencies in Europe* (London: Jessica Kingsley, 1998), p. 355.

37. Charles Sabel, "The Re-Emergence of Regional Economies" (1987) (mimeograph). Cited in Haynes et al., "Regional Governance and Economic Development."

38. Haynes et al., ibid.

39. P. McDonagh and P. Commins, "Governance and Institutional Innovation: The Need for Strategic Management." Paper presented at the 38th European Regional Science Association (Congress, Vienna, 1998).

40. Halkier, Danson, and Damborg, eds., *Regional Development Agencies in Europe*, p. 18.

41. Ibid.

42. Stöhr, *Global Challenge and Local Response*.

43. The concept of synergism was first used in chemistry and pharmaceutics, where it denotes that the "effect obtained from the combined action of two distinct chemical substances is greater than that obtained from their independent action added together." See *Encyclopedia Britannica* (1978), p. 740. In regional development, this concept would denote that not only the presence of specific agents and institutions within a region, but also their mutual dynamic interaction, is a prerequisite for optimizing regional creativity and innovation under conditions of structural instability.

44. Stöhr, "Regional Innovation Complexes."

45. Bengt Johannisson, "The Nordic Perspective: Self-Reliant Local Development in

Four Scandinavian Countries" in Stöhr, *Global Challenge and Local Response*, pp. 57–89.

46. A. Birner et al., *Lokale entwicklungs-initiativen—ein interkultureller vergleich: lebensstratgien und globaler struktureller wandel* (Frankfurt: Peter Lang Verlag, 1998). See English summary: "Local Development Initiatives—An Intercultural Comparison: Life Strategies and Global Structural Change" (Discussion Paper 51) (Vienna: Institute for Urban and Regional Studies, University of Economics and Business Administration, 1998).

47. John Friedmann, *Empowerment: The Politics of Alternative Development* (Cambridge, MA: Blackwell, 1992).

48. Halkier, Danson, and Damborg, *Regional Development Agencies in Europe*, p. 18.

49. G. Hennings and K. R. Kunzmann, "Priority to Local Economic Development: Industrial Restructuring and Local Development Responses in the Ruhr Area—The Case of Dortmund" in Stöhr, ed., *Global Challenge and Local Response*, pp. 199–223.

50. Halkier, Danson, and Damborg, *Regional Development Agencies in Europe*.

51. Denis Maillat, "Role of the Milieu in the Evolution of the Territorial Production System of Two Border Regions: The Case of the Watch Industry in the Swiss and French Jura Arc" (paper presented at the International Conference on Urban Development: The New Challenge of the Frontier, University of the Negev, Beer-Sheva, 1998).

52. P. Roberts, C. Collis, and D. Noon, "Local Economic Development in England and Wales: Successful Adaptation of Old Industrial Areas in Sedgefield, Nottingham and Swansea" in Stöhr, *Global Challenge and Local Response*.

53. H. Goldstein and M. Luger, *Technology in the Garden: Research Parks and Regional Economic Development* (Chapel Hill: University of North Carolina Press, 1991).

54. W. Stöhr, "Regional Policy, Technology Complexes and Research/Science Parks" in Maria Giaoutzi and Peter Nijkamp, eds., *Informatics and Regional Development* (Aldershot: Gower, 1988), pp. 201–14; and W. Stöhr and R. Pönighaus, "Towards a Database based Evaluation of the Japanese Technopolis Policy: The Effect of New Technological and Organisational Infrastructure on Urban and Regional Development," *Regional Studies* 26 (July: 1992): 605–18.

55. Camagni, *Innovation Networks*; and Roberta Capello, "Spatial Transfer of Knowledge in High-Tech Milieux: Learning vs. Collective Learning Processes" (paper presented at the 38th European Regional Science Association Congress, Vienna, 1998).

56. Capello, ibid, p. 14.

57. Ibid, p. 16.

58. Stöhr, "Regional Innovation Complexes."

59. Camagni, *Innovation Networks*.

60. Capello, "Spatial Transfer of Knowledge in High-Tech Milieux."

61. Keeble et al., "Collective Learning Processes."

62. Stöhr and Taylor, *Development from Above or Below?*

63. See also W. Stöhr, "Local Development Strategies to Meet Local Crisis," *Journal of Entrepreneurship and Regional Development* 1 (1989): 293–300. Spanish translation: *"Estrategias de desarrollo local para hacer frente a la crisis local," Revista Latinamericana de Estudios Urbano Regionales* 18 (May 1992): 5–11.

64. P. M. Romer, "Increasing Returns and Long-Run Growth," *Journal of Political Economy* 94 (1986): 1002–37. Cited in Feser, "Old and New Theories of Industry Clusters."

65. Stöhr, "Regional Innovation Complexes"; and Stöhr, *Global Challenge and Local Response*.

66. P. Nijkamp and W. Stöhr, eds., *Technology Policy* (Special issue of *Environment and Planning C: Government and Policy* 6 (Spring 1988); Stöhr, "Regional Innovation Complexes"; and Stöhr, "Regional Policy."

67. Organisation for Economic Co-operation and Development (OECD), "Best Practices Selected, Programme Leed and Their Partners" (http://www.oecd.org//tds/docsword/bestpracticesleed.doc).

68. *Der Standard* (Vienna, 1/2 August 1998).

69. *MUNICIPIA Newsletter* (2/1998) (www.municipia.at).

70. A. V. Ganesan, "Strategic Options Available to Developing Countries with Regard to a Multilateral Agreement on Investments" (Discussion paper no. 134) (Geneva: UNCTAD, 1998). Cited in Barry Coates, "Developmental Implications of the MAI: WDM Critique of the Fitzgerald Report to DFID" (London: World Development Movement, 1998).

71. Y. E. Amaizo, "Is ACP Economic Sovereignty Just 'Virtual Reality'?" *EU-ACP Courier* 169 (May–June 1998). Cited in Coates, ibid.

72. Coates, ibid.

73. Coates, ibid, p. 7.

74. Coates, ibid, p. 8.

REFERENCES

Higgins, B., "From Growth Poles to Systems of Interactions in Space," *Growth and Change* 14 (1983): 3–13.

Hirschman, A. O., *Exit, Voice and Loyalty: Responses to Decline in Firms, Organizations, and States* (Cambridge, MA: Harvard University Press, 1970).

4

From Sophisticated Plans to Daily Business in Regional Development Planning: Experiences of GTZ

Petra Stremplat-Platte

INTRODUCTION

The approach to Regional Rural Development (RRD) at Deutsche Gesellschaft für Technische Zusammenarbeit (GTZ)[1] promotes cross-sectoral development in regional development planning that incorporates support to programs and projects in the following areas:

a. Planning, coordination, and management;

b. Development and testing of appropriate innovations;

c. Development of an overriding planning process interlinking initiatives of the communities with expedient measures from above; and

d. Promoting key actors in the development process with particular emphasis on improving knowledge, skills, and exchange of information as part of human resource development in a region.

The spatial focus is on a given region, which may be a subdistrict, district, province, or any administrative or functional area at the subnational level.

Subject matter specialists in the different departments of GTZ, at the headquarters and in the field, are contributing to various aspects of regional development.

OBSOLETE AND ACTUAL APPROACH

Within the last decade, there has been fundamental change in the advisory approach of GTZ-supported projects and programs with a planning component.

Some years ago, technical assistance in the field of regional planning was concentrated on the production of master plan documents. The regional aspect was often treated as a technical issue in a centralized planning system and conceived in its essence by the planning departments of the relevant ministries. The perception of planning was mainly a very technical one, and there was the belief that the application of technical methods would solve regional development problems.

For some years, there were no projects with a special focus on planning. Planning was rather a component in the last RRD during one or more phases of a project or program. In recent years, the demand for regional planning is rising again due to the decentralization policies of several countries as well as the transformation process of some economies. The shift of competence and responsibility to different subnational levels of administration, however, is not always followed by corresponding budget allocation.

Today, the planning approach is process-oriented with an emphasis on the involvement of many actors at different levels. The daily business in regional development planning is characterized by planning as an ongoing activity that includes feedback from implementation, whenever possible. For this purpose, permanent structures are required. Hence, the change from implementation-oriented planning to advice-oriented planning must encompass the actors involved and their respective structural environments. Regional planners are no longer technocrats believing in the making of everything; now their competence is more and more in an advisory capacity for the decision-making process of politicians.

Regional development planning as part of the RRD strategy was further developed by the end of the 1980s as a concept promoting the development of a particular region. A critical factor was the emphasis on the spatial dimension of development. Regional development planning was based on principles that ensured sustained economic, social, and ecological development of a given subnational area. Strategy guidelines were developed that were critically dependent on decentralized arrangements. Although classical master planning is still requested by some partner countries, for the time being, the option is to provide advice in line with the actual approach.

THE KEY ELEMENTS OF THE ACTUAL APPROACH

Participatory Approach for Sustainable Development

The target groups were rather passive subjects but active participants in the earlier planning approach. The result of this way of thinking was that many of the established objectives were never met or accepted by the target groups. Planning, nowadays, is a process in which the target population must participate actively. Planning has gradually become a process of dialog between the various participants.

Several constraints have been observed. For example, it does not make sense to apply sophisticated participatory tools at the village level to generate a bottom-up planning process if the structures at district or regional levels are missing to adequately harness those proposals coming from the local level. If there is no political will to give feedback to local-level proposals or even consider a prioritization among these, most local target groups will refrain from an active role in regional development planning very quickly. Experience in some projects has shown that only a few rules and regulations of the planning process are relevant to an individual and therefore, do not demand the participation of all citizens for each and every planning aspect. To encourage equivalent participatory processes at the subdistrict or regional level remains a challenge for many project teams.

Regional development planners should be professional in facilitating the participation of groups and individuals in innovative processes. The importance of involving local and regional stakeholders in regional development has been underestimated in project design for many years.

Process-oriented Planning

With the earlier approach in a master plan project, a team of experts elaborated comprehensive documents and after the master plan was accepted, implementation followed. For the next planning period, the same procedure was followed in preparing a new master plan. The direction in planning was mainly top-down. As a consequence, all actors involved made the upper levels responsible for all the problems they faced.

In contrast to the earlier classical master planning, the actual approach in regional development planning is based on step-by-step progress and relies on planning as an ongoing activity, which involves all actors in the concerned region. All planning activities need to be tailored to the unique problems of the regions and their population.

The process orientation is often designed to start at the local level and to involve subsequently different levels (public and private stakeholders, municipalities, nongovernmental organizations [NGOs], and local government units [LGUs]) at an early stage of planning. To bring all these levels together from time to time, even if they are not very eager to cooperate, leads to a common understanding of regional development planning and forms a solid basis for the implementation of planned and agreed upon action (see Figure 4.1). During implementation, the updating of the planning document should be envisaged in order to enhance a smooth revision based on monitoring and evaluation of the actual implementation phase.

A critical aspect of the actual approach is that it is a time-consuming procedure and probably the identified core problems or bottlenecks in the development of a region may change before the envisaged measures become operational. The loss of manipulative power for some local or regional elites and the lack of

Figure 4.1
The Key Elements of the Actual Approach

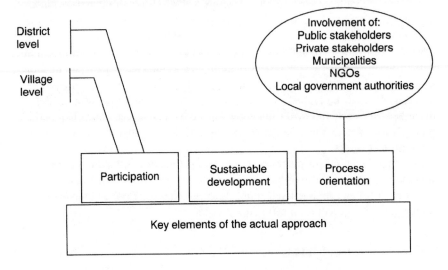

forecasted possibilities of how the process will develop may become a constraint in the planning process as well.

TOOLS AND PROCEDURES

The following discussion focuses on some of the different tools and procedures applied in a planning process.

Land-Use Planning

One of the major tools in participatory planning applied at the local level in GTZ-supported projects is land-use planning. Experience shows that there is a tremendous advantage in starting a process in a small community and showing results within an adequate time horizon. Many projects started with village-level land-use planning but acquired considerable experience with different issues as well by applying the whole range of participatory rural appraisal (PRA) techniques such as village surveying and mapping, seasonal analysis, demarcation of village boundaries, transect walks, wealth ranking, Venn diagramming, workshops, identification of key actors, and gender analysis. This has become a standard tool in GTZ-supported regional development projects. The projects faced some constraints in the planning process. Sometimes, village people were diffident in moving on from appraisal to participatory planning. This is partly due to the lack of an appropriate method, as PRA techniques are mainly geared toward appraisal and provide little assistance in planning. Although officials accept participatory concepts during training courses, once they return to their offices, they revert to their previous styles and behavior. The changes required to realize participatory planning are fundamental. Sufficient time and resources must be provided in order to give the approach a fair chance to survive the early stages of planning.

Recently, there has been a shift from community-based land-use planning to collaborative land-use planning. This means that considerable effort is needed to integrate the local and regional stakeholders' different objectives into the land-use planning process. Examples are those who would rather see exploitation of a forest than sustainable management as the main objective. This has been applied with success in some project areas of the Mekong River Commission Support Programme.[2]

Geographic Information Systems

The application of geographic information systems (GISs) is increasingly acknowledged in regional development planning. However, the introduction of an innovative application can only be effective if it becomes an integral part of the structure and working procedures. Apart from GISs, typical problems are data availability, data standards, and transformation into useful information. GISs have an impact on work patterns, management of information, and staff roles in the planning process. A major concern often mentioned by projects is the reluctance of GIS staff in providing services to other departments or organizations involved in planning, that is, a lack of service orientation in order to maintain their unique role in data access and processing.

Business Promotion

An example of GIS application and service orientation is in the field of business promotion in Sri Lanka.[3] In order to channel technical, marketing, and financial support to small and medium enterprises (SMEs), a business service-providing entity has been set up within the regional information system of the provincial planning unit in the Central Province. It is a joint venture between the Provincial Ministry of Industries, the regional banks, and the local Chamber of Commerce. The benefits of the private sector having access to the GIS database and maps are manifold. Enterprises can base their marketing plans on an improved database, which provides data indicating the spatial distribution of family income and purchasing power, transport facilities, and other communication infrastructure. They can locate potential customers, site businesses, target marketing campaigns, optimize sales territories, and model distribution systems. A state-owned bank operating a dense network of branch offices in the province required a GIS to identify overlapping and nonserviced areas, provide socioeconomic data for individual branch service areas, and visualize area maps to evaluate customers' potentials better. The results revealed that the nonserviced area was greater than expected, the percentage of unreached customers was high due to the lack of proper service area delimitation, and there was substantial overlap of branch areas. Since then, the bank management has initiated a reorganization of the branch service areas, which has immediately shown positive effects in enterprise promotion in the region.[4]

Communicative Planning

Participatory techniques can be used to moderate conflicts. For example, if a decision about using land for agriculture or tourism has to be made, joint trekking and mapping by local people and planners can create the beginning of a sustainable planning process. Planners have to be prepared to moderate a meeting, listen, and be able to reconcile their different interests. Sometimes the planning team plays a role in conflict resolution in order to maintain the involvement of all the actors in regional development in the planning process. Mediation between sectoral and political levels can be achieved through regional conferences and roundtable meetings. There is evidence that the subsequent steps of initiating the process, coordination, moderation, and mediation including proper problem-solving proposals are helpful in the elaboration of plans as well as in the implementation phase.

Human Resource Development

Human resource development requires continuous support by training, advisory services, and strengthening independent responsibility (such as ownership of the planning process). The GTZ-supported Decentralized Development Planning Unit of South Africa in Pretoria identified best-practice planning methods that can be undertaken by local authorities.[5] Training is, for example, not exclusively directed toward planning institutions but includes related sectoral staff from other public and private institutions that are (or should become) engaged in the regional development process.

Capacity-Building Support at the Subnational Level

The role and responsibilities of planners and their advisors have changed as well. Many partner countries follow a strict top-down planning procedure. The planning organizations are fairly large and hierarchically organized, and their institutional culture is based on traditions. They are often resistant to change. There is a danger that the transition to more participatory approaches is merely following a fashion and in practice, little may have changed. In addition, there is pressure to achieve targets from different sides—from planners as well as implementing institutions and politicians. However, participatory planning can only be carried out with a significant shift in many areas including role reversal and this will take a long time. It should be made clear to all decision-makers that participatory planning is a time-consuming process and not a blueprint approach applicable at any time, anywhere.

In order to support decentralized decision-making and strengthen local and regional capabilities, the approach involves LGUs (as coordinators), NGOs, self-help organizations, the private sector (as technical support to implementation), and local communities as initiators and owners of the process.

Support to a regional planning project in Eastern Cape, South Africa, for example, has shown that capacity-building must ensure that:

a. Implementing institutions in the province are familiar with strategies and methods for self-help promotion, needs orientation, and gender-specific planning;

b. Communities apply participatory planning methods for developing local-level structures under the guidance of facilitators from the government, NGOs, and community-based organizations (CBOs);

c. Selection procedures will be drawn up for assistance measures at the local authority and local infrastructure level;

d. Participatory planning methods will be incorporated as a regional development planning tool; and

e. The role that regional and local NGOs and CBOs play in the planning process as facilitators between communities and responsible government authorities must be recognized and institutionalized.[6]

Ideally, all these tools and procedures contribute to alleviate urgent problems and to achieve the long-term objective of regional development.

THE FRAMEWORK

Political-administrative frame conditions affecting regional development differ considerably among GTZ-partner countries. A variety of interventions aimed at frame conditions has been developed by a network of regional development projects supported by GTZ. These interventions have a common goal of contributing to necessary changes in the frame conditions with an anticipated enhancement of the results of the planning process. Some interventions are as follows:

a. Marketing of field successes at the decision-making level;

b. Support for policy formulation or formulation of regulations;

c. Exposure of decision-makers to field successes and field conditions;

d. Providing forums for exchanges between regional and national (or central-level) actors;

e. Assisting the national level in monitoring, evaluation, and benchmark setting;

f. Assisting in the formulation of government pilot projects;

g. Linking regions to form associations to give greater voice to reforms;

Figure 4.2
Interrelationships between the People and the Local and Central Governments

h. Linking local actors directly with international bodies to give greater voice and support; and

i. Training policymakers in participatory policy development.

Tested in the Indonesian context, a framework has been developed by the Support for Decentralization Measures Project in Jakarta (see Figure 4.2). In the planning process, interrelationships between the people and the local and central governments are analyzed.

The involvement of the central government in the planning process at the regional level is a prerequisite for sustainability in regional development. At present, it is only rarely possible for the subnational governments to implement plans with their own resources. In many GTZ-partner countries, at the subnational level, funds are insufficient and official procedures allowing access to public funds are ill-defined. Within the regional development process, it is essential to carefully examine the type of planning and the skills required at each level in order to avoid a mismatch between the two.

Another important frame issue is the extent to which economic objectives dominate ecological objectives.

Incentives that guide individual behavior are often inconsistent with the overall system goals. Those directly concerned are the most important actors in sustainable regional development. They are the only ones who can make real choices concerning the direction of development planning. Their concerns must be taken into consideration for both ecological and economic reasons. This means that ecologically important measures must also be economically feasible and economic targets must be ecologically compatible. A dialog orientation in planning with all the actors involved gives sustainable development a chance to meet both economic requirements and ecological necessities in the process of making local and short-term goals and incentives consistent with regional, national, and long-term goals.

Land tenure and property regimes increasingly play an important role in the sustainability of regional development planning measures. Thus participation, certainty of law, and access to resources are of major importance in the formulation of regional development policies.[7] The Bondoc Development Project in the Philippines aims to speed up the land reform process in close cooperation with the Department for Agrarian Reform (DAR) and the facilitation of regular consultation between the involved public organizations, NGOs, and governmental organizations (GOs). The project continues to provide legal advice free of charge on property rights and tenancy problems as well as legal assistance to agrarian reform beneficiaries in cases of harassment of people and violation of the law by the landlords. After years of disappointing performance, the land reform program has accelerated, despite the difficult frame conditions and strong resistance by influential landlords.[8]

SUMMARY

In regional development planning, GTZ promoted a change from a technocratic orientation to a process orientation.

The role of technical assistance experts has changed as well. The role of an expatriate team fulfilling a task for (or instead of) a national planning institution is shifting to an advisory function by an expert working with a national team of planners at different levels, ranging from local target groups to the cabinet.

Supported projects are oriented toward the impact of regional development planning measures derived from a participatory planning process.

The Swiss writer Max Frisch in 1953[9] had the vision that freedom in the world could be saved only by planning for the future. That was an untimely modern view of planning as a task of innovative experts. Although there is much practical evidence of the failure of plans and planners in the past, planning stands for the option to influence the development of the spatial environment in a desirable direction. To deny this, being aware of all the urban and rural problems we face, would be a rather cynical option.

NOTES

1. GTZ acts as an executing agency for the German Federal Ministry for Economic Cooperation and Development. Being organized as a private firm, GTZ is mainly contracted by this ministry, but is working for other donors as well, such as the Asian Development Bank (ADB), World Bank, United Nations High Commission for Refugees

(UNHCR), and other German ministries. In partner countries, GTZ supports bilateral programs and projects in the fields of design, implementation, and evaluation. GTZ is not a donor and the contributions are mainly in kind in the form of advice as well as equipment for counterpart organizations or institutions.

2. Mekong River Commission/GTZ, "Mekong Info" (Hanoi, 1998).

3. GTZ, "Experiences of Land Use Planning in Asian Projects—Colombo, Sri Lanka" (Colombo, 1996).

4. Regional Rural Development Project, R. Riethmueller, and GTZ, "Development and Utilization of a Spatial Information System in the Central Province of Sri Lanka" (Kandy, 1998).

5. Decentralized Development Planning Unit, GTZ, "Training the Trainers" (Pretoria, 1998).

6. Department of Housing and Local Government, Eastern Cape, GTZ et al., eds., *Planning Handbook for Eastern Cape Local Authorities* (Bisho, 1997).

7. GTZ, *Land Tenure in Development Cooperation—Guiding Principles* (Wiesbaden, 1998).

8. Bondoc Development Program, GTZ, "Reports—Catanauan, Philippines" (Catanauan, 1998).

9. Max Frisch, *Bund schweizer architekten* (Vortrag: Zürich, 1953).

REFERENCE

Support for Decentralization Measures, Ministry of Home Affairs, and GTZ, eds., *A Tool for Analysing Political-Administrative Frame Conditions for Development Co-operation* (Jakarta, 1998).

5

Governance and Sustainable Regional Development: The CIDA-IOG Canada-ASEAN Governance Innovations Network Program

Kathleen Lauder and Joaquin L. Gonzalez III

Around the world, governance, or "the way in which power is exercised, decisions are made, and citizens have their say," is in a state of transition. Governments, businesses, organizations of civil society, academics, the media, and private citizens are asking difficult questions about the nature and impact of this transition. Some believe that sustainable development can only occur with a vibrant, vocal, and engaged civil society. Others argue that business is the engine of economic growth and prosperity and that the regulatory and policy environment must be supportive of business with minimal government interference. Some feel that a strong government is critical to peace, security, and prosperity and must maintain ultimate power and the responsibility for public policy, programs, and services, even if this means checking the power of civil society and the market.

There are no models of effective governance in either the west or the east, the north or the south that are universally respected. The way in which a society, nation, or region exercises power and makes decisions must be decided within the community and in response to its social, cultural, political, and economic context.

However, sharing experiences on governance can be useful when governance is seen in the context of practical community issues and community processes and mechanisms that are used to address those issues.

THE CANADA-ASEAN GOVERNANCE INNOVATIONS
NETWORK (CAGIN) PROGRAM: SIX GOVERNANCE PILOT
INNOVATION PROJECTS

The CAGIN Program, funded by the Canadian International Development Agency (CIDA) and managed by the Institute on Governance (IOG), provides an opportunity to learn from six pilot projects in four Association of Southeast Asian Nations (ASEAN). Each pilot project involves the creation of a new process and mechanism through which government, civil society, and business share power and make decisions in new ways. For each of these pilot projects, local action researchers are collecting information to shed light on new ways of sharing power and engaging more stakeholders in decision-making.

This chapter describes the CAGIN participatory action research project and discusses preliminary findings.

DEFINITION OF GOVERNANCE

For purposes of the CAGIN Program, "governance encompasses the traditions, institutions, and processes which define how power is exercised; how important decisions are made; and how citizens have their say. With effective governance, the public sector, the private sector, and civil society work together as partners in building a stronger economy and a better society. Qualities of effective governance include: efficiency, integrity, equity, transparency, accountability, predictability, and participation." CAGIN emphasizes promoting a strong partnership between government, civil society, and business.

CAGIN PARTICIPATORY ACTION RESEARCH
FRAMEWORK

The primary purpose of the CAGIN participatory action research is to develop insights and understanding on governance, that is, on how power is shared, important decisions are made, and different people are accorded a voice in decision-making. It also seeks to understand how effective partnerships are developed among key stakeholders such as the public sector, the private sector, and civil society.

The process of developing effective partnerships is understood by attempting to answer the following questions:

First, *what is the nature and structure of the governance mechanism or process being piloted?* Each of the six pilot innovation projects involves the development of a new governance process or mechanism with new ways of power sharing between the state and society. The structure, function, and operation of the mechanism, and the development of the partnership are analyzed.

Second, *how are attitudes changed and knowledge developed?* The CAGIN team considered that the first step in enhancing the effectiveness of the governance partnership is ensuring that individuals in the community develop the attitude that they are important players in governance and are responsible for the quality of life in their communities. Associated with the development of this attitude is the acquisition of knowledge regarding how to most effectively input into the governance process and how to effect desired changes in public programs and services. Therefore, the CAGIN team considered it important to study the dynamics of attitudinal change and the development of knowledge in the pilot projects.

Third, *how are networks developed to address governance issues?* An individual with a sense of responsibility for his/her community is not likely to attain much power by himself or herself. On the other hand, a group of people, organized or *networked* around a particular issue, can influence decisions and plans. Therefore, this participatory action research studies the development, activities, and impact of various networks involved in the pilot projects.

Fourth, *how are "change agents" developed and nurtured?* For networks to be effective in influencing policy, they must have champions, who may be leaders such as presidents, chairmen, and directors of groups or organizations, or ordinary members of the group whose commitment to the objectives and whose reputation is such that they are powerful agents of change. Because of their critical role, the participatory action research studies how change agents are identified, their characteristics, and means to support and nurture them through the project implementation process.

Fifth, *what is the impact of the governance mechanism on some practical aspects of development?* Governance is a process, mechanism, or tradition that impacts on public policies and programs. For the governance partnership to be sustained, it must lead to practical improvements in the community. Therefore, the participatory action research seeks to identify and quantify the impact of the governance process or mechanism on some practical issues in the community such as waste management, development of laws, and generation of income.

The CAGIN Program studies these questions through a variety of participatory action research methodologies guided by a coordinator and implemented, in each pilot project, by a local action researcher. A team of international research advisors provides overall direction to the research. Participatory action research methodologies include:

- Participant observation;
- Structured interviews with stakeholders;
- Questionnaires and surveys completed by participants who are involved in various aspects of the process;
- Focus groups with stakeholders;
- Stories depicting events and people involved in the process; and
- Collection of quantitative data such as number of people involved by gender and sector.

DESCRIPTION OF PILOT PROJECTS

CAGIN pilot projects were selected based on a call for proposals, reviews of proposals against criteria, and approval of the most successful proposals by an advisory committee of public and private sector practitioners in ASEAN. All proposals were submitted by the community itself, based on specific issues identified within the community.

In order to be selected as a CAGIN pilot innovation project, proposals must show evidence of:

- *Leadership.* The project must be undertaken under the leadership of key individuals and organizations who are in a position to effectively implement the proposed project;
- *Partnership.* The project must aim to develop a process or mechanism that will support government, citizens, and/or business to more effectively work together to address a particular problem or challenge in the community; and
- *Relevance.* The proposal must address a clearly articulated problem or issue in the community.

Other criteria used in the selection of pilot projects include the following:

- *Impact.* The proposed process or mechanisms will develop government, citizen, and/ or business partnerships that will become self-sustaining and are likely to have a measurable impact on addressing the defined problem within a two-year period;
- *Management.* Competent project management resources must be available within the proposing organization(s);
- *Work plan.* The proposal must include a detailed work plan that outlines a timeline or schedule and roles and responsibilities of each partner in the project;
- *Resources.* The project proposal must demonstrate that it can be implemented within the budget available and must include some resource commitment from sources other than CAGIN (such resources could be in kind, e.g., services provided by members of the community, government officials, or academics);
- *Evaluation of results.* The proposal must include a viable approach for measuring the results and impact of the project; and
- *Adaptability.* Proposals that are able to contribute to solving similar problems in other jurisdictions are especially encouraged.

CAGIN offered funding for successful proposals of up to US$70,000 as well as linkages with other relevant organizations and individuals, international exposure, and the opportunity to be a part of a participatory action research process aimed at learning from their experience.

The appendix provides a summary of the six CAGIN pilot projects, which are listed below:

1. Tambol Civil Society Participatory Local Governance Project, Thailand;
2. Eco-Walk: Environmental Awareness Program for Children in Baguio City, Philippines;
3. Vietnam Business Council (VBC);
4. Multi-Stakeholder Strategic Planning and Implementation of Solid Waste Management in Guimaras, Philippines;
5. Sustainable Penang Initiative (SPI), Malaysia; and
6. Democratic Planning: Civic Assemblies in Khon Kaen, Thailand.

LESSONS LEARNED

Some preliminary findings of the participatory action research are highlighted in this section.

What Is the Nature and Structure of the Governance Mechanism or Process that Is Being Piloted?

The CAGIN projects have demonstrated that one of the most critical features of effective governance processes or mechanisms is that they are clearly *developed around a specific, critical issue in the community*. The issue itself helps to galvanize the group and suggests how they should organize to address specific subissues. For example, the SPI is organized around five overall themes: cultural vibrancy, social justice, ecological sustainability, economic productivity, and popular participation. For each of these, a number of subgroups have been formed. Within social justice, separate groups have been formed to address specific topics including health care, workers, disabled persons, family, social services, education, housing, public amenities, governance, and civil society. Because of the participants' personal interest and knowledge of the issues, they are motivated and effective at producing results. For example, the Sustainable Independence Livelihood Access (SILA) group managed to get the Botanical Gardens in Penang retrofitted for disabled persons.

The CAGIN projects have also demonstrated that there must be *committed membership* in the process or mechanism for it to be effective. Participants are not passive actors but critical stakeholders in ensuring that the initiative meets its objectives. For example, in the Eco-Walk Project in Baguio City, the committed members forming the core group include the bishop, the mayor, and other representatives from government, business, and civil society. All of these people are committed personally to saving the watershed and are highly motivated by the opportunity provided by the project to develop in children a stronger awareness of the environment and the need to protect it.

Moreover, in order to have committed membership, participants *must have the time required*. Almost all of the participants in the CAGIN projects are participating in a volunteer capacity, which is hard to sustain when there are so many other demands on volunteers' time. Projects that were most successful were those that had some paid staff, or where participants saw their involvement in the project as relevant to their jobs or immediate needs. For example, members of the VBC recognize that an important part of their job is to participate actively in the reform of laws and they see the VBC as a means through which they can do this more effectively and efficiently.

All of the projects demonstrate the critical importance of creating a *venue for frank, open, and constructive dialog and deliberations.* If participants sense that they cannot speak openly, that other participants are pushing their own agenda rather than that of the group, or that the meetings are dominated by vested interest groups, the power of the process will be dissipated. In Guimaras, for example, special attention is paid to ensuring that the dynamics of the meetings are participatory, that all views are heard, and that every speaker is respected. Questionnaires completed after each meeting provide feedback on the extent to which participants felt they were able to participate openly and freely.

In short, for the partnership to be effective, the process or mechanism must galvanize participants around issues of personal importance to them and allow an opportunity for equal and committed involvement by a variety of stakeholders.

How Are Attitudes Changed and Knowledge Developed?

Citizens *wish to have a voice in the shaping of their community.* This is seen in the quantity and quality of participation in the CAGIN projects, and the fact that the majority of the participants participate without remuneration, and in addition to their work and family responsibilities. A preliminary estimate indicates that more than 3,000 volunteers have been involved in the six projects.

The projects have also revealed a number of barriers to participation. There is a value in Asian cultures, which encourages loyalty, respect, and obedience to elders and "leaders." In addition, very often the education and training of government officials is perceived to be more relevant to the development of public policies and programs than is that of the majority of the citizens.

The projects have explored how representatives of civil society, including marginalized groups and villagers, can be encouraged to assume responsibility for public policies and programs and how government officials can learn to value the input of citizens. This has been addressed quite effectively in all the projects by *creating an environment and a culture for dialog that is seen as constructive* by representatives of both state and society. The roundtables in Penang actively seek ideas from both state and society on topics on which citizens have a lot to contribute such as social justice and cultural vibrancy. Both the Khon Kaen Civic Assembly and the Tambol Administrative Organization (TAO) projects in Thailand involve the conduct of "town hall"–type meetings that bring people together to discuss practical issues in their community such as transportation and income generation. The discussions are structured so that all participants feel that they have something useful to offer on the topic.

The projects have also revealed that even if you can create an environment where all stakeholders feel that they have a role and responsibility in the process, there are some stakeholders who simply lack the knowledge and experience of the subject area or of the process of decision-making, to provide effective inputs. The projects have shown that this lack of knowledge can be at least partially addressed by *learning from successful experiences elsewhere.* The SPI began with a seminar on a related experience called Sustainable Seattle. The VBC started by inviting speakers from Singapore, Malaysia, and Canada to speak about similar councils in those countries. The core group creating the Khon Kaen Civic Assembly traveled to the Philippines to study decentralized governance mechanisms there before developing a strategy for their civic assembly. The study tour exposed them to the actual workings of the Local Government Code of 1991. This was a useful input for Thailand in revising its constitution. These experiences provided useful and practical ideas on how to develop and implement the mechanism. They also provided motivation by demonstrating the positive practical impact of the mechanism.

How Are Networks Developed to Address Governance Issues?

All the CAGIN pilot projects involved the development of various groups with specific roles and responsibilities related to the overall objectives of the project. Moreover, all these projects involved the development of a core group or a steering committee, which essentially steered the project. They also had a working group, which sometimes involved paid staff to undertake specific tasks. Many of the projects involved the development of subgroups and often sub-subgroups around particular themes and issues in the project. For example, in the Sustainable Penang Initiative there were five roundtables. For each roundtable, an average of ten groups were developing indicators on specific aspects. These networks, or groups, are critical in getting things done in the project and ensuring sustainability of the initiative.

What makes the new networks effective? One of the key components of effective networks is that they *involve representatives from government, business, and civil society.* In Guimaras, for example, the Municipal Implementation Task Forces draw their strength from the fact that they include not only government, which has the formal authority for waste management, but also citizens and businesses that can identify issues and participate directly in implementation.

The CAGIN experience indicates that *informal networks* are very important in making the new governance mechanism effective. In Penang, for example, the main drivers of the SPI are a group of people with shared interests in sustainable development, preservation of the cultural and environmental heritage, equity, and participation. These people meet frequently at various events and gatherings. They have participated in many of the same activities and programs in Penang over the past years. They have a common language, understanding, and values. They also trust and respect each other. This makes it very easy to move the project forward.

How Are Change Agents Developed and Nurtured?

Perhaps one of the most important factors in the successful pilot projects was the emergence of change agents who could motivate people around them, set direction, and involve their team in producing results.

The CAGIN experience indicates that change agents can emerge from unlikely places. They are *often ordinary citizens* who have not had a long experience in community work, nor do they necessarily assume leadership roles in their families or workplaces. For example, the leader of the group representing the disabled in Penang had no previous experience in a leadership role. Similarly, the person who took the lead in organizing the night market in Khon Kaen is a bank employee who had no previous involvement in civic activities.

Common characteristics of these new change agents are their *commitment to address a specific issue, their belief in the importance of the issue, and the trust and confidence with which their group regards them.*

The CAGIN project has also shown that change agents can often *come from marginalized groups.* In Baguio City, important change agents are the children involved in the eco-walks. The children learn about the importance of the environment in general and the importance of trees to their water supply. They use this knowledge to raise the awareness of their families and to inspire them to get involved in environmental management. In the TAO project in Thailand many of the village activities are organized and run by women's groups. These children and women are discovering new power to mobilize others and change power behavior, which may have always been present but which is mobilized through the new governance mechanisms and processes supported in the CAGIN project.

All participants in the project are, to some extent, change agents. The mechanism or process provides an opportunity to harness and direct their energies. To stimulate change agents, the CAGIN projects have shown that *incentives are important.* These can take the form of recognition, salary, and skills training. Stimulating change agents requires a lot of capacity development, helping them to learn to resolve problems rather than just complain about them. In Penang, a ten-day training program has been mounted for the group representing the disabled, to teach them facilitation and leadership skills.

What Is the Impact of the Governance Mechanism on Some Practical Aspects of Development?

The CAGIN pilot projects have shown that for the new governance mechanism to be sustained and the government-citizen-business partnership to be strengthened, it is important to be able to point to practical and useful impacts of the mechanism.

In some cases, it is too early to assess the impact of the new governance process or mechanism on development. There are some exceptions however. The VBC will lead to less bureaucracy and red tape for entrepreneurs. The council has also increased the level of predictability of policymaking. In Guimaras, the project has had a strong impact on improving coordination in the public service. In Penang, some physical improvements that have actually been made, for example, have increased access to certain areas for people with physical disabilities. In Baguio City, the core group is already taking steps to expand its environmental activities beyond the Busol watershed. This is an indicator of the impact of the project on sustainable development. Environmental issues have been incorporated into the government agenda, particularly in the area of education. These practical and concrete results are critical in motivating and reinforcing the transition of power and the strengthening of partnerships.

Each of these "successes" resulting from the governance mechanism is a reward and an incentive to the new partnerships to continue their work together.

IMPLICATIONS FOR POLICYMAKERS AND PRACTITIONERS

The implementation of the CAGIN Program has taught a number of lessons about building capacity to govern that may be of interest to practitioners or donors seeking to enhance governance effectiveness. These are summarized below.

Governance in the Context of Development

The experience of the CAGIN Program indicates that an effective way of connecting with local partners, building commitment, and attracting resources to address governance is by working on governance in the context of a specific, practical development issue that is a priority for local partners. Partnerships among government, business, and civil society are more readily developed in response to common issues that are a priority in that community, such as waste management, job creation, and cultural vibrancy.

The importance of the issue brings various stakeholders together and suggests the need for a particular governance process or mechanism. The motivation of the group to address the issue results in effective partnerships and encourages the development of processes and mechanisms that demonstrate qualities of effective governance such as accountability, transparency, participation, and equity.

Facilitator—Not Implementer

The role of the facilitator in governance programming is a particularly sensitive one. The facilitator should see him/herself as a catalyst for processes that are essentially locally driven. Changes in governance must come from within the community. The facilitator must let the partner do the leading. He/she should be prepared to work with multiple stakeholders and have the requisite skills.

Participatory Action Researcher and Communicator

One of the most powerful motivators for change in the area of governance is viewing the positive experience of others. Examples of experiences in which new governance processes or mechanisms have resulted in practical improvements in communities can play an important role in facilitating change. A useful role for the facilitator therefore, is in reflection, documentation, and dissemination of information and experience on governance.

CONCLUSION

Around the developing world, questions are being raised by civil society, business, and government about how they can most effectively share power, develop public programs and services that are sustainable, and provide an effective process for hearing the voice of all stakeholders. Arguments are being made that where there is accountability, transparency, equity, and participation there will be stronger and more sustainable development.

The CAGIN Program is based on a belief that governance is important for development. Those who share that belief and who want to learn how they might enhance the effectiveness of governance in their communities might find the results of the CAGIN participatory action research useful.

Highlights of the findings are as follows:

- Governance comes from within and governance initiatives must be driven and implemented by community members;
- People in all walks of life generally want to have a voice in decisions affecting their lives. However, in some cultures and traditions, strong value is placed on respect, honor, and loyalty for official leaders. This can be an impediment for citizens with views different from those of government. Moreover, many citizens, especially those in villages, have not been trained or educated in the process and knowledge related to the development and implementation of public plans, policies, or laws. The CAGIN pilot projects have demonstrated that changing attitudes of citizens, especially marginalized groups, so that they see themselves as partners with government and important stakeholders in the planning of their communities, takes time and effort. Moreover, for citizens to be effective in the process they must climb a steep learning curve. Processes that support changing of attitudes and development of relevant knowledge are more likely to result in more effective partnerships among state and society stakeholders;
- Similarly, in many of the communities in which the CAGIN projects have been implemented, there is a long tradition of government seeing itself as the decision-maker. It has the training, knowledge, and experience to weigh alternatives and to develop and implement public policies and programs. In many cases, it also has the mandate

and accountability for public programs and services. It may not, therefore, be easy for government to seek the views of citizens and to carefully consider their input;

- Governance is relevant and meaningful only in the context of real and practical issues and priorities such as waste management, development of new laws on trade, and water supply in a community; the more clearly those issues can be defined, the more likely they are to galvanize multiple stakeholders toward action;

- Effective partnerships can only be developed in an environment of trust and respect, where open and frank dialog is encouraged and where there is no suspicion that certain members of the group have vested interests. This environment can be best created by ensuring that leaders are trusted, that the venue for meetings is neutral, and that the facilitators of the process are skilled in identifying and addressing problems as they arise and ensuring that everyone has an equal opportunity to express himself;

- Informal networks involving people with shared interests and values and who are already associated through other activities are often just as important as the formal structures within new governance processes and mechanisms. These informal networks play a key role in setting direction, solving problems, and achieving meaningful impacts. One of the strengths of these informal networks is often in the inherent trust and respect that exists among the members;

- Development of effective government-citizen partnership depends on the development of a new kind of change agent: one who can effectively motivate and guide groups toward specific goals. These change agents may come from formerly marginalized groups such as the socially challenged and women. Even children can be powerful agents of change. These change agents can be supported through incentives such as recognition, salary, and skills training; and

- An important factor in the sustainability of new governance mechanisms or processes that are based on a government-citizen-business partnership is the achievement, by the new partnership, of practical results or impacts such as increased income generation, improved waste management, and improved environmental management.

APPENDIX: SUMMARY OF SIX CAGIN PILOT INNOVATION PROJECTS

Democratic Planning: Civic Assemblies in Khon Kaen, Thailand

The broad objective of the pilot project is to strengthen the capacity of the newly created Khon Kaen Civic Assembly (KKCA), the Northeast's experiment with democratic planning. Led by Khon Kaen University's Institute for Dispute Resolution, the specific objectives are to:

- Develop an agreed-upon vision, mandate, structure, and mode of operating of the KKCA;

- Expose KKCA to multistakeholder consensus-building processes in other jurisdictions;

- Experiment with a process of multistakeholder consensus building on a specific issue in Khon Kaen and assess its effectiveness in terms of both process and result; and

• Channel the results of the consensus process to determined authorities for the purpose of influencing the planning process.

The pilot project was designed to evolve iteratively. Since launching the KKCA at the August 1997 Khon Kaen Vision 2550 Workshop, the KKCA has organized regular monthly meetings on different policy and community issues, as well as supported several activities. Meetings have been held on issues such as waste management, urban transportation, and the new constitution.

A study tour of the Philippines exposed the group to other models of multistakeholder consultation and consensus building. KKCA's biggest highlight in recent months was the KKCA Weekend Market. Approximately 3,000 people attended this first-time event that created a direct link between rural producers and provincial consumers. The weekend market became a symbol of the presence of the KKCA, and the ability of the government and the KKCA to work together. Thus far, however, the KKCA has been unsuccessful at transferring responsibility for organizing the weekend market to the government.

The KKCA continues to define and strengthen its mandate as a mechanism for multistakeholder participatory planning and action on provincial development issues. Although there is wide agreement on the KKCA as a mechanism for strengthening people's participation, how to reach this vision is still being defined. In particular, there is a question of whether the KKCA should be a functional body or purely an advisory one. The latest consensus is that the KKCA should be a provincial forum that concentrates on drawing in marginal voices. The project will close with a workshop for collective reflection on the experiment, the dissemination of research products including a case study and a "how-to" guide for setting up a Civic Assembly, and a pilot training workshop.

Eco-Walk: Environmental Awareness Program for Children in Baguio City, Philippines

The Eco-Walk pilot project is the culmination of an innovative partnership between the Baguio Regreening Movement (BRM), a local environmental nongovernmental organization (NGO), and the City Mayor's Office. The Department of Environment is also a critical player, as are several other government agencies and civic groups. The major actors in the project are thousands of Baguio's schoolchildren, with support and guidance from teachers, NGOs, foresters, and other volunteers. The project promotes regular and organized walks by schoolchildren in the forest areas to explore, plan, and tend seedlings under the guidance of forestry volunteers and personnel. Aside from being a watershed rehabilitation program, it was designed to address the need for children to be exposed to and to help rehabilitate the environment they will inherit. Value formation, with the forest as an open classroom, is a critical part of the project.

Before CIDA-IOG-CAGIN arrived on the scene, the Eco-Walk project had already been pilot tested in the Busol watershed with much success. The objectives of the pilot project are to expand the activities by:

• Continuing to promote regular and organized walks by schoolchildren;
• Strengthening the institutional capacity of the BRM and its partners in effectively managing the project through participatory workshops, training seminars, and membership recruitment;

- Disseminating information to more children, parents, visitors, and local officials;
- Sharing lessons and benefits of this successful pilot project with the seven other watersheds in the Baguio City area as well as other cities (both in the Philippines and elsewhere in the ASEAN) that are experiencing the same problems as Baguio;
- Institutionalizing eco-consciousness as a permanent module in the school curriculum; and
- Deepening the networking with other environmental groups in Baguio and elsewhere through dissemination of the experience.

The Eco-Walk project yields results for both environment and governance as follows:

- Rehabilitation, restoration, and protection of water sources, increase in the number of trees in the watershed, and increased water availability;
- Coordinated effort among government and NGOs to address the problem of the destruction of Baguio's watersheds and forest resources; and
- Firmer and more sustainable implementation of forestry laws, ordinances, and passage of quality laws on environmental protection by the local legislature.

A total of 1,127 people have participated in hikes and tree planting in the watershed from January to June 1998. In addition, twenty-four volunteer eco-walk guides underwent training in April 1998 on issues related to forest conservation and management. The trainees have now organized themselves into an association. Although the Eco-Walk project has already had much success, project proponents have never been able to share their experiences regionally, nationally, and internationally. As a result, the project will produce several products in order to upscale the Baguio experience. A fact sheet on the Busol Watershed and Eco-Walk has already been produced, as has the first issue of a newsletter on environmental developments in the Cordillera. Teachers' guides for the classroom have already been piloted. In the next several months, a training manual for volunteer guides and a Radio/TV Program on Environment called "Eco-Walk on the Air" will also be produced. Much of the project has also been captured through video and photos. Finally, the project will produce a case study, and will close with an internal reflection and an outreach workshop.

Multistakeholder Strategic Planning and Implementation of Solid Waste Management in Guimaras, Philippines

Led by the Provincial Government of Guimaras and the Canadian Urban Institute, the project is a proactive intervention to address the potential problem of solid waste. The project aims to institutionalize coordinated, participatory, and multistakeholder planning and implementation of solid waste management (SWM) services in the five municipalities of the province.

Before the pilot project, a number of workshops were held to examine SWM and numerous activities were undertaken, albeit with limited results because of poor coordination between the concerned departments at the provincial and municipal levels. Moreover, citizens were not fully engaged in developing an integrated strategy and in implementing it.

The specific objectives of the project are to:

- Build the capacity of government, business, and citizens in assessing, developing, and implementing a SWM strategic action plan;
- Promote community awareness regarding what households and industries can do to improve waste management;
- Implement recycling-reuse-reduce demonstration projects designed, developed, and monitored by people's organizations, NGOs, and small business entrepreneurs; and
- Formulate comprehensive and coordinated policies and ordinances to support the SWM system in provincial and municipal governments.

The project yields results in terms of: functional and coordinated planning and implementation of solid waste projects in the province and five municipalities; increased knowledge of the key personnel of local government units (LGUs), farmers' cooperatives, entrepreneurs, resort owners, and people's organizations in assessing and developing SWM strategic action plans; implementation of solid waste demonstration projects in five municipalities that result in better waste collection, disposal, and recycling; establishment of a solid waste monitoring report card system for the municipalities and the province to monitor performance of the LGUs in SWM; and coherent and comprehensive policies and ordinances supporting the SWM system in the provincial and municipal governments.

Five municipal and one provincial multistakeholder Project Implementation Task Forces (PITFs) lead the project. Activities include a participatory waste assessment, study tours of innovative SWM sites, provincial and municipal strategic action workshops, policy review and ordinance formulation, preparation of strategic action plans, design and implementation of a solid waste demonstration project, establishment of a report-card monitoring system of the demonstration projects, and a public involvement information campaign. The project will produce a case study on its experience, as well as a how-to manual on planning and implementing solid waste projects for other LGUs.

The project has already had significant results in terms of changing the attitudes of different stakeholders toward the issue of SWM. Further, the project has triggered the creation of the Council on Sustainable Development, a new umbrella institution that will oversee all development activities in the province.

Sustainable Penang Initiative, Malaysia

Development planning in Malaysia has typically been a top-down process that relies almost entirely on conventional macroeconomic measures. There is little by way of an integrated approach toward development, and there is increasing realization that such fragmented planning with the use of limited indicators does not give a clear and holistic picture of what is happening within and to the society and environment.

Led by the Socio-Economic and Environmental Research Institute (SERI), a new think tank supported by the Penang State Government, the project's objectives are to:

- Develop a series of indicators for gauging sustainable development;
- Develop a model for a holistic and sustainable development plan that takes into consideration social, cultural, and environmental dimensions besides conventional economic ones;
- Establish a mechanism for public input and consensus building based on a partnership between government, the business sector, and civil society; and
- Channel the output of the consensus process to relevant authorities in order to influence development planning and policy formulation.

The key activities of the project are a series of roundtables on five different dimensions of sustainable development including: ecological sustainability; social justice; economic productivity; cultural vibrancy; and popular participation. Through a creative and participatory process, each roundtable defines Penang's "burning issues" for the challenge at hand. Roundtable participants also begin to create a series of indicators that are refined and monitored by smaller working groups involving people from various sectors including business, the academe, government, and NGOs. The indicators and findings of monitoring will be incorporated into a *People's Report on the State of Penang*, produced annually. A Penang Popular Assembly will meet annually to discuss and debate the report, and will constitute a formal forum for citizens' input to state government.

Modeled loosely on the Sustainable Seattle experience, the SPI is the first community indicators project of its kind in Asia. The case study will carefully document the processes undergone in the course of the project in order that the methodology and experience can be shared with other states in the country that might wish to set up similar think tanks or formulate more holistic and sustainable development plans.

The project has created a platform to voice development change, and has increased awareness in Penang on different aspects of development. All roundtables have been implemented, and the indicators were compiled and edited for the *People's Report on the State of Penang*. Working groups met actively to develop indicators related to: air, hill, and forest ecosystems, urban development, pollution, health care, housing, family, and workers. One other significant result of the project is the "spin-off" groups that have been created. For example, Penang Water Watch was created at the ecological sustainability roundtable to monitor indicators related to water. Further, since transport issues emerged at every roundtable session, a Sustainable Transport Environment Penang (STEP) network has also emerged. Finally, SILA (Sustainability, Independence, Livelihood, Access), a network of "socially challenged" people, has been created.

Tambol Civil Society Participatory Local Governance Project, Thailand

In 1994, the parliament approved the Tambol Council and Tambol Administrative Organizations (TAOs) Act. These new local bodies can determine their own development policy, implement a wide range of development programs, and collect taxes and retain them for local development. By 1998, approximately 7,000 TAOs and Tambol Councils were to be established as the main mechanism for local development.

The overall objective of the pilot project is to mobilize the participation of local people in planning, implementing, and monitoring local development activities. The project aims to establish and strengthen "Tambol Civic Groups," comprising representatives from informal groups such as farmers, women, youth, community forest groups, and occupational groups, linked with formal bodies such as the Tambol Councils and TAOs.

The project is led by the Local Development Institute, along with a network of other NGOs spread throughout the country. There are various project outputs including short books, case studies, and pilot projects.

Short books highlight topics such as: Thai law concerning TAO structure, authority, and budgets; links between civil society and *tambol* councils; how to encourage participation in *tambol* councils; participatory learning techniques; and the techniques for the development of civil society.

Four case studies highlight the creation and functioning of strong civic groups and reasons for their effectiveness at the local level.

Finally, four *tambol*-level pilot projects function as demonstration models and "learning centers" from which experience can be shared with the Ministry of Interior and various provincial civic groups. Each pilot project includes the creation and operationalization of a community action plan, developed through a participatory process. The objectives of individual subpilot projects and case studies range from community forestry, management of water and wetland resources, women and community enterprises, and microcredit.

The significant results of the project are the creation of an effective research analysis, a better understanding of the context of civil society-LGU collaboration and partnership, and the creation of cases to highlight local capability in the government.

Vietnam Business Council

Led by the Vietnam Chamber of Commerce and Industry (VCCI), this pilot project supports the creation of the VBC. Other supporting organizations, which form a coordinating committee, include: the Prime Minister's Research Commission (PMRC), the Government Committee of Organization and Personnel (GCOP), and the Central Institute for Economic Management (CIEM).

The project addresses two highly relevant issues in Vietnam: the development of policies, laws, procedures, and regulations that support business development, especially the development of small- and medium-sized enterprises (SMEs); and the involvement of people outside of the traditional, primarily governmental, power holders in the policy development process.

The VBC is a forum for business-government consultation on economic and trade policies. For the business community, it opens a regular, effective, and coordinating channel to participate in legislation and policy development. For the government, the VBC is a mechanism to relate to business and understand its issues, as well as a mechanism for improved accountability in government policymaking. Membership in the council includes approximately twenty carefully selected representatives from government, business associations and entrepreneurs, and research institutes.

VBC-VCCI conducted a survey of 400 local businesses on their perceptions on the business environment in Vietnam including a description of their working relationship with the various government ministries and provincial governments.

The VBC is now officially institutionalized under the Prime Minister's Research Commission and has a direct reporting relationship with the prime minister and deputy prime ministers, as well as with relevant ministries on significant issues.

6

Regional Development through Rural-Urban Linkages: The PARUL Program in Indonesia

Hugh Emrys Evans

INTRODUCTION

To achieve broad-based economic growth in a region, two conditions must be met. First, the region must succeed in selling its products and services to markets in other regions elsewhere in the country and abroad. Second, earnings from exports must generate additional rounds of income within the local economy through the purchase of inputs and household spending on consumer goods by those involved in export production.[1] But for this to happen, the region must possess an efficient set of economic linkages connecting producers, traders, and suppliers in rural and urban areas throughout the region and farther afield.[2]

Like any business enterprise, a region prospers when it competes effectively in the marketplace. Its economy grows when it succeeds in selling its products and services to a broad range of markets. Any strategy to promote local economic development (LED), therefore, must start from a basic economic resource with an export potential. Exports here are defined as sales outside the immediate area of production to large cities, other regions in the same country, and other countries. In a more developed country, the export base is likely to be located in the city and comprises tourism, assembly plants, or a major manufacturing activity. In less developed countries, the export base is more commonly found in rural areas and contains activities such as mining, fishing, forestry, or agricultural commodities.

The intention underlying such a strategy is that production for export will generate multipliers throughout the rest of the local economy. In the first round, producers of exports receive income from buyers abroad. In the second round, producers spend a large part of this income on inputs required to produce the exports, such as seeds and fertilizers, raw materials, semimanufactured items, services, machinery and equipment, and, of course, labor. Suppliers of these inputs likewise make similar purchases, much of it going eventually to labor. In the third round, the workers engaged directly or indirectly in export production spend their wages and salaries on a wide range of household consumption items. Depending on the nature of the purchases, part of this spending in turn accrues to other farm and nonfarm households within the region, and so on through successive and gradually diminishing rounds of spending. In less developed regions where incomes are still low, and where the greater part of household income normally goes to purchases of food, a significant share of spending eventually accrues to farm households in rural areas.[3]

While this is the intention, it does not always happen. In some instances, the export activity sputters and fails. In others, it survives, may even prosper, but behaves largely as an enclave, particularly where a large modern multinational corporation (MNC) is involved in an activity such as drilling oil or mining, with the result that limited benefits accrue to the population of the surrounding region.

Whether the multipliers materialize or not, and whether the initial impetus from export production leads to sustained growth across a broader front or not, depends in part on how the economic base is linked to the mainstream economy. The ability of local producers to compete successfully in outside markets depends crucially on the linkages that connect the region to the rest of the world. The extent to which initial earnings are multiplied into further rounds of income within the region depends crucially on linkages connecting producers of exports to local suppliers of inputs and consumption goods. As is now becoming better understood, an export base is a necessary but insufficient condition for generating self-sustaining growth in a region. Equally important is a set of efficient economic linkages, which connect producers, suppliers, traders, and consumers in rural and urban areas throughout the region and farther afield.[4]

A STRATEGY TO STRENGTHEN RURAL-URBAN LINKAGES

This perspective suggests that to promote LED it is necessary to strengthen rural-urban linkages associated with production and trade both within the region and between the region and more distant markets. The question arises as to how such a strategy may be put into practice.

One approach is to focus on linkages and transactions between urban areas and their rural hinterlands within a particular region or physical space. This approach tends to lead to proposals for a range of investments in infrastructure designed to support local production and trade in general, such as improved roads, power, telecommunications, marketplaces, storage facilities, and the like, most of which require public funding. While this approach is useful, it tends to underplay the role of the private sector and key issues of demand, production, marketing, and the manner in which the local economy is functioning.

Another approach is to focus on clusters of related economic activities within a region, and the set of linkages that connect producers, suppliers, traders, exporters, and consumers associated with that cluster. Typically, a cluster might be defined as those activities that revolve around an important element in the local economy, such as tourism, garment production, fishing, timber, or agricultural commodities such as coffee, tea, rice, cocoa, or horticulture. This approach is more conducive to identifying specific bottlenecks or opportunities facing those engaged in the cluster. It also explicitly highlights issues of demand, production, and marketing, and the role of farmers, fishermen, traders, small businesses, larger firms, and other actors in the private sector.

As explained later, this approach is also likely to lead to a wider range of proposals for potential interventions to strengthen linkages. Broadly speaking, in predominantly rural regions, it may imply expanding linkages associated with adding value to production and trade in agricultural commodities. In newly emerging regions, it may involve building linkages between a modern enclave activity (such as oil, gas, minerals, or forestry) and the more traditional local economy. In more heavily urbanized regions, it may point to improving the competitiveness of manufacturing and services and expanding backward linkages to suppliers of semimanufactured inputs.

OPERATIONAL ISSUES IN IMPLEMENTATION

In operational terms, three key issues need to be considered in implementing this approach to strengthening rural-urban linkages for LED.[5] These are:

- Establishing an institutional framework for planning and execution;
- Identifying actions to strengthen rural-urban linkages; and
- Mobilizing resources to execute these actions.

The Institutional Framework

The mix of potential interventions implied by a strategy for strengthening rural-urban linkages will require complementary actions by a wide range of actors. Thus, an institutional framework is needed that facilitates the participation of numerous actors in the planning and execution of the strategy. Typically, these are likely to include central government agencies and their local offices at the provincial or district levels, local authorities, business organizations, producer groups, traders' associations, nongovernmental organizations (NGOs), community-based organizations (CBOs), and possibly many others.

Given the high profile of the private sector in a cluster approach to strengthening linkages, this framework must allow for effective partnerships between the government and the private sector in order to secure the full commitment of those whose collaboration is needed for implementation. While scattered precedents exist for public-private partnerships for economic development in less developed countries, it is not widely practiced at the local level. Where it is practiced, the government commonly occupies the driver's seat and the private sector the passengers' seats, often with inconclusive results. However, if the private sector is to be fully engaged in such an initiative, the institutional framework must provide clear incentives for participation by treating it as an equal, not subordinate, partner with government in the process of planning and implementation.

The design of an appropriate structure for an institutional framework in a given situation will clearly depend on local political factors, administrative arrangements, and cultural traditions. The aim is to empower public-private coalitions to prepare action plans for strengthening rural-urban linkages and to facilitate the implementation of these plans.

Issues to Resolve

Issues that must be resolved are the following:

- What kind of framework likely promotes most effective collaboration between the actors concerned?
- What responsibilities and tasks should be assigned to the unit responsible for a rural-urban linkage approach to planning and development (autonomy for planning and decision-making)?
- Who should provide primary leadership—government or the private sector?
- How can active and sustained participation of the private sector be ensured?
- How can adequate representation of small-scale producers and traders be ensured?
- What procedures are most effective in building broad support for initiatives?

Actions to Strengthen Linkages

A second issue has to do with identifying actions to strengthen linkages associated with clusters of economic activities. This first requires an analysis of trade and production linkages within the cluster itself, and particularly the nature of export demand for the goods and/or services involved. One purpose of this analysis is to assess the extent to which local producers are currently integrated into the mainstream national economy, and to identify opportunities for enhancing their ability to compete in major markets within the region and elsewhere. The specific nature of the studies to be completed obviously depends on the cluster of economic activities in question, but broadly speaking, analysis needs to address the following kinds of topics:[6]

- *Export demand*—the destination of current exports out of the region to other parts of the country and the rest of the world, likely future trends in world prices and changes in consumer demand, and the impact of any recent or foreseeable changes in currency exchange rates.

- *The regulatory and fiscal environment* within which trade takes place—rules and regulations of central and subnational government affecting trade and production, including quotas, tariffs, and taxes, and particularly the role of parastatals and de facto monopolies.

- *Primary production*—trends in the quantity and quality of primary production, employment, investment, the productivity of land, labor, and capital, and the spatial distribution of production within the region.

- *Inputs for production*—the backward linkages associated with primary production, the spatial incidence of these linkages, suppliers of inputs, and accessibility to the same.

- *Initial processing*—existing postharvest processing, such as grading, cleaning, packing, milling, and potential opportunities for new activities.

- *Secondary processing*—existing forward linkages to manufacturing and industrial establishments using primary products as inputs, the potential for expanding local processing and adding value, and implications for increasing employment and raising incomes.

- *Marketing*—current and potential markets for raw materials, semiprocessed, and processed products associated with the sector, marketing channels and networks, price markups along the chain, marketplaces, and storage facilities for assembly, retailing, and wholesaling.

- *Supporting services and facilities*—extension services and technical assistance for production methods, marketing, and business management; transportation services by road, sea, and air; repair of machinery and equipment; banking and insurance services, and credit programs; vocational training institutes, courses and content; and research institutes.

- *Principal actors and institutions*—agencies of central and local government, business organizations, associations and cooperatives of producers and traders, NGOs supporting cluster activities, research institutes, and other relevant groups directly or indirectly involved in the cluster, particularly those representing small-scale farmers and businesses, women, and others with a traditionally weak voice in planning and decision-making.

These analyses are a prelude to the task of preparing proposals for strengthening rural-urban linkages associated with a cluster. Generally speaking, these should aim to raise productivity, increase production and trade, and add value locally to products associated with the cluster. Typically, proposals might include a mix of interventions related to infrastructure improvements, supporting services, facilities to add value, policy reforms, and capacity building. In designing proposals, attention needs to be given to initiatives that likely yield a greater overall impact, can be implemented swiftly, and are most effective in benefiting specific target groups.

Resources for a Rural-Urban Linkage Strategy

Once proposals have been formulated, the next major issue is to mobilize the human and financial resources needed to execute proposed initiatives. Infrastructure improvements are sometimes funded by private corporations, but more often by government agencies or public utility companies, which means proposals need to be incorporated in the relevant agency budgets. Supporting services may be offered by government agencies, NGOs, commercial banks, or private firms. In many instances, these are provided on a fee-for-service basis, which partially eliminates the need for special financing, but may require mobilizing resources from relevant firms and organizations. Where this is not possible, funding may be needed from public agencies to subsidize the service.

Facilities to add value provide opportunities for producer cooperatives and private firms, and as such will require efforts to attract private investors. Policy and regulatory reforms do not normally need funding as such, but will require the collaboration of relevant government bodies. Capacity-building initiatives are most likely to be supported through donor programs or larger NGOs, though some organizations might be willing to pay for certain kinds of technical assistance themselves, particularly when this yields direct benefits.

In terms of activities and initiatives that require funding from public sources, there are a number of options to consider. Three are discussed here: funding from regular budgets of government line agencies; financing through local government; and a special-purpose fund. Each has its merits and drawbacks.

Funding through Line Agency Budgets

One option for financing public sector activities of a rural-urban linkage program is simply to rely on existing budgets of central government. This is probably the most common approach, and was used, for example, some years ago in Bolivia in the departments of Potosi and Oruro, where infrastructure for a program entitled "Urban Functions in Rural Development" was funded either by the Regional Development Corporation, which received most of its funding from national sources, or by line agencies of central government ministries.

The great merit of this approach is that it relies on existing processes for public sector budgeting and is, therefore, more sustainable in the long run. However, it does mean that proposed activities of a rural-urban linkage program have to compete with other demands on available resources and funding is likely to be harder to secure, especially from agencies with other priorities. Given the potentially wide range of activities to be included in such a program, special procedures will be required to obtain the collaboration of the numerous, different agencies involved and to ensure that proposed actions are incorporated in relevant public sector budgets.

This has often been a major stumbling block for integrated programs, especially those that rely mainly on line agencies of central government, even more so where regional offices must defer budget decisions to headquarters. Better results may be achieved where decision-making authority is delegated to the regional level, and where there is an effective mechanism for interagency coordination within the region, as, for example, the District Development Committees in Malawi and Kenya, and the Provincial Development Planning Agencies (BAPPEDAs) in Indonesia. Nevertheless, special measures will still be needed to integrate the rural-urban linkage program closely into public sector processes for planning and budgeting at the regional level.

Financing through Local Government

A second option is to finance a rural-urban linkage program through local government. Depending on the country, the appropriate local government unit (LGU) may be the state, province, district, municipality, or something similar. While a few larger LGUs with substantial fiscal resources may be able to finance a rural-urban linkage program on their own, most will probably need to rely on fiscal transfers of some kind from central government. One example is the State of Paranà in Brazil, which is currently implementing a rural-urban program with partial funding from the Federal Government. Another example are the Local Development Funds set up through the United Nations Capital Development Fund (UNCDF) in a number of low-income countries around the world. These provide multipurpose block grants for capital investment to local governments, most of which possess few or no other resources for the purpose.

The main advantage of this approach is that by placing funds directly in the hands of local government, it transfers responsibility for planning and decision-making to the local community, giving them greater choice and control. It also makes it easier to coordinate funding for the diverse activities of a rural-urban linkage program, since all decisions are made by a single body, the local government council.

A local government development fund may not be difficult to set up initially, particularly, if it is largely or entirely financed by donors. It is much harder to institutionalize such an arrangement since it requires the commitment of central government to an ongoing system of fiscal transfers to local government, which it may not be ready to support. Furthermore, once such a fund is established, a rural-urban linkage program will likely have to compete with numerous other claims for the use of its limited resources. This option may also not be viable where a substantial proportion of activities in a rural-urban linkage program extend beyond the physical jurisdiction of the local government authority, a particularly severe constraint for urban authorities. It is most viable in countries where LGUs encompass urban centers and surrounding rural areas, such as the *municipios* in many countries of Central and South America.

A Special-Purpose Fund

A third option is to establish a special-purpose fund specifically for a program to strengthen rural-urban linkages. Depending on the country concerned and the scale of the program involved, this might be administered directly by the ministry responsible for the program, or by its offices at the subnational level (say state, province, or district) that are responsible for the region(s) in which the program is to be implemented. One example of this approach is the Fund for Rural Trade and Production Centres set up under the Ministry of Finance and Planning in Kenya in the late 1980s, which financed packages of projects prepared by District Development Committees for selected market towns considered to offer superior prospects for economic development.

The big advantage of this option is that by providing a single source of finance it greatly simplifies the process of securing funds for a potentially wide array of initiatives likely to be proposed under a program for strengthening rural-urban linkages. Such a fund may also be attractive to donors, as was initially the case in Kenya, since it is directly associated with an easily identifiable set of activities, and donor funds can, if necessary, be targeted to specific regions.

But it does have drawbacks. In many countries no single ministry is an obvious candidate to administer such a fund, and those that might be, such as a Ministry of Planning or Economic Development, usually lack experience or capacity in directly executing programs themselves. Such a fund will also likely duplicate existing sources of finance for similar activities from regular line agencies. They may oppose the idea, especially if allocations for the special-purpose fund might otherwise have gone to them. If donors are to support the fund, it may be difficult to sustain once that support ends.

APPLICATION IN INDONESIA

Some idea of how these issues play out in practice may be gleaned from an attempt to implement a strategy to strengthen rural-urban linkages that is currently ongoing in Indonesia through the PARUL[7] program. This program is funded by the United Nations Development Programme (UNDP) and the Government of Indonesia (GOI), receives technical assistance from the United Nations Centre for Human Settlements (UNCHS) (Habitat), and is executed by the National Development Planning Agency (BAPPENAS). It is structured in two phases: a recently completed one-year Development Phase, and a three-year Implementation Phase that began in January 1999.

The original impetus for the PARUL program came from BAPPENAS. On the one hand, it wanted to devise a more effective approach to regional development planning. As is often the case, this is undertaken by two separate units, one responsible for urban development, the other for rural development. Instead of designing separate programs for each sector, it sought ways to reinforce potential complementarities between the two. On the other hand, lessons from extensive experience with earlier poverty alleviation programs indicated that one of the reasons why backward regions lag behind is that they are often inadequately linked to the mainstream economy. Out of these two concerns evolved the search for a strategy to strengthen linkages between urban and rural areas as a means to better promote development of a region as a whole. The aim was to devise a framework for a rural-urban linkage approach to planning and development, which GOI could incorporate in the next five-year development plan, REPELITA VII, that began in 1999.

In a nutshell, the PARUL program is a pilot project that aims to test concepts and approaches for strengthening rural-urban linkages in selected provinces and districts of Indonesia. By developing an innovative methodology focusing on the links between urban and rural markets within a region and beyond, the project aims to generate action plans to promote production and trade for clusters of associated economic activities. Initially, the program is operating in three provinces of Eastern Indonesia—South Sulawesi, North Sulawesi, and Irian Jaya (Sorong district). Eventually, the plan is to expand activities to five other provinces.

The longer-term development objectives of the PARUL programs as a whole are three:

1. To promote a more balanced pattern of urban and rural development;
2. To promote economic development of selected regions of Indonesia that are particularly underdeveloped; and
3. To raise incomes and create productive employment opportunities for poorer households in these less developed regions.

It is recognized that these objectives cannot be met quickly, but will require sustained support over a far longer period than the four years envisioned for PARUL.

The Development Strategy

During the development phase, the main goals were to develop a better understanding of the nature of rural-urban linkages in the local economy and the interventions needed to strengthen them, and to build a consensus on a rural-urban linkage approach to planning and development. Towards this end, several reports were prepared and presented at national and provincial workshops. Among other things, these reports examine the nature of trade linkages between the three provinces and the rest of the world, rural-urban linkages within each of the three provinces, and linkages associated with key commodities in each province that constitute important elements of the local economy.[8]

Based partly on these studies and partly on a well-established body of theoretical and empirical literature, the PARUL team has evolved a development strategy for the program that aims to integrate lagging regions into the mainstream economy. Briefly stated, this is to be achieved by strengthening linkages between local producers and markets within the region, in the country and beyond, focusing on clusters of economic activities associated with key local export commodities. Central to this strategy are provincial and district coalitions whose function is to facilitate collaboration between government, private firms, small businesses, and others in designing and implementing action plans to strengthen linkages and promote production and trade.

Economic Clusters

For reasons indicated earlier, the focus of analysis in the PARUL program is not a physical region but a cluster of economic activities that constitute a key element of the regional economy. Typically, a cluster includes large firms, small businesses, households, and supporting institutions engaged in production, processing, and trade associated with an export commodity. Here, exports are taken to mean commodities sold to other countries as well as to other provinces in Indonesia and larger urban markets outside the region of origin.

The selection of commodity-related clusters is based on four main criteria that reflect:

- Potential external demand;
- Potential for continued future growth;
- Potential for involving small-scale farmers and nonfarm businesses, raising incomes, and creating productive employment opportunities for poorer households; and
- Potential for multiplying initial earnings from exports into further rounds of spending and income that benefit local households.

Based on studies in each of the three provinces, the PARUL team has initially selected clusters associated with cashew nuts in South Sulawesi, coconuts in North Sulawesi, and fish in the Sorong district of Irian Jaya. To keep the program manageable, activities are also being restricted initially to only two or three districts in each province. Once the PARUL team has tested and gained experience from pilot applications, other districts and clusters will gradually be added.

Public-Private Coalitions

To implement the strategy, PARUL is setting up public-private coalitions to facilitate collaboration between government and the private sector. Initially, for each cluster, this takes the form of a Cluster Development Partnership (CDP) at the provincial level, with supporting units in each district, called Kabupaten Implementation Teams (KITs). In each case, the coalition includes representatives of key actors involved in the cluster such as: producers, traders, exporters, manufacturers, local government, line agencies of central government research institutes, NGOs, and other relevant organizations. The aim is to empower the private sector to share with government in the ownership and responsibility for generating and promoting action plans.

Later, as PARUL expands to cover other clusters, the intention is to build Provincial Economic Development Coalitions (PEDCOs) comprising members of the CDPs and KITs, which would assume broader responsibilities for planning and promoting economic development in the region.

Action Plans

Under PARUL, the public-private coalitions are given the task of preparing action plans. These are intended to strengthen rural-urban linkages associated with each cluster, raise productivity and incomes, add value to local products, and thereby expand production, exchange, and employment.

Typically, action plans include a mix of initiatives (see Table 6.1) covering:

- Infrastructure improvements (such as roads, power, telecommunications, and market-places);
- Supporting services (such as technical assistance, credit, marketing, and transportation services);
- Facilities to add value (such as storage, sorting, packing, processing, and associated manufacturing);
- Regulatory reforms (such as government policies, rules, and regulations affecting production and trade); and
- Capacity building (through training and/or technical assistance to create or strengthen organizations associated with the cluster to support production and trade).

While action plans are intended to address the cluster as a whole, particular emphasis is to be given to poorer districts within each province where much of the population is engaged in primary production of the commodity concerned. The preparation of action plans is not envisioned as a one-time exercise but rather as an ongoing activity to be revised as circumstances and opportunities arise. Some elements of action plans might be carried out right away, while others may need more time. The aim is to speed up implementation of simple measures while developing more complex initiatives requiring feasibility studies and outside funding.

Human and Financial Resources

The PARUL program requires human and financial resources to prepare and promote action plans, and later to execute initiatives contained in the plans. For

Table 6.1
The Mix of Initiatives

Infrastructure: • Farm-to-market roads • Mini-irrigation projects • Local power generation • Telecommunication hookups • Rehabilitated marketplaces	**Development budgets of:** • Local council (town, village) • Midlevel government (province, district) • Line agencies of central government
Supporting services: • Technical assistance for production methods • Technical assistance for business management • Credit programs linking commercial banks to small-scale businesses • Market information services • Marketing cooperatives • Revised curricula for vocational training programs	**Local government programmes:** • Not-for-profit NGOs • For-profit private firms • Commercial banks
Facilities to add value: • Plants for sorting, grading, and packaging • Storage facilities and cold stores • Transportation services • Plants for secondary food processing	**Private investors:** • Commercial banks
Fiscal and regulatory reforms affecting: • Production • Trade and marketing • Investment, etc.	**Undertaken by:** • Central government • Midlevel government • Local government
Capacity-building initiatives: • Producer groups • Export and trader groups • Local government agencies	**Public and private agencies covering:** • Management information • Marketing and sales

the first step, UNDP provides funds for technical assistance through PARUL to assist the public-private coalitions in their tasks. Owing to other commitments and obligations, most members of coalitions are able to contribute only a limited amount of time. Their main role is to create ideas, evaluate proposals, and decide on priorities. The more detailed work of elaborating plans, designing specific proposals, and following through on these is done by others, including members of the PARUL team, consultants hired through PARUL, and professional staff of the government agencies involved.

In terms of executing initiatives contained in action plans, resources will be needed from both public and private sectors, depending on the kind of activity proposed (see Table 6.1). For the public sector, PARUL initially intends to rely on resources available from existing programs of local and central government agencies. This means that PARUL will have to compete with other programs in obtaining a share of limited public funds. To ensure that PARUL initiatives are given due consideration in the process of government budget allocations, the public-private coalitions will include representatives of key government agencies whose collaboration is needed for executing elements of action plans.

Proposals are also under discussion for setting up a separate PARUL Development Fund, which would be used to finance specific initiatives generated by the program. As mentioned earlier, there are arguments for and against this idea but ultimately it will depend largely on the interest of donors.

PARUL will also need resources to finance activities undertaken by the private sector. Particularly important here is access to credit for small- and medium-sized firms to invest in new ventures that add value through processing selected commodities. To attract private investment and facilitate funding by commercial banks, PARUL includes funds to hire consultants to prepare feasibility studies, and aims to collaborate with local offices of the Ministry of Trade and Industry in promoting small and microbusinesses.

CONCLUSION

Many issues remain to be resolved. The more important ones relate to public-private coalitions, accessing public resources, private investment, program expansion, and sustainability.

Public-Private Coalitions

Since public-private coalitions are to play a leading role in the PARUL program, it is critical that they function effectively. In the past, government has assumed leadership of such coalitions, leaving the private sector as more or less a passive spectator, with the result that initiatives have tended to be supply driven. In PARUL, the aim is to reverse this tendency, and to encourage private actors to set the pace, creating demands for the government to respond to. This assumes that private sector members are willing to act in concert to achieve goals of promoting production and trade. In practice, this may be difficult to accomplish, especially if proposed initiatives designed to benefit some parties (for example, farmers) are perceived to injure others (for example, traders). This is a problem faced by any democratic institution and as such it should be possible to forge initiatives that gain general support.

Another challenge will be to maintain the support and participation of private sector participants in these coalitions during the lengthy period required to formulate plans, mobilize resources, and execute actions. To achieve this, PARUL will have to move fast to demonstrate the utility of the process by producing concrete results quickly.

Accessing Public Resources

Since PARUL will rely heavily on public resources to execute elements of action plans, public-private coalitions will have to prove themselves successful in obtaining government support and access to these resources. Without special-purpose funds for the program, government agencies may be reluctant to allocate their own scarce funds for PARUL initiatives.

Several factors should alleviate this risk. This inclusion of representatives from key government agencies in coalitions is one measure to ease possible resistance and win support. A recent decision by central government to increase fiscal transfers to local government will greatly help transfer decision-making to those who have the most interest in promoting PARUL initiatives. BAP-PENAS also has the power to allocate certain discretionary funds for the use of local governments. Assuming the ministry decides to use part of these funds to support PARUL, local governments will have an incentive to include elements of action plans in their requests for supplementary budget allocations. Either way, PARUL staff will need to work closely with coalitions and government to ensure that program initiatives are taken into account and that due provision is made in forward budgets.

Private Investment

Another uncertainty concerns the willingness and ability of the private sector to invest in PARUL. Recent political and economic events in Indonesia have seriously undermined business confidence and weakened the capacity of commercial banks to lend money. Reportedly, many firms are on the brink of bankruptcy or are reluctant to engage in new activities in face of civil unrest, while numerous banks burdened with bad loans are unable to extend further credit. Meanwhile, rapid inflation has pushed up interest rates to levels that discourage borrowing. Some of these problems are being addressed by the infusion of donor funds into the commercial banking sector for lending at subsidized interest rates, although it is unclear what effect this will have on borrowing and investment.

Another factor in PARUL's favor is the sharp depreciation of the *rupiah*, which has opened up opportunities for new and increased exports to other countries.

Even under more normal circumstances, however, it may be difficult to persuade commercial banks to lend funds to private firms interested in PARUL projects. Many avoid investing in unfamiliar activities that they feel they know little about, particularly in agriculture and industry, and few are equipped to handle the special needs of microenterprises. This implies PARUL should aim to work with more specialized banks and NGOs catering to such activities.

Program Expansion

A further issue faced by PARUL is strong pressure from BAPPENAS to expand the program rapidly across the country. This is prompted in part by the government's concern to demonstrate speedy and effective responses to the present crisis that is affecting the entire population and swelling the ranks of the poor. Although the title of the program includes the words "Poverty Alleviation," it is emphatically not designed as a short-term remedial exercise but as a longer-term, broader-based attempt to reduce poverty by strengthening the underlying local economy and building coalitions for this purpose. Given the heavy emphasis on institution building, it is not a program that can be replicated rapidly. The PARUL concept of public-private coalitions is lesser known in Indonesia and it may take a while for government and the private sector to embrace it locally.

Nevertheless, there are ways to expand the program in the provinces where it is already operating. Once the CDPs and KITs are up and running, it should not be difficult to incorporate other districts into action plans. Once the process has been tried and tested for one commodity, it should be possible to reduce the time needed to launch clusters for other commodities. And once the PARUL approach has been demonstrated successfully in one province, it should make it easier to replicate the approach in other provinces.

Sustainability

The ultimate test of the PARUL approach over the longer term is whether program activities will continue after donor support terminates. Will public-private coalitions survive? Will Provincial Economic Development Coalitions have the capacity to generate and promote action plans for other commodity clusters? Will resources be forthcoming to execute initiatives? Although it is far too early to answer these questions, they do serve to highlight the importance of key tasks for the implementation phase. These relate specifically to strengthening the capacity of public-private coalitions and devising effective mechanisms for mobilizing resources from both the public and private sectors.

NOTES

1. Harvey Perloff and Lowdon Wingo, "Natural Resource Endowment and Regional Economic Growth" in J. Friedmann and W. Alonso, eds., *Regional Policy: Readings in Theory and Applications* (rev. ed.) (Cambridge, MA: MIT Press, 1975), chapter 12; and Charles M. Tiebout, "Exports and Regional Economic Growth," *Journal of Political Economy* 64 (April 1956): 160–69.

2. Hugh E. Evans, "Rural-Urban Linkages and Structural Transformation (Report INU 71) (Washington, DC: Infrastructure and Urban Development Department, World Bank, 1990).

3. Hugh E. Evans, "A Virtuous Circle Model of Rural-Urban Development: Evidence from Kenya," *Journal of Development Studies* 28 (July 1992): 640–67; and Blane D. Lewis, "District-Level Economic Linkages in Kenya," *World Development* 20 (June 1992): 881–97.

4. T. Carroll, B. Lentnek, and R. Wilkie, "Exploration of Rural-Urban Linkages and Market Centres in Highland Ecuador," *Regional Development Dialogue* 5 (Spring 1984); Barbara Harriss, "Regional Growth Linkages from Agriculture," *Journal of Development Studies* 23 (February 1987); and D. A. Rondinelli, "Cities as Agricultural Markets," *Geographical Review* 77 (April 1987).

5. Hugh E. Evans, "Rural-Urban Linkages: Operational Implications for Self-Sustained Development" (A Report for the United Nations Development Programme (UNDP)) (New York, 1994).

6. Ibid.

7. National Development Planning Agency (BAPPENAS) and UNDP, "Poverty Alleviation through Rural-Urban Linkages (PARUL)" (Project document) (Jakarta, 1997).

8. BAPPENAS and UNDP, "An Analysis of Trade Linkages between Selected Provinces and Markets Elsewhere" (Jakarta: PARUL, 1998); their "Analyses of Linkages Associated with Clusters of Economic Activities" (Jakarta: PARUL, 1998); and their "Analyses of Rural-Urban Linkages within Selected Provinces" (Jakarta: PARUL, 1998).

7

Decentralization in Africa: Trends and Prospects for the Twenty-First Century

Walter O. Oyugi

INTRODUCTION

After more than three decades of debate, decentralization as a method of organizing government administration still lacks conceptual clarity. Decentralization is defined alternatively as:

- Devolution, that is, the legal ceding of power to political bodies operating at the subnational level—in which local representatives are given formal power to decide on a range of public matters[1] or

- Deconcentration, which includes both political and administrative aspects.[2]

Decentralization sometimes includes delegation of tasks to public enterprises and privatization.[3] To avoid further conceptual confusion, Conyers suggests that decentralization be analyzed in terms of certain dimensions to include a wider variety of forms.[4]

In this chapter, decentralization is defined as "the transfer of authority on a geographic basis, whether by deconcentration (i.e., delegation) of administrative authority to field units of the same department or level of government, or by the political devolution of authority to local government units or special statutory bodies."[5] Devolution and deconcentration are accepted as "satisfying" subconcepts.

This chapter compares the postindependence decentralization experiences of select Anglophone African countries using devolution and deconcentration.

The analysis is restricted to forms of decentralization including the design of decentralization. The financial, resource, and management aspects of decentralization such as central-local relationships are also touched upon. The conclusions attempt to assess what the future portends.

THE CASE FOR DECENTRALIZATION

The call for decentralization as a strategy of local development during the early phase of independence was necessitated by the politicoadministrative problems associated with the overcentralized nature of the inherited colonial state—a situation that worsened as a result of the centralizing tendencies of the new leaders.

The struggle for complete control of the state, initially between top rival political parties and later within ruling parties gave rise to three kinds of developments: militarization of politics, emergence of the authoritarian one-party system, and concomitantly the emergence of "personal rulers."[6] Individually or in combination, these developments provided the ideal climate for the continuation and growth of centralizing tendencies in the body politic of many African states with direct negative effects on the structure and behavior of state bureaucracies.

To begin with, the one-party system as practiced at different times in many African countries (Tanzania, Malawi, Ghana, Guinea, and Zimbabwe) operated on the basis of total subordination of all the institutions and organs of the state to the ruling party and its leader. Totalitarian tendencies similar to those existing at the time in the communist states were its common ingredients. The omnipresence of the state was felt in every walk of life, and the state-party system acted on the people who complied out of a sense of fear and insecurity. In these circumstances, the civil bureaucracy continued to play its old role as an instrument of penetration and control of the localities and its operations remained as centralized as they had been during the colonial period. The center was assumed to be all-knowing and the state emerged soon after independence as the engine driving the development process.[7]

The struggle among the ruling elites in some countries (especially the former French colonies) gave rise to a spate of *coups d'état* and, consequently, to the institutionalization of militarism in the body politic of many states. It would soon extend to some former British colonies (Ghana, Nigeria, Sierra Leone, and Uganda). The advent of militarism was *ipso facto* accompanied by the disappearance of competitive politics and power-sharing between the center and the localities. The emergent rigid military structures eliminated all forms of local initiative in the governance process. And even with the transformation of some of the military regimes through manipulated elections, in which the former military rulers acquired civilian status, the authoritarian/hierarchical systems associated with militarism remained intact (e.g., Ghana and Uganda). Decentralization efforts in such countries would turn out to be devices by the center to continue the "old" penetration and control of the subnational units of government.

Regardless of the form of political system that exists, one phenomenon that most African states share in common is that of "personal rule," where "political and administrative actions are not rooted in the state institutions and organizations but in friendship, kinship, factional alliances, ethnic fellowship . . . that are . . . at odds with the state institutions . . . and . . . tend to undermine them."[8]

In such a system, democratic participation is rendered irrelevant unless it serves the interests of the personal ruler and those around him.

Throughout the period between independence and the late 1980s, efforts aimed at power sharing between the center and the localities through programs of decentralization have been frustrated by singular political ideologies, which in turn led inevitably to the accentuation of monocratic organizational culture[9] in every sphere of activity of public organizations.

The situation has not changed much since the resurrection of pluralistic politics in the late 1980s and early 1990s. In some cases, militarism has reared its ugly face once again (Congo-Brazzaville, Togo, Niger, Burundi, and Central African Republic) or the phenomenon of personal rule has refused to give way to institutional functioning (Kenya, Zambia, Tanzania, and Malawi). The net effect has been the lack of democratic consolidation that would have provided fertile ground for the sustenance of pluralist politics and power sharing. Meaningful decentralized governance in Africa has so far lacked an ideal environment for its development and institutionalization. Efforts aimed at decentralizing the state and its bureaucratic apparatus must take cognizance of the obstacles, while determining strategy and alternatives.

The advantages of decentralization can be realized only if factors that have sustained the centralizing ideology in the governance process are adequately addressed.

FORMS OF DECENTRALIZATION

Colonial Roots

The forms that decentralization assumed at independence in many African countries were directly influenced by their colonial heritage. The policy of identity pursued with zeal by France in its African colonies resulted in the establishment of politicoadministrative structures shaped in the image of similar ones in metropolitan France. Thus, the prefectural system that operated in field administration throughout the colonial period and after was a direct import of the French system with the prefect representing the authority of the central government and having control over all public institutions and personnel.

A common pattern emerged among the former British dependencies. Throughout the colonial period, the British had encouraged a partnership system in which some services were rendered by field units of central agencies and others by local authorities.[10] Right from the inception, the British were intent on building the two systems concurrently while allowing for variations dictated by the circumstances of individual colonies.

In settler colonies such as Kenya and Rhodesia, the ideology of separate development of the races dictated the institutionalization of structural-functional duality in the society. A hierarchy of authorities was established in the "native" areas that linked them to the center through the office of the Chief Native Commissioner. Separate structures were developed for the areas settled by the whites. In the area of local government in Kenya, local native councils emerged in the African reserves and European district councils (later county councils, during 1952–62) in the settled areas. In Rhodesia, local government in African areas revolved around the institution of chieftainship. A chief embodied local government as well as development authority. Rural councils were established in white settled areas.[11] Until independence, local authorities in Kenya and Rhodesia remained separate entities. In the meantime, the center was busy establishing ministerial departments in the field for the control of native affairs. Thus, devolution and deconcentration were encouraged simultaneously.

A different mode of devolution took place in the territories where the British opted to apply the so-called "direct rule," where the decision was influenced by the conspicuous presence of strong traditional authority such as a king or chief.

Direct or indirect rule did not cover the entire territory but only sections of it. A combination of direct and indirect rule created other dualities in institutional development, as seen in Nigeria and Uganda. The Hausa-Fulani Emirates were ruled indirectly. So were the Yoruba Kingdoms and a few other entities in the East.[12] Uganda, Buganda, Bunyoro, Toro, Ankole, and to some extent Busoga were ruled indirectly. The rest of the country was subjected to direct administration. There were other countries also where local authority centered around the chief: Malawi, parts of Ghana, parts of Tanzania, and Northern Rhodesia. Even after the establishment of modern-type district councils, the chiefs continued to be recognized as traditional authorities and wielded a lot of power.

Throughout the colonial period and regardless of the form of decentralization in operation, the British colonial administration exercised considerable control over subnational institutions. On the eve of independence, the system of elective councils had been introduced in many former British colonies. But they were still subject to control both by the parent ministries (of local government) and also, by the field political administrators who ensured that their political behavior was in conformity with the norms established centrally.

Local authorities wherever they existed were required to participate in development management. Their powers were derived from the colonial legislature. Normally, they would be given specific functions to perform on behalf of the state if their resources allowed. Sources of revenue were often identified along with modes of collection. Success or failure in collection determined what a council could or could not provide. Often, the center would provide specific and general grants to ensure the functions performed on its behalf did not grind to a halt. The experience varied from one council to another and from one country to another. But in general, the picture that emerged on the eve of independence was one of dependable partnership between the local authorities and the state, especially in service provision.

Postindependence Trends

African countries have a lot in common with regard to institution building during the postindependence period, albeit with variations influenced by factors internal to individual countries.

The partnership between central government and local authorities was well established at independence throughout Africa. Two forms of local authorities had been in operation in the terminal years of colonialism: elective and/or partially elective district councils and traditional authorities. Where elective or partially elective councils had been put in place at independence (as in many former British colonies), the institutions were inherited by the incoming authorities and used as instruments for providing basic services in their areas of jurisdiction. Where the independence constitution continued to recognize the authority of traditional leaders, as in Nigeria and Uganda, a dual local government system continued to operate—the elective councils in the formerly directly administered areas and chief-centered authorities in the formerly indirectly administered areas. Only political upheavals changed the *status quo* as when, for instance, the traditional authorities were abolished in Nigeria in 1966 after the coup[13] and in Uganda in 1966–67 following the overthrow of the 1962 constitution by Obote.[14]

In the former settler colonies, a major concern on the eve of independence had been the rationalization and subsequent unification of the hitherto dual system of local authorities. In Kenya, a winding-up commission was set up in 1962, which recommended that a unified system be established throughout the country, with the new councils being named as county councils, and having jurisdictions largely coterminous with the administrative districts.[15] In Zimbabwe, the colonial institutional duality survived independence in the rural areas, where the settler-controlled rural councils remained undisturbed to avoid antagonizing the settlers who were perceived as the backbone of the national economy.

Decentralization, through the devolution of limited powers to elective district councils, emerged as the dominant form of political decentralization in most Anglophone African countries at independence.

But there was also the concern that these institutions might become alternative political power centers—to be used in the mobilization of the peasantry in articulating local demands. The experience varied from one country to another. But two strategies of control seemed to have emerged, the political and the

Figure 7.1
Approaches in Devolution

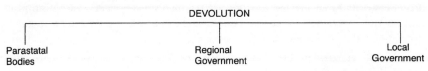

Source: G. Hyden, *No Short Cut to Progress: African Development Management in Perspective*
(Berkeley: University of California Press, 1983).

bureaucratic. The former involves subjecting local authorities to close party control. The experience of Tanzania best illustrates this strategy. A hierarchy of
party structures was put in place that at once subordinated all other institutions
to the party. Five years later (1966) the party's (Tanganyika African National
Union's) district chairmen were made chairmen of district councils. All council
candidates would at once be required to face a preselection by the party and a
final vetting at higher levels.[16]

Following independence in Zambia, the appointment of politicians as resident
provincial ministers with executive powers was the United National Independent
Party's (UNIP's) and the government's attempt to consolidate their power in the
field under the slogan of "decentralization in centralism."[17]

The district councils established in 1965 to replace the colonial ones headed
by traditional chiefs were at once subjected to control. UNIP had then
emerged as the dominant party and began behaving as if Zambia had already
become a one-party state (that status was not achieved until 1 December
1972). From 1972, there was a deliberate attempt by UNIP to transform local
institutions into structural extensions of the party.[18] In Zambia and Tanzania,
the idea was to penetrate and control district councils without necessarily destroying them.

Elsewhere, a more bureaucratic mode of control was preferred. The local
government acts in Kenya, Botswana, Malawi, and Uganda gave the central
government statutory powers in the constitution of the authorities, budgetary
matters, making of bylaws, and appointment of senior staff. The center also
exercised the right to nominate councilors—in some countries up to one-third
of the total. In a multiparty system, this power was bound to be abused.

In states where the institution of provincial administration or regional administration still operated along the old colonial lines (e.g., Kenya, Botswana, and
Uganda under Obote [I]), the district commissioners were made ex-officio members of the councils for the sole purpose of ensuring central government sur-
veillance and control of council activities.

Other Devolution Options

Devolution includes federalism and cession of powers to statutory authorities
(see Figure 7.1).

Delegation to parastatals or statutory authority cannot be regarded as an independent type of decentralization.[19] Parastatals are created by acts of parliament and have parent ministries just like local authorities. Both have a lot in common including dependence on the center and therefore operate at the same level.

Several countries created statutory authorities at the regional level for development projects aimed at providing basic services. Examples are the Lake Basin Authority and Kerio Valley Development Authority in Kenya. These authorities have tended to duplicate the functions of existing local government agencies and in some instances generated unintended "bureaucratic imperialism" and conflict. Their weakness in income generation left them exposed and consequently, the center has tended to move in and treat them as mere extensions of the parent ministry.[20]

Federalism as a form of political decentralization is by its very nature quite removed from the people and, therefore, not a suitable framework for involving the local people in their own governance. Indeed, where the practice has been resorted to in Africa (e.g., Nigeria and to some extent Uganda), it has been used to address a peculiar colonial heritage. As a result, the form of devolution that has been widely adopted in Africa is local government based initially on traditional forms of authority, and later on popularly elected councils at the district level and below.

Bureaucratic Decentralization

Bureaucratic decentralization (i.e., deconcentration) involving delegation of responsibility to ministerial/department units in the field as well as to centrally initiated development committees and area-based programs has been the most preferred form of decentralization in Africa.

At independence, some African countries inherited relatively well-established departmentalized administrative systems, reflected in the presence of many departments at the provincial, district, and in some cases even at the subdistrict and locational (frontline) levels. Where an elaborate structure had not been put in place, doing so became a major preoccupation of the incoming regimes. Institution building was regarded as a basic prerequisite for nation building. Initially, the center received more attention but with success recorded at that level soon after independence, attention was immediately directed to the field. Functional congestion at the center soon necessitated sharing responsibilities with field-level units and personnel.

A well-managed system of delegation was put in place. It involved a power-sharing system in which the center provided broad guidelines within which field-level units performed their responsibilities. Decisions involving policymaking remained the exclusive prerogative of the center. In practice, how much was actually delegated depended on the center's perception of what the field units could do. The experience varied between areas and between ministries and departments.

The irony of departmentalization is that often it leads to "departmentalism,"[21] which discourages the sharing of resources and ideas. Agencies become inward-looking as they intuitively promote and protect their own interests and discourage cooperation and coordination essential for development management.

Factors Affecting Bureaucratic Decentralization: Lessons of Experience

Rondinelli, Nellis, and Cheema[22] identified four factors that usually affect decentralization:

a. Degree of political commitment and administrative support;
b. Attitudinal, behavioral, and cultural conditions conducive to decentralization;
c. Effective design and organization of decentralized programs; and
d. Adequate financial, human, and physical resources.

Quieti and Maetz suggest that decentralization could be analyzed by focusing on:[23]

a. Administration and organization: the administrative, political, and legal will, and efforts undertaken to promote decentralization;
b. Finance: the extent to which subnational levels have the liberty to use financial resources to promote decentralization;
c. Planning: the degree to which subnational units are engaged in planning in terms of local preparation of plans; and
d. People's participation: the extent to which the local people have an input in planning and implementation of projects at the local level.

The overlap between the two formulations is quite apparent. Therefore, the framework used below is a consolidation of the two.

The Degree of Political and Administrative Support. Decentralization is an organizing strategy for the sharing of responsibilities between the center and the localities. It involves power sharing between two unequal partners with the center being in a stronger position to dictate the terms of the transaction. Therefore, for any program of decentralization to succeed, the support that the lower units receive from the center has to be both *strong* and *sustained.* Two groups of actors are critical in this dispensation: the political leadership and the top bureaucratic managers. This is so regardless of the form of decentralization.

Lessons of the African experience suggest that the center is usually reluctant to engage in meaningful decentralization, preferring instead to engage in symbolism. This partly explains the marginalization of local government authorities as partners in governance and development. But even in the case of administrative decentralization (i.e., deconcentration) preference for *monocratic* management has remained strong since independence. Indeed, the higher bureaucracy in Africa has, without exception, been the major source of frustration for decentralization schemes. During 1970–76, a donor-led experiment in Kenya in area-based development (the Special Rural Development Programme [SRDP]) was tried in six subdistricts to ultimately replicate the successes in other areas. The ministerial headquarters were required to fully delegate responsibilities for planning and implementation of their projects in the selected areas. A local coordinator was appointed to coordinate the activities of all the ministries in the area and given authority over development resources. SRDP failed largely because most ministries refused to delegate responsibilities and authority to the program.[24] Similarly, district planning in Kenya, lacking political and bureaucratic support, performed poorly throughout the 1970s because ministry headquarters chose to ignore the exercise—preferring instead to plan for the districts from the center.[25]

Tanzania's famous decentralization scheme of 1972–82 suffered a similar fate. Ministry headquarters continued to retain strong links with their field units and often interfered with the decisions made within the context of decentralized management. The office of the prime minister, which was responsible for the decentralization program, established links and relationships that ensured the program remained under the guidance of the center.[26] In Malawi, the decentralization program introduced in 1993 has faced many frustrations because of lack of central political and administrative support. Known as the District Focus for Rural Development (DFRD) and introduced initially in six districts, its main objective was the strengthening of the district as the focal unit for planning and development coordination. Operationally, it involves staff strengthening, financial decentralization, integrated district planning, and the enhancement of popular participation in development.[27] The financial mainstay of the program is the newly established District Development Fund (DDF). Unfortunately, the fund relies wholly on donor support. A midterm evaluation undertaken in 1996 established that although some good progress had been made in getting the program off the ground, it still faced a lot of problems. Many ministries saw DFRD as a donor's program and owed no loyalty to it. Some went as far as instructing their field staff to have nothing to do with its activities. With the Ministry of Local Government and Rural Development (MLGRD) as its parent ministry, the program lacked political support at the center. The fear was generally expressed that the program would collapse as soon as donor support ended due to the lack of central ownership.[28] If that were to happen, its recorded achievements would be woefully sacrificed.[29]

That strong central political and administrative support is critical to the success of a program of decentralization was at one point positively demonstrated in the case of Kenya's DFRD initiated in 1983. Designed to achieve the same objectives as the Malawian one (in fact the Malawian program was a direct replication of the Kenyan one), it began on a sound footing with the full support of the president, who personally presided over its launching and subsequently popularized it in his many speeches to the nation. The program also received energetic support from the permanent secretary in charge of development, who continued to support the program even after leaving the ministry to become the head of the civil service between 1984 and 1988. The support that the program received from these two sources was largely responsible for breaking the initial resistance to the program by some sections of the higher bureaucracy responsible for development policies and the disbursement of development resources to the districts.

By the late 1980s, the program was an example of strong deconcentration.[30] However, toward the end of the decade (especially after the departure of the former holder of the Office of Development Coordination), support for the program at the center began to wane. His successor, who lacked the stature, enthusiasm, and drive that had kept the program on course, allowed the situation to slowly return to the old bureaucratic order. By the beginning of the 1990s, little had been heard of the program and indications are that the center has regained the control it supposedly lost to the districts during the 1980s.[31]

The disregard of institutional rules and the inclination toward monopolitic governance characteristic of personal rule regimes in contemporary Africa has meant that programs of decentralization can succeed only when there is strong personal intervention at the highest political and bureaucratic levels.

Sociocultural Influences. Since decentralization involves power sharing in the conduct of government business, its success must depend on the prevailing attitudes, orientation, and behavior in the society toward the notion of power sharing as a basis of governance. To understand traditional African attitudes toward power sharing, the precolonial period has to be studied.

The prevalence of monistic political orientation in the body politic of contemporary Africa is largely attributable to the sociopolitical policies pursued by the various colonial powers. The policies of assimilation, identity, and paternalism pursued by the French and the Portuguese in varying degrees were inherently centralistic. The so-called "empirical" approach employed by the British in the administration of its African colonies was a façade intended to hide the real intentions and practices, namely, the complete subordination of the indigenous institutions and authorities to the new colonial order.[32] Throughout Africa, colonial states were bureaucratic states with hierarchies of authority that linked the capital towns with the localities. The latter operated according to centrally determined norms and practices regardless of whether the mode of administration was direct or indirect. The administration was not only centralized but also authoritarian in its orientation and behavior.

Whereas parochial traditional culture could still find some expression in the governance process, the dominant culture that affects the relationship between the center and the localities is politicoadministrative. But there are also class-based interests.

In theory, decentralization is widely accepted because of its assured advantages. In practice, however, centralization is preferred, as it is feared that decentralization could strengthen ethnic blocks and other centrifugal forces in society. Also feared is a loss of politicoadministrative authority. Decentralization efforts in many African countries indicate the tendency of the center to insist on referral of important decisions to it at the various stages of planning or implementation of development programs.[33] In particular, the authority allocating resources is highly valued because quite often monopoly over this authority serves personal material interests as well.

A study of decentralization experience in Botswana revealed that "the strongest barrier to genuine decentralization is the vested interest of a small but entrenched socioeconomic elite. The elite recognize the need to create the impression of helping the rural poor and encouraging participation, but they also know that strong local institutions controlled by the poorer elements of society might jeopardize their interests in capital accumulation in the rural areas."[34]

Indeed, the operative centralizing administrative culture has meant that decentralization remains in practice a myth and a façade under which the real behavior of the higher bureaucracy is camouflaged.

The Design of Decentralization. Rondinelli, Nellis, and Cheema identified the major design variables influencing the outcomes of decentralization efforts as:[35]

- Clarity and simplicity of the structure and procedures used to decentralize;
- The ability of the implementing agency staff to interact with higher-level authorities; and
- The degree to which components of decentralized programs are integrated.

Of course, these are important variables. But there are other more basic ones that ought to be highlighted here as well, such as:

a. The feasibility of the chosen form of decentralization;
b. The extent to which the decentralization goals are realistic; and
c. The structural configuration in terms of vertical and horizontal relationships.

During the first decade after independence, little thought seems to have gone into the need to design appropriate decentralization systems. Many countries embarked on decentralization schemes because others were doing so. That may explain why identical structures seem to have emerged in many African countries.

The choice of appropriate forms of decentralization is important if the venture is to succeed. Devolution of power would not work where the center lacks political confidence in the subunits of the political system. Similarly, decentralization to an integrated field administration would not work unless there is a strong coordinating authority in the field, who wields both political and bureaucratic authority similar to that of the prefect in the French model.

The goals of decentralization have also to be realistic in terms of the framework of power-sharing capabilities between the center and the localities. What the center decentralizes must be capable of being performed at the level to which decentralization or delegation is directed.

Within the operative structure of field administration, decentralization to lower-level units requires putting in place a structure of functional relationships that links the various departments vertically and horizontally. This is what Rondinelli, Nellis, and Cheema seem to be referring to in their previously mentioned second and third points. Our conceptualization goes a little beyond theirs by including in the horizontal linkage the beneficiaries of development.

In administrative decentralization, three forms of decentralization have been used in practically all countries: delegation within the ministerial/departmental hierarchy, the use of the committee system, and the establishment of area-based programs. It will be recalled that many new ministries and departments were created immediately after independence in virtually all African countries. Some of them did not immediately have field representatives. But over the years, and as the scope of their activities expanded, the need to establish field units was felt. What logically followed was the decision about the functions and associated powers that needed to be delegated to them. However, in the practical sense, the field units under such an arrangement continued to refer upward all the important decisions about development management. Thus, delegation within a ministerial hierarchy is the weakest form of administrative decentralization. But in the context of the political and management administration at that time, it was the most feasible form of decentralization. What such field units of the parent ministry were required to perform was quite consistent with the doctrine of departmental delegation.

The important development in the decentralization movement was the realization that development goals in the field could not be effectively pursued in situations in which departments operated in isolation of one another in the development process. The need for coordination and integrated development led to the creation of structures to give expression to that concern. It was against that background that development committees were created (or strengthened in cases where they had existed before independence in weak *ad hoc* forms).

From the mid-1960s, the establishment of development committees became a fashionable preoccupation of development managers. In some countries, a plethora of such committees was established within a hierarchy that began at the lowest administrative unit (e.g., sublocational level in Kenya) and went all the way up to the national level. By the close of the first decade of independence they would exist in practically all Anglophone Africa. The functions they were required to perform varied little between the various levels of government as well as among different countries. Indeed, the common practice was for one country to replicate the structures in operation in a neighboring country. Often there would be a consultant from a donor country initiating such replication.

Since for many African countries, the district is the most important unit in field administration linking the field to the center, the development committees at that level emerged as the focus of development activities, and all the lower-level committees were made responsible to it in a well-established hierarchy. The nomenclature—district development committee—was universalized as it were. Therefore, an analysis of the design of decentralization in Africa has to address, for the greater part, the structure and performance of development committees at the district level.

Development Committees: Organs of Participation or Instruments of Central Control?

The idea of development through planning was popularized by the Labour Government in 1945 through the Colonial Development and Welfare Act (1945) requiring colonies to produce ten-year development plans (1946–1956) as a guide to their own development.[36] Even after 1956, development plans continued to be produced on a short-term basis (about three to four years) until the eve of independence. But no permanent planning organs were established, and planning committees that drew up the colonial plans were largely *ad hoc*. Soon after independence, many countries established agencies or ministries for development planning that felt the need to establish structures in the field to assist the center in project identification. These committees were established at different times for different countries, depending on the date of each country's independence. But once established, the committees tended to acquire common characteristics.

Characteristics of the Committees

The level at which the committees have been created has varied over the years from country to country. Some countries established them at all the existing administrative units in the field (e.g. Kenya, Tanzania, and Zimbabwe). Elsewhere (e.g., Malawi and Botswana), the district has been the highest level. In some countries (e.g., Kenya), two sets of committees—one supposedly advisory and the other executive—were established in the mid-1960s. The advisory committee consisted of elected and ruling party political leaders as well as a few representatives of interest groups. The other committee was made up exclusively of provincial or district heads of departments. Below the district level, membership was mixed. These committees operated in a vacuum wherever they existed in Africa.

Functions

The general-purpose committees were expected to coordinate overall planning and implementation of development programs within their jurisdiction. Although the experience varied from country to country, on the whole, the problems that the countries experienced in trying to discharge their functions were by and large similar.

To begin with, these committees did not have any legal personality. They had been created by presidential decrees or through ministerial pronouncements and were without political or bureaucratic powers. In Kenya, they were moribund for a long time, for neither the line ministries nor other agencies involved in rural development took them seriously.[37] The advisory committees were later merged with the development committees and the membership rationalized and streamlined. At the provincial level, they now exist as Provincial Monitoring and Evaluation Committees, with the district retaining the old name—District Development Committee (DDC).

As planning organs, these committees continued to rely on their parent ministries in the capital cities. In Zimbabwe, they controlled no resources and, therefore, had no control over the planning behavior of line ministries.[38] Even after the posting of a provincial governor for development coordination, vertical linkages remained dominant because the ministries still controlled effective resource flows from the center.[39] Indeed, even after introducing a fund specifically earmarked for rural development, MLGRD continued to control the fund centrally and release it on centrally determined criteria.[40]

In Uganda, the DDCs of the 1960s were mere appendages of the Ministry of Planning. With their recent revival following many years of institutional lethargy between 1971 and 1986, central control persists. The ministry's technical committee made up of departmental heads is supposed to draw up plans for its approval but the fact that the departmental heads are still directly responsible to their own ministries in Kampala is inherently limiting. Limiting too is the presence of the president's representative at the district, whose functions include "advice especially on matters of national nature that may affect the councils in their planning."[41]

In Botswana, the DDCs operate according to centrally determined guidelines. They are under the control of the district commissioner who, administratively, is responsible to the Office of the President, and on development matters, to the Ministry of Local Government, Lands, and Housing (MLGLH). It has been observed that the DDCs are administrative creations without statutory powers or budgets of their own. They are not implementing agencies and are not directly responsible for the expenditure of development funds.[42]

Botswana's DDCs have been under the guidance of a district officer (development) since 1970. But in discharging his duties the district officer works very closely with the Rural Development Unit in the Ministry of Finance and Development Planning and also with the District Plans Committee based in the same ministry. In district planning, MLGLH, whose deputy secretary chairs the plans committee, is represented by the council planning officer. The exercise of district planning, begun in 1971 and scaled up in 1977, still remains a top-down exercise. Sharma adds: "Development plans are essentially formulated at the centre where policies are determined and decisions are taken with regard to the allocation of resources. The contribution of district-level organizations has increased steadily, but remains limited."[43]

A further weakness of district planning in Botswana is that it is still highly dependent on expatriates who occupy critical planning positions both in Gaborone and in the districts.[44]

Committees: Do They Facilitate Popular Participation?

One design weakness of the DDCs that needs special consideration is the weakness or absence of horizontal links with the beneficiaries. In countries where political parties play a subordinate role in the governance process, they have been dominated by civil servants (e.g., Kenya and Botswana). In such situations, popular participation in the development process through the DDCs has been marginal and yet that is a major component of horizontal relationships in the development process. Where leftist ideologies have had some influence on the structure of the committees, political activists have tended to dominate the membership of the committees (e.g., Zambia under Kaunda, Tanzania under Nyerere, and Uganda under Museveni). The result has been tactical retreat by the professionals, who have instead preferred the use of technical committees. Their participation in the DDC meetings has been symbolic. In 1971, Montgomery and Esman drew a distinction between genuine and symbolic participation,[45] where the former implies real influence while the latter is manipulated or controlled to ratify rather than influence official behavior.

The question, then, is why should it be that at one point participation is genuine and at another it is manipulated? The answer to this question lies in what participation entails by its very nature. Essentially, the act and process of participation is a political one. Participation involves power sharing in decision-making. The assumption behind power sharing is the existence of a balance of forces between the interacting parties. Where the relationship is characterized by imbalance, the more powerful actor will arrogate unto himself as much power as he can possibly master.

Indeed, James Riedel is right in observing that in real life, no one gives up power to others unless he no longer needs it, can no longer sustain it for personal reasons, or is forced to do so.[46] He observes further that if the power involved is transferable and useful, there is almost always an heir-apparent in the wings. In this light, talking of community control groups as if the governments were about to surrender anything more than nominal power is to entertain a dangerously false expectation.[47] Here then lies the limitation of popular participation.

By its very nature, popular participation implies introducing the citizens or the masses into the act of power sharing in the governance process. For decades now, questions have been asked about whether and how the citizens should be involved not just in decision-making about those issues that affect their lives directly, but also how these decisions, once made, should be implemented with their participation.

As presently constituted, the local development committees lack the incentive structure and strong operational posture that would make them an instrument of local participation in the development process. The national politicoadministrative culture is monistic and therefore, local-level institutions lack sufficient authority to undertake their tasks. The fear that popular participation might lead to loss of state control over the citizens explains why the notion remains largely symbolic in the realm of decision-making.

The missing link in many countries remains the absence of an integrating national-level development committee responsible for ensuring that DDC matters are centrally coordinated and with sufficient power and authority to force compliance on reluctant line ministries.

Area-Based Development

Another type of deconcentration was tried in a number of African countries. Between 1970 and 1976, largely in response to donor initiative, Kenya experimented with the SRDP. Botswana's Accelerated Rural Development Programme (ARDP) was tried between 1974 and 1976 and Zimbabwe's Integrated Rural Development Programme (IRDP) was conceived on the eve of independence and generated a lot of ideas but remained unimplemented.[48]

In a nutshell, these programs involved the selection of a development area on criteria agreed upon at the center with the donors. A special organizational arrangement was created that removed the program from vertical control by the cooperating central ministries. The authority was vested in the program leadership in the field, with project funds being managed in the project area. The funds were to be exempted from the routine budgetary release procedures. If implemented as conceived, this would have represented a high degree of bureaucratic decentralization.

It is precisely the freedoms they were supposed to enjoy that became the source of their frustrations. The project staff were to be responsible to the project but not employed by it. In some cases (e.g., Kenya), they found themselves responding both to project demands and to demands of their routine departmental responsibilities. They controlled a vote, but had no power to decide about its replenishment—the center did.

The projects stood like islands within a wider environment yawning for similar attention. Soon politicians from the excluded areas complained. The original experimental character of the projects was lost as expatriates working on them pushed for visible signs of success, thus transforming projects into areas of development per se. There was also reluctance and resistance by many ministries, especially in Kenya and Botswana, to accept the principles associated with the program. This led to delays in program implementation or distortions in the implementation process.[49] The programs were viewed as a threat to the existing management procedures in government. The way out for both the Kenyan and Botswanan governments was to claim that enough lessons had been learned in the program that would be used in launching (in the case of Botswana) or strengthening district planning (in the case of Kenya).[50]

Area-based development has high potential for meaningful role playing in decision-making at the local level, but it also has high potential for conflict generation considering that the participating ministries and agencies have dual and often multiple loyalties. In Zimbabwe, the interest as well as conflict that it generated at a time of uncertainty led to its abandonment without trial. In Kenya and Botswana, it had to be wound up as a way of dissipating an assault on it from a variety of sources.

RESOURCES FOR DECENTRALIZATION

Financial

A major missing link in deconcentration efforts in many African countries has been the lack of locally controlled resources for development. Decisions involving the commitment of financial resources in the field are made in a vacuum, and procedures for the release of approved funds are cumbersome and bureaucratic.

After decentralization, funds continued to be controlled from the center and were released to individual departmental units in the field instead of to an integrated fund at the local level. The DDCs could not perform their coordination functions because, lacking control over development funds, no departmental head paid any attention to them.

After some years the need to create special funds to spur the committees into action was realized (Kenya, Tanzania, and Malawi). Special grants were made to the committees to be spent on projects identified by the local people and approved by the DDCs and ultimately, by the ministry in charge of district planning. Because of the availability of such funds, the departmental heads at the district level began to take the deliberations of the committees seriously and attendance at committee meetings improved markedly.[51]

In Zambia, and more recently, in Ghana and Uganda, where an integrated decentralization system is being tried, the districts' own funds derived from local taxation contributed to the strengthening of the local financial base. But still budgets have to be centrally approved.

More recently, the transformation of the district as the hub and focus of local development management has resulted in substantial funds being controlled at the district level. As a result, better and more realistic project proposals have been made.[52] In the case of Malawi, however, the situation remains fluid as the funds in question have come mainly from a donor source.

Staffing Situation

Decentralization is also affected by the staffing situation in the decentralized units. In many countries, the less qualified staff members are posted to the districts. Ironically, this has been partly responsible for the reluctance by the center to delegate important responsibilities to the districts. The absence of qualified professional staff with relevant experience in the fields of planning, project design, implementation, and monitoring and evaluation has been a major missing link. The hierarchical structure of the ministries, according to which staff operating in the field depend on the higher levels for recognition and reward, tends to encourage dependence mentality in the interaction between the center and the field-level staff. In that sort of situation, field-level staff shy away from taking initiative in the management process; yet the success of decentralized development to a large extent depends on the capacity of the local staff to be creative, innovative, and proactive.

Even in situations where integrated local administration has been the option—Zambia in the 1980s, Tanzania during 1972–82, Uganda[53] since 1993, and Ghana under Rawlings (mark II)—the departmental working norms were marginally changed and local-level staff continued to rely on the higher levels of departmental hierarchies for recognition and professional mobility.

There is evidence (e.g., Kenya and Malawi) to show that decentralization works better when resources, funds, and staff are made readily available to support the program, and more so when the funds are controlled locally through a well-established system of release from the center; and that the upgrading of the level and quality of staff creates a sense of confidence that encourages the center to extend discretionary powers to the lower units of administration.

THE SEARCH FOR ALTERNATIVE FORMS

The frustration with the partnership form of decentralization in which central government ministries operated alongside local authorities in the field, sometimes without clear separation of functions and responsibilities, ultimately led in some countries to the search for alternative forms of organization. Three countries have been selected to illustrate this case: Tanzania, Zambia, and more recently Malawi (still pending final authorization).

From the documents establishing these policies,[54] the purpose of creating a unified system[55] or prefectural system[56] appeared to aim at rationalizing and unifying government authority at the district level.

Maro's study categorized the Tanzanian government's objectives into three:[57]

a. *Political*, to achieve wider and more constructive popular participation, an enhanced role for the party, and more equitable redistribution of resources;

b. *Administrative*, to attain increased efficiency and effectiveness in operation of the government, more effective integration of government programs, and increased accountability of the bureaucracy; and

c. *Economic*, to ensure increased government ability to mobilize the people and successfully implement productive projects; greater capacity to assist villagers and other local institutions in their production efforts, and facilitation of rural development in the broad socioeconomic context.

Appropriate institutions were established in the field to facilitate the implementation of the stated objectives: creation of development directorates at regional and district levels; reorganization of the district council into a development council and rationalizing its membership to include district heads of departments, members of parliament (MPs), and other interested groups; and creation of a development planning committee answerable to the newly created district council. Other development committees were created at administrative levels below the district. No elective committee was put in place at the provincial level, but a regional development committee under the newly appointed regional director was established to coordinate regional planning—especially the activities of the district development planning committee. At the center, the Office of the Prime Minister was reorganized and charged with providing a link in the development process between the districts and the center.[58]

Because the new councils did not have the powers to raise revenue, the center held the leverage over budgetary matters. The control exercised by the Prime Minister's Office over the regions and the regions in turn over the district was comprehensive and detailed.[59] Mawhood writes: "Although labeled decentralization this was of course a well known formula of deconcentration plus advisory committees, a management reform with little political content. It set out to concentrate the allocation of resources at each level in a single authority which would itself be effectively controlled from the centre."[60]

The program did not enhance popular decision-making in the development process. Ideologically, decentralization was conceived to enable the state to act on the people through *mobilization* not participation. The villagization program launched at about the same time was inherently authoritarian in all its manifestations. The role of the state was enhanced at the cost of popular support. This would over the years (1972–81) influence the economic performance especially in agriculture.[61] Baregu is forthright: "It was realized in the early 1980s that the system of decentralization which had relied on coercion to secure increased output had in fact resulted in the overall decline of production."[62]

The decentralization policy in Zambia[63] envisaged the district as the focus of development activities and the creation of an integrated administrative system at the district level.[64] The 1980 Decentralization Act provided for the establishment of a plethora of management units at the provincial, district, and other lower levels of administration. At the provincial level, the act provided for the establishment of a provincial council, provincial committee, and provincial secretariat. The three organs were also established at the district level. Except for the secretariat, membership of councils and committees at both levels was confined to UNIP members, drawn from elected politicians, party functionaries, women's groups, mass organizations, trade unions, security forces, and chiefs. Whereas the provincial secretariat was to be made up of provincial heads of departments, the same was not the case at the district level. Here, membership was to be determined by the district council, with the minister empowered to prescribe, by statutory order, the functions of each member of the secretariat.

Apart from reference to the minister, the Decentralization Act is silent about the links between the province and the center of the district and the center. Functions prescribed for the provincial and district councils and committees (Schedules I–VI) reveal functional duplication and overlap. In practice, these were bound to create confusion and conflict.

The situation was compounded by the presence of provincial and district planning units that were functionally linked to the National Commission for Development Planning and to the Ministry of Decentralization established in 1985.[65] In practice, however, the ideology of *decentralization in centralism* that took place after 1981 implied that the field-level units would continue to behave as appendages of the center.[66]

Malawian Move

Currently, the Government of Malawi is in the final phase of experimenting with the District Focus Strategy for Rural Development. The strategy is similar in many respects to the one Kenya has been implementing since 1983 under the same name. It involves the delegation of planning and implementation decisions concerning district-specific projects to the district level. The project is coordinated through the DDC chaired by the district commissioner and the technical professional decisions are handled initially by the district executive committee (DEC) made up of departmental heads with the district development officer as chairman. DEC reports to DDC. To strengthen district planning, planning units have been set up in the six districts where the project is under trial. A District Development Fund—subscribed to by donors (mainly the United Nations Development Programme (UNDP)) and the Government of Malawi—has been established to support district-specific projects identified at the district level. This has allowed the project to be taken seriously by district heads of departments. As presently set up, the project has not interfered with the activities of district councils, whose chairmen and chief executives are both members of the district committees.

Although there was some indifference in some quarters at the central level and, in a few cases, even hostility and resistance to this mode of deconcentration, the program appears to have performed quite satisfactorily so far.

While implementing this strategy, the Government of Malawi also considered the long-term organizational structure that needs to be put in place to support local governance. From comparative studies of existing options in Africa, an integrated administrative setup was selected to be "a single unified representative and autonomous body combining the merits of local authorities and DDCs," and called the district council.

MLGRD would provide primary guidance and support to district councils. The creation of a cabinet committee on decentralization to provide political leadership on decentralization has been suggested. The proposal is attractive in its formulation. The question, however, is: Will it work in practice?

What is contained in the document represents the ideal situation. Writing on the subject, Selznick once suggested that decentralization would be incomplete in a situation in which the following powers were not decentralized:[67]

- Discretionary power over decision-making;
- Power to raise and commit revenue; and
- Power to hire and fire.

The proposed Malawian Decentralization Act has adequately addressed these issues and it is the struggle over the control of the three that usually breaks the letter and spirit of decentralization. At present, the district commissioner, the integrating generalist at the district level, is responsible to the Office of the President and Cabinet Affairs. Under the proposed structure, that office (of the DC) will cease to exist and the task of guiding the districts will revert to the MLGRD. Will that arrangement not deprive the executive of a direct link with the localities through the districts? And considering that Malawi is relatively a small country, how will the staff react to the "localization" of their service with no prospects for upward mobility beyond the district? Is that not what has created staffing problems for local authorities all over Africa? These are questions that any country contemplating setting up such a system has to address—not just Malawi. Indeed the experiences of Tanzania and Zambia offer many lessons.

EMERGING ISSUES: A SUMMARY

Decentralization is both an ideal and a way of organizing government operations. As an ideal, there are certain associated assumptions that are now platitudes. We can, nevertheless, restate them here. Decentralization:

- Reduces overload and congestions in channels of administration and communication;
- Reduces delays; and
- Improves government's responsiveness to the public and increases the quality and quantity of services it provides.[68]

With special reference to devolution through local government, Olowu adds the following assumptions. Decentralization:

- Is a training ground for democracy;
- Promotes accountable government; and
- Is an instrument of social and other types of development.[69]

Olowu does not claim that these services are necessarily provided by local government. What has been done is simply to restate them for purposes of analysis.

Local Government: Lessons of Experience

In many African countries, there has not been any deliberate attempt to strengthen local governments as instruments of either political participation or socioeconomic development. The functions of local governments have always been closely defined and the manner of carrying them out prescribed. A closer examination of the acts creating the local governments (e.g., in Kenya, Tanzania, Uganda, Botswana, and Zambia) revealed that there are no functions that they can perform independently. There is a web of structural and functional stipulations that often leaves the power leverage with the center.

Personnel Matters

We have referred to the absence of discretionary powers over employment through a system of approval by the central government council budgets and estimates. Many countries have established a Local Government Staff Commission (e.g., Tanzania, Nigeria, and Botswana) to recruit, deploy, and fire senior council staff. In addition, there are senior posts such as clerk to council and treasurer that need to get the approval of the parent ministry. The net effect of this situation is that senior staff are rarely loyal to the councils they serve.

Financial Resources

The laws relating to financing local government activities have changed many times over the years. At independence, when the councils used to provide many basic services such as primary education, health, and rural roads, they received a lot of funds locally through fees and other charges. The center also provided specific grants to support these services. The situation changed soon after independence with the growth in demand of services and the inability of the councils to provide the services. Transfer of services to the center simultaneously deprived the councils of sources of revenue. In Kenya, for example, the problem persists to this day.

Elsewhere, efforts have been made to earmark a percentage of the national budget for local governments. In Nigeria, the percentage was increased in 1992 to 20 percent and regulations were put in place to ensure that this share would not be diverted by the concerned state governments for their own use.[70]

Financial dependence on the central government remains a major bottleneck in the councils' efforts to exercise their little autonomy. In Zambia, for example, a 1987 budget of local councils revealed that they could mobilize only 20 percent of their needs from local sources.[71] In Zimbabwe, up to 85.3 percent of the councils' funds come from the central government with councils raising only 14.7 percent from their own sources.[72]

Deconcentration Experience

The ministries have been reluctant to meaningfully involve field-level officers in policymaking. As a result, policies are still centrally determined and the field units are merely expected to implement them. Where district planning has been put in place, it operates on centrally determined principles and guidelines. In some countries, even model plans are prepared centrally—usually by expatriate advisers—as guides to district planning.

Under district planning, development plans are being produced that do not have any influence on what the sectoral ministries implement or on what is contained in the national development plans.[73]

Even in area-based development (e.g., Kenya's SRDP, Botswana's ARDP, and Tanzania's RIDEP), decentralization of resources was strongly resisted by some ministries and only partial delegation to the areas had been achieved. Similar resistance has been experienced in both Kenya and Malawi in their efforts to make the district the focus of rural development. In the case of Kenya, however, some impressive results were realized in the formative years largely because the head of state and the then chief secretary (head of the public service) took keen personal interest in the program. In Malawi, unlike Kenya, the main push has come from the donor community which has played a major role in its financing. In spite of resistance from some quarters, the program has so far recorded many achievements: reactivation of hitherto dormant committees; strengthening of district planning capacity; and creating the spirit of departmental cooperation. But the fact still remains that throughout Africa, decentralization has been preached more than it has been practiced. What is the problem and what is the way out?

SOME CONCLUDING REMARKS

The problem with decentralization in Africa is that it has been approached as an ideal and therefore, its limitations have not been seriously considered. Maddick reminded us many years ago that governments will not decentralize power unless they had full confidence in the field units.[74] In regimes that lack legitimacy or in military and personal rule regimes, the fear is further compounded.

The other issue relates to the absence of allocation of powers between the center and the localities. What can the various government agencies and units meaningfully do? To answer this question, one would have to consider the political and economic maturity of the individual states as well as the availability of men and women to whom technical and professional responsibilities are to be delegated.

As for now, the purpose of decentralization remains not *"political"* in the sense of power sharing, but bureaucratic and efficiency-oriented. Kasfir is right in suggesting that in Africa today decentralization means distributing authority and power horizontally rather than vertically.[75] Mawhood adds: "The purpose of central-local relations as seen from the national centre can be summarized as follows: political control; economic regulation; common minimum standard of operation; administrative efficiency."[76]

As presently constituted, decentralized organizations—whether political or administrative—must be seen as the center's agents, discharging whatever functions have been delegated to them. The right to alter, modify, or withdraw the delegated powers remains the prerogative of the center. That is likely to continue into the twenty-first century. Africa is not alone. This attitude still prevails in some developed countries as well.

NOTES

This chapter brings together the author's ideas developed in two unpublished papers on the subject: "Decentralization Policy and Its Implementation in Post-Independence Africa" (Paper presented at the African Association of Public Administration and Management [AAPAM] Roundtable Conference, Nairobi, 1997); and "Decentralization and Local Development in Africa" (Paper presented at the Africa Regional Development Policy Forum, Nairobi, 10–11 June 1998).

1. Philip Mawhood, ed., *Local Government in the Third World: Experience of Decentralization in Tropical Africa* (2nd ed.) (Pretoria: Africa Institute of South Africa, 1993), pp. 2–3.

2. Henry Maddick, *Democracy, Decentralization and Development* (London: Asia Publishing House, 1963); Brian Smith, *Field Administration: An Aspect of Decentralization* (London: Routledge & Kegan Paul, 1967); and P. de Valk and K. H. Wekwete, "Challenges for Local Government in Zimbabwe" in P. de Valk and K. H. Wekwete, eds., *Decentralization for Participatory Planning: Comparing the Experience in Zimbabwe and Other Anglophone Countries in Eastern and Southern Africa* (London: Avebury Publishing, 1990).

3. D. A. Rondinelli, J. R. Nellis, and G. S. Cheema, "Decentralization in Developing Countries: A Review of Recent Experience" (World Bank Staff Working Paper No. 581) (Washington, DC: World Bank, 1983).

4. D. Conyers, "Decentralization and Development Planning: A Comparative Perspective" in de Valk and Wekwete, *Decentralization for Participatory Planning.*

5. United Nations, *Decentralization for National and Local Development* (New York, 1962).

6. C. G. Roseberg and R. Jackson, "Personal Rule: Theory and Practice in Africa," *Comparative Politics* (July 1984).

7. Goran Hyden, *No Short Cut to Progress: African Development Management in Perspective* (Berkeley: University of California Press, 1983).

8. Roseberg and Jackson, "Personal Rule."

9. Victor A. Thompson, "Administrative Objectives for Development Administration," *Administrative Science Quarterly* 9 (June 1964): 91–108.

10. E. Sady, "Improvement of Local Government and Administration for Development Purposes" in Raphaeli Nimrod, ed., *Readings in Comparative Public Administration* (Boston: Allyn & Bacon, 1967).

11. de Valk and Wekwete, "Challenges for Local Government in Zimbabwe."

12. Alex Gboyega, *Political Values and Local Government in Nigeria* (Lagos: Malthhous Press, 1987).

13. Ibid; and Ronald Wraith, *Local Administration in West Africa* (London: Allen & Unwin, 1972).

14. G. Kanyeihamba, *Constitutional Law and Government in Uganda* (Nairobi: East African Literature Bureau, 1975).

15. Walter O. Oyugi, "The Unification of the Local Government System in Kenya: An Historical Note" in de Valk and Wekwete, eds., *Decentralization for Participatory Planning*.

16. Mawhood, ed., *Local Government in the Third World*; and L. Cliffe and J. Saul, "The District Development Front in Tanzania" in L. Cliffe and J. Saul, eds., *Socialism in Tanzania* (Nairobi: East African Publishing House, 1972), p. 312.

17. K. Kaunda, *Zambia's Guide for the Next Decade* (Lusaka: Government Policy, 1998), p. 180 as cited in B. L. Mwape, "Party and Local Government in Zambia: Decentralized Planning, 1964–1985" in de Valk and Wekwete, *Decentralization for Participatory Planning*, p. 180.

18. Mwape, "Party and Local Government in Zambia," p. 183.

19. Rondinelli, Nellis, and Cheema, "Decentralization in Developing Countries."

20. Walter O. Oyugi, "Local Government in Kenya: A Case of Institutional Decline" in Mawhood, ed., *Local Government in the Third World*.

21. B. Schaffer, *The Administrative Factor* (London: Frank Cass, 1973).

22. Rondinelli, Nellis, and Cheema, "Decentralization in Developing Countries."

23. Maria Quieti and M. Maetz, *Training for Decentralized Planning: Lessons from Experience* Volume 1 (Rome: Food and Agriculture Organization [FAO] of the United Nations, 1987).

24. Walter O. Oyugi, *Rural Development Administration* (New Delhi: Vikas, 1981).

25. P. Delp, "District Planning in Kenya" in Tony Killick, ed., *Papers on the Kenyan Economy* (Nairobi: Heinemann Educational Books, 1981); and John Cohen and Richard Hook, *District Development Planning in Kenya* (Nairobi: Rural Planning Unit, Ministry of Finance and Economic Planning, 1986).

26. J. R. Finucane, *Bureaucracy and Rural Development in Tanzania* (Uppsala: Scandinavian Institute of African Studies, 1974); G. Munishi, "Development Administration in Tanzania" (unpublished paper submitted as a chapter of a manuscript being considered for publication in Walter O. Oyugi, ed., *Bureaucracy and Development Management in Africa*, 1960–1990 (forthcoming)).

27. Ministry of Local Government and Rural Development (MLGRD), Government of Malawi, "National Decentralization Policy" (Draft) (Lilongwe, 1995).

28. MLGRD, Government of Malawi, *Mid-Term Evaluation Report of Programme IV: Management for Development* (Lilongwe, 1996).

29. J. Mbeye, "Implementing Decentralization: Financial Resource Consideration" (AAPAM Roundtable, Nairobi, 17–21 March 1997).

30. Walter O. Oyugi, "Decentralization and Its Implementation in Post-Independence Africa: An Analysis" (AAPAM Conference Paper, Nairobi, 1997).

31. Ibid.

32. J. N. Paden and E. Q. Soja, eds., *The African Experience* (Evanston: Northwestern University Press, 1970); and L. H. Gan and Peter Duignan, eds., *Colonialism in Africa, 1870–1960* (Cambridge, UK: Cambridge University Press, 1969).

33. Mawhood, ed., *Local Government in the Third World*; and de Valk and Wekwete, "Challenges for Local Government in Zimbabwe."

34. Wyn Reilley and W. Tordoff, "Decentralization in Botswana: Myth or Reality" in Mawhood, ed., *Local Government in the Third World.*

35. Rondinelli, Nellis, and Cheema, "Decentralization in Developing Countries," p. 62.

36. J. M. Lee, *Colonial Development and Good Government* (Oxford: Clarendon House, 1967), p. 113.

37. H. Jackson, "Provincial Planning in Kenya" in G. Hyden et al., *Development Administration: The Kenyan Experience* (Nairobi: Heinemann Educational Books, 1981); Walter O. Oyugi, "Kenya: Two Decades of Decentralization Efforts," *African Administrative Studies* 26 (1986): 133–61; and Oyugi, "The Unification of the Local Government System in Kenya."

38. K. H. Wekwete and A. Mlalazi, "Provincial/Regional Planning in Zimbabwe: Problem and Prospects" in de Valk and Wekwete, *Decentralization for Participatory Planning.*

39. Ibid.

40. de Valk and Wekwete, "Challenges for Local Government in Zimbabwe."

41. Government of Uganda, "Resistance Council Statute, 1993," *New Vision* (15 April 1994).

42. Brian Egner, *District Councils and Decentralization, 1978–1986* (Report to SIDA by Economic Consultancies) (Gaborone, 1987).

43. K. C. Sharma, "The Role of Local Government and Decentralized Agencies in Local Level Development: Lessons from Botswana," *African Journal of Public Administration and Development* 1 (2:1992).

44. W. Reilley, "District Development Planning in Botswana" (Manchester Papers on Development; No. 3) (Manchester, 1981), pp. 28–69.

45. J. D. Montgomery and Milton Esman, "Popular Participation in Development Administration," *Journal of Comparative Administration* 3 (3:1971).

46. James A. Riedel, "Citizens' Participation: Myth or Reality" in Mawhood, ed., *Local Government in the Third World.*

47. Ibid.

48. Wekwete and Mlalazi, "Provincial/Regional Planning in Zimbabwe."

49. Oyugi, *Rural Development Administration.*

50. Government of Kenya, *National Development Plan, 1974–78* (Nairobi: Government Printer, 1974); Reilley, "District Development Planning in Botswana"; and Gov-

ernment of Botswana, Chapter 40: District Councils, *Local Government* (Gaborone: Ministry of Local Government, Lands, and Housing, 1992).

51. On Kenya, see Oyugi, "Kenya"; and his "The Unification of the Local Government System in Kenya"; on Tanzania, see G. Munishi, "Development Administration in the Tanzanian Experience" (Dar es Salaam: University of Dar es Salaam, 1984).

52. On Kenya, see Oyugi, "The Unification of the Local Government System in Kenya"; and on Malawi, see Mbeye, "Implementing Decentralization."

53. Government of Uganda, Local Administration Act 1997.

54. J. K. Nyerere, *Decentralization* (Dar es Salaam: Tanzania Publishing House, 1972); Government of Zambia, *The Local Government Act* (Gazette Notice No. 15 of 1980) (Lusaka: Government Printer, 1980); and MLGRD, Government of Malawi, "National Decentralization Policy."

55. Smith, *Field Administration.*

56. Sady, "Improvement of Local Government."

57. These descriptions benefit from P. S. Maro, "The Evolution and Functioning of Local Government in Tanzania" in de Valk and Wekwete, *Decentralization for Participatory Planning*; and Nyerere, *Decentralization.*

58. Maro, ibid.

59. Maro, Ibid.; Mawhood, ed., *Local Government in the Third World*; and D. Conyers, "Decentralization for Regional Development: A Comparative Study of Tanzania, Zambia and Papua New Guinea," *Public Administration and Development* 1 (1981): 107–20.

60. Mawhood, ibid.

61. See for example, G. Hyden, *Beyond Ujamaa in Tanzania: Underdevelopment and Uncaptured Peasantry* (Berkeley: University of California Press, 1980); and M. Baregu, "Conflict and Collaboration in Party/Government Relations in Tanzania" in Walter O. Oyugi, ed., *Politics and Administration in East Africa* (Nairobi: East African Educational Publishers, 1994).

62. Baregu, ibid.

63. Government of Zambia, The Local Government Act.

64. K. K. Kaunda, Speech on the Launching of 1980 Decentralization Act; see National Institute of Public Administration (NIPA), *Decentralization in Zambia: Readings on the New Local Government System* (1981).

65. D. Noppen, "Decentralization and the Role of District and Provincial Planning Units in Zambia" in de Valk and Wekwete, *Decentralization for Participatory Planning.*

66. Mwape, "Party and Local Government in Zambia"; Noppen, ibid; and C. H. B. Muleya and Mbilikita, "In-Service Training in Agricultural Project Analysis" in Quieti and Maetz, *Training for Decentralized Planning.*

67. P. Selznick, *TVA and the Grassroots* (Berkeley: University of California Press, 1949).

68. Rondinelli, Nellis, and Cheema, "Decentralization in Developing Countries."

69. Dele Olowu, *African Local Governments as Instruments of Economic and Social Development* (Publication No. 1415) (The Hague: International Union of Local Authorities [IULA], 1988).

70. Alex Gboyega, "Local Government Reform in Nigeria" in Mawhood, ed., *Local Government in the Third World*, p. 247; and Said Adejumobi, "The Military and Local Government Autonomy: Some Reflections" in Said Adejumobi and Abubakar Momoh,

eds., *The Political Economy of Nigeria under Military Rule, 1984–1993* (Harare: Sapes Books, 1995).

71. Muleya and Mbilikita, "In-Service Training in Agricultural Project Analysis," p. 76.

72. Wekwete and Mlalazi, "Provincial/Regional Planning in Zimbabwe," p. 93.

73. Walter O. Oyugi, "Decentralized Development Planning and Management in Kenya: An Assessment" in L. Adamolekun et al., *Decentralization Policies and Socio-Economic Development in Sub-Saharan Africa* (Washington, DC: Economic Development Institute of the World Bank, 1990); and Cohen and Hook, *District Development Planning in Kenya.*

74. Maddick, *Democracy, Decentralization and Development.*

75. Nelson Kasfir, "Designs and Dilemmas of African Decentralization" in Mawhood, ed., *Local Government in the Third World.*

76. Mawhood, *Local Government in the Third World.*

8

Decentralization and Local Autonomy: Regional Planning in Ethiopia

Getachew Mequanent and D. R. Fraser Taylor

INTRODUCTION

In the 1990s, many African countries underwent profound socioeconomic and political changes. Hyden and Bratton state that many Africans are inclined to see the 1990s as the period of the second liberation.[1] The "one leader, one ideology, and one political party" slogan of the 1960s had apparently encouraged leaders to take virtual control of state power. "Development became a top-down affair, and politics increasingly an activity confined to a small clique of people. The latter ran away with politics ... turning the public matter into private and making a mockery of political accountability."[2] By the mid-1980s, however, international financial institutions and bilateral aid agencies had begun putting pressure on African national governments to reform centralized political systems and economic planning. As a result, many governments adopted measures such as market liberalization, state decentralization, and a move toward political pluralism. In addition, emerging civil society has increasingly challenged the dominant structures of power and institutions that had hitherto dictated the terms and conditions of economic and political governance. McGee and Edgington state that such entities often bypass national institutional channels to build relational networks that enhance their capacity to promote regional/local interests.[3] Consequently, governments have been forced to create a political space that would allow groups, communities, and civic organizations to have a say in the decision-making processes. Finally, as the economies of many countries are increasingly integrated into the global economy, centralized planning has declined in importance both as a concept and as a method of policy formulation.

Issues pertaining to the decentralization of power and organizational resources to regional/local levels and the creation of institutional conditions that allow flexible and adaptable decision-making have emerged as a popular theme in the African development debate.

Managing change no doubt presents a critical challenge for policymakers but equally, it creates many opportunities to introduce new policy formulation methods, institutional arrangements, or a new culture of organization and decision-making. But such opportunities are better used if policymakers are able to equip themselves with hands-on conceptual and methodological tools that help to improve their understanding of social phenomena, to develop a range of choices of alternative strategies, or to enhance their ability to predict the future. Here, we want to draw on a recent major study in Ethiopia—political decentralization in the Amhara National Regional State, North-Central Ethiopia[4]—to propose a flexible approach for regional planning. Ethiopia has had a long history as a centralized state whose organization revolved around feudalism and monarchical traditions. In 1974, the feudal state collapsed as a result of rising discontent within both the urban areas and the military. In fact, the military overthrew Haile Selassie's regime and instituted a socialist-military state that turned out to be even more centralized and repressive. This led to decades of civil war and caused the deterioration of the country's economy and social infrastructure. In 1991, the Ethiopian People's Revolutionary Democratic Front (EPRDF) toppled the socialist-military state. The EPRDF immediately transformed itself into a Transitional Government and worked toward the formation of the new federal state in 1995, with nine ethnically defined regions. Although this political setting may have the potential to encourage separatist movements, the EPRDF believes that giving regional autonomy to different ethnic groups curtails the emergence of centrifugal forces. The Ethiopian constitution strongly advocates the transfer of adequate powers to regional and local governments, especially in the area of planning and administration of development programs. Our intention here is thus to examine this decentralized politicoadministrative structure and to assess the prospects and problems for initiating regional planning processes.

Decentralization is often intended to correct inefficiencies in the public sector by transferring management responsibilities and resources to the lower levels of the state hierarchy. This is supposed to improve the efficiency and effectiveness of planning and budgeting decisions as well as the implementation of programs or projects, so that: (a) planners are better able to identify proper strategies of policy, program, or project formulation and implementation; (b) bureaucratic red tape can be reduced thus increasing the speed of budgeting and resource allocation decisions; and (c) the provision of institutional support mechanisms and adequate resources will increase the responsive capacity of local-level agencies to address problems. However, the debate has now extended from technical and managerial issues to structural imbalances in geographic, material, political, and organizational power relationships. In this respect, decentralization is supposed to create the conditions that enhance local autonomy. In doing so, it enables people to manage their own affairs, including asserting a greater degree of influence over program/project formulation and the budgeting and resource allocation processes.

However, decentralization policies have often failed to achieve their goals. The problems are mainly attributed to the lack of genuine political commitment to support decentralization initiatives; the absence of local capacity to accommodate the demands induced by decentralization policies; and the lack of "operation theory"[5] to plan and implement initiatives effectively. In their comprehensive study of the experience of decentralization in five African countries (Botswana, Kenya, Tanzania, Zambia, and Zimbabwe), de Valk and Wekwete argue that decentralization was intended to improve administrative efficiency instead of transferring resources and decision-making powers to local-level agencies.[6] In a sense, it simply has meant expanding the state apparatus by creating many new organizational layers and multiple reporting relationships in the state system that subsequently impeded rather than facilitated popular participation. Local-level decisions were simply "confined to a limited functional area and a limited part of the decision making process."[7] Policy choices and financial decisions were still made at the center. In addition, decentralization initiatives did not generally focus on people's real needs, such as access to resources, public services, and asset building. The deployment of state structures to the local society has tended to increase "legitimation and control." Thus, although participation was more intense in Tanzania, Zambia, and Zimbabwe than in Botswana and Kenya, this had much to do with enhancing the state's control of society through local-level party branches. Botswana did better because of the greater involvement of local bodies, more adequate resources (material, manpower, and organizational), and strong political commitment. It should also be recognized that local bodies have different capacities to meet the tasks demanded by a decentralized system. For instance, local authorities must deal with rigid expenditure rules and regulations from above. They must also create attractive incentives that will induce local participation and encourage the emergence of a consensus. Based on the experience of four countries (Nigeria, Sudan, Tanzania, and Zambia), Olowu draws similar conclusions: the outward expansion of state structures has often created difficulties for coordinating development activities, mainly because resources and institutional support mechanisms were not sufficient; the lack of local capacity has often led to the transfer of tasks to central agencies, which has subsequently reinforced the supremacy of state agencies; central bureaucrats have been reluctant to relinquish power, since the "political and administrative offices at the local level as well as contracts and other public organizational resources constitute veritable sources of spoils to sustain the regime";[8] and elitist values and practices have been embedded within the state structure, a situation where "development was perceived by central officials very much in the mould of their colonial predecessors as the application of 'modern' knowledge and techniques to traditional societies. Given such a mindset, local people especially in rural areas are presumed to be ignorant."[9]

Even under improved political conditions and institutional arrangements, operationalizing planned initiatives (policies, programs, or projects) is a complex task. Plans generally deal with abstract ideas and action strategies that provide us only with a conceptual framework for deciding what to do and how to do it, whereas policy, program, or project implementation deals with the actual reality—the social, personal, institutional, and political/ideological dimensions of "doing things." Thus, for example, in the course of plan implementation, there will be social pressures to do, or not to do, things as they are stipulated in the plans. The degree to which social or institutional actors are committed to the plan's implementation will depend on their perception of the social, organizational, and political environment, including perceived remuneration (social and material), the fear of authority, job security, shared values, and participation. The values of the organization (participation, for example) and its technical and material resources will determine its capacity to execute the plan. Ideology and politics are the most important factors in the implementation process—ideology shapes the policy discourse, while politics defines the priority areas. All this calls for a strategic approach that facilitates the application of a flexible and adaptable method of planning and implementation.

As Uphoff points out, the development planning debate has been dominated by the fallacies of top-down and bottom-up planning.[10] The former often reduces people's needs to the mere consumption of program or project services, while the latter exaggerates the local community's capacity to find real solutions for its problems. The fact of the matter is that sustainable results can be produced by initiatives that combine both top-down and bottom-up strategies, or if all agencies in the development field combine their energy and resources to carry out multiple tasks in the development process.[11] Can regional planning provide a middle ground between the two contesting approaches? This issue has generated a heated debate,[12] in part because the subject of regional planning is too broad. As Friedmann and Weaver point out, regional planning is both a concept of development and a method of procedure.[13] As a concept, one regional planning approach advocates the idea of promoting self-reliant and equitable development through selective spatial closure.[14] This includes regional control of resources, decentralized planning, the application of appropriate technology, utilizing local skills, redirecting investment priorities to basic needs, and taking strategic advantages of trade. As a method, regional planning has four broad functions: "the implementation of national plans; the facilitation of popular participation; the coordination of sectoral activities; and the reduction of inequalities."[15] However, as noted earlier, development planning and implementation involve maneuvering through a web of relationships at the personal, social, institutional, and political interface at different levels of hierarchy in the government. Therefore, unless there are practical procedures to deal with the organization and methodology of planning, regional planning will not fare better than either bottom-up or top-down approaches. Indeed, our thesis is that, to be effective, regional planning should be seen as what Stöhr refers to as a multilevel process.[16] Stöhr argues that such an approach is embedded in the principle of subsidiarity, which means that "those processes and decisions which can be best performed at local or regional levels should be executed there; only those that cannot be performed there satisfactorily should be delegated to higher levels." Stöhr views clusters, networks, and innovative milieus as the principal actors in the process. As they possess a high degree of flexibility and adaptability to the rapidly changing environment, these entities have a comparative advantage over national-based agencies in areas of activity related to: the articulation of the problems and needs; the conception and formulation of plans and implementation strategies; galvanizing a spirit of cooperation; the facilitation of horizontal and vertical flow of information; and the exchange of resource and experiences. Development from within[17] can be supplemented or complemented by national policies if national-based agencies play a facilitative role through the provision of resources and technical and organizational support.

Note that Stöhr is writing from a European perspective and there may be limits to the extent to which the concept of subsidiarity can be relevant to countries such as Ethiopia. For instance, unlike the flourishing networks, clusters, or innovative milieus of Europe, regional or local functional entities in Ethiopia will have little resource and organizational capacity to meet the task requirements. In fact, as we illustrate here, as financial and organizational resources are concentrated at the center, all the requirements of planning (access to resources, participation, and control) will be dependent on the kind of relationships between the state and society. The notion of complementing or supplementing local initiatives with national policies ought to be seen in the context of the existing capacity and the institutional arrangements that define the relationship at the macro-micro interface. Bearing this in mind, we aim to show that various planning functions and different areas of responsibility can be identified at each level of hierarchy in the Ethiopian government (federal, regional, zonal, *woreda* or district, and *kebele* or local levels). The chapter will draw on empirical evidence from Mequant's study of North Gondar Zonal Administrative Zone (NGZ), Amhara National Regional State, North-Central Ethiopia.[18] The first section briefly discusses the political history of Ethiopia and then proceeds to examine the new federal structure, which was formulated by the EPRDF in the 1990s. The second section looks at the decision-making practice in NGZ within the context of the new politicoadministrative structure. The third section proposes a regional planning approach in the light of the issues outlined above. The final section draws some conclusions.

POLITICAL TRANSITION IN THE 1990s

Background

Ethiopia has an effective form of polity dating back more than 2000 years.[19] In the 1850s, Emperor Tewodros II ascended to the throne and forced regional nobilities into submission. He also introduced some remarkable reforms that reduced the influence of the church in state affairs and liberated the peasant population from exploitation by the feudal landlords. But his ambition to create a united Ethiopia was continuously hampered by powerful regional nobilities and the church. Even though Tewodros failed to create a united empire, many regard him as the founder of modern Ethiopia.

Tewodros' successor, Emperor Yohannese, attempted to establish effective control of the imperial territory but with only limited success. It was Emperor Minilik II, Yohannese's successor, who established a strong, central state and expanded the territory southward to include what is today's Southern, South-Western, and Eastern Ethiopia. His military power ensured the supremacy of the imperial state throughout the country. But, a more effective central state was established during the reign of Haile Selassie I. Beginning in 1930, Haile Selassie systematically destroyed all regional power throughout the country and created a centralized administrative system. The Italian occupation (1936–41) also resulted in the dramatic weakening of regional power. Selassie abolished all feudal forms of tribute and instead instituted a land tax and an agricultural income tax,[20] which increased the central government's revenues while weakening the economic base of the regional powers.

Haile Selassie's rule collapsed in 1974 when deteriorating social and economic conditions culminated in an urban uprising that led to the end of the 2000-year-old Solomonic dynasty. At that time, all training and educational institutions and most new industries were concentrated in the capital, while the rest of the country provided the resources to support this modernization process. Other regions in the country received little industrial investment. The mass of the peasantry was totally ignored, especially in the North where a growing population and environmental degradation required government action.

The revolutionary military government that overthrew Haile Selassie immediately took radical measures to abolish all feudal forms of production by nationalizing the land and distributing it to the peasants. This government allied itself with the Soviet-community block and increasingly followed a socialist-oriented development strategy. It created mass organizations—such as peasant associations, agricultural producers cooperatives, and rural marketing cooperatives—which later became integrated into the structure of the central military-socialist state.[21] Any opposition to the new order was outlawed and members of the opposition groups were imprisoned, tortured, and executed.[22] Many of the opponents fled to the countryside and formed strong-armed resistance movements. One of these, the EPRDF, succeeded in toppling the government in May 1991.[23]

The New Federal State

Shortly after rising to power, the EPRDF organized a national conference that created the charter that asserted the right of nationalities to self-determination and also established local and regional councils along ethnic lines. Thirty-one political groups, mostly under the tutelage of the EPRDF, signed the charter. The EPRDF transformed itself into a Transitional Government, with a mandate to create conditions that would pave the way for the formation of a federal state under a new constitution. It also won thirty-two of the eighty-seven seats in the Council of Representatives of the Transitional Government and controlled the key organs of the state, such as foreign affairs and defense.[24] There was a lot of controversy, however. Many argued that the charter could lead to the breakup of the country, while regional political groups, notably the Oromo Liberation Front (OLF) and even those ethnic groups that were orbiting around the EPRDF, felt that they were once again to be dominated by another "Northern" political elite. The various opposition groups in exile, particularly the Coalition of Democratic Forces (CODEF) and MEDHIN, made it clear that they would have no dealings with EPRDF unless it changes its policy of ethnic division. Soon many of the organizations withdrew from the Transitional Government, leaving the EPRDF and its political allies to take complete control of state power.

In 1995, the EPRDF inaugurated the Federal Democratic Republic of Ethiopia (Proclamation No. 1/1995). The federal constitution recognizes all languages in the country and gives regional states the right to determine their respective working languages. However, Amharic would remain the national language. There would be no state religion and no state interference in religion or vice versa. Articles 11 to 44 set out the fundamental principles of Universal Human Rights, such as human dignity, protection against cruelty, rights of the arrested, rights of the accused, equality before the law, respect for privacy, freedom of religion, freedom of expression of opinions and beliefs, freedom of association and movement, marriage, status of women, property rights, right to development, right to environment, and so on. Article 39 is very sensitive. It states: "Every Nation, Nationality and People in Ethiopia has an unconditional right to self-determination, including the right to secession." And paragraph 3 of this article also states that every nation, nationality and people has the right to "establish institutions of government in the territory that it inhabits and to equitable representation in the State and Federal government."

Articles 45 to 49 define the form of the federal government (see Figure 8.1). The government is made up of ethnically based regional states: Afar; Amhara; Oromo; Tigray; Somali; Benshangul-Gumuz; Southern Nations, Nationalities and Peoples (SNNP); Gambella Peoples; and Harari Peoples. Moreover, nations,

Figure 8.1
The Ethiopian Federal Structure

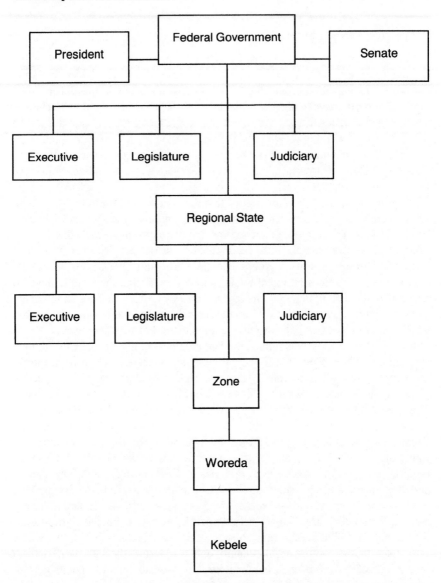

nationalities, and peoples within these states have the right to create their own state if this is the popular will and with the approval of the regional state. Both federal and state governments shall have legislative, executive, and judiciary power (Articles 50 to 52). The federal government shall be responsible for "formulating and implementing the country's policies, strategies and plans in respect

Figure 8.2
Zonal Hierarchy

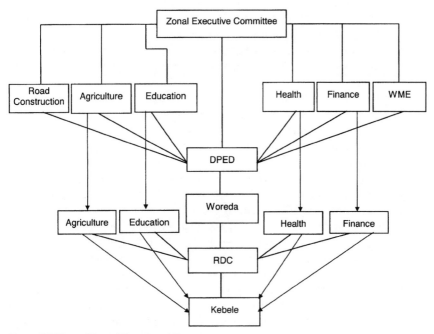

Notes: WME = Water, Mineral, and Energy
DPED = Department of Planning and Economic Development
RDC = Rural Development Committee

of overall social, economic and development matters (Articles 51 to 52)," including maintaining standards for the provision of social services. It shall formulate and execute the country's fiscal and monetary policy, enact legislation in the area of investment, the utilization of natural resources, interregional and foreign trade, defense, public security and immigration. The state council is the highest organ of the regional states and is accountable to the people of the region. States shall have power on matters falling under state jurisdiction and adequate power shall be given to local-level governments.

The Regional State

The constitution of the Amhara National Regional State (proclamation No. 2/ 1995) organizes the state into four administrative hierarchies: regional, zonal, *woreda*, and *kebele* (see Figure 8.2). The constitution gives the state legislative, executive, and judicial powers. The regional council has the power to make laws that do not contravene the federal laws, including preparing plans, administering land and natural resources, levying taxes from employees, profits, and agricultural income, control of the civil service, collecting fees from licenses and other services, and maintaining public security. The chairperson of the executive committee is the head of state; the council of the Amhara State elects him or her. The state also has a deputy president, secretary, and commissioners who oversee economic, social, and administrative institutions.

The next level in the regional state is the zonal administration. A zonal administration has an executive committee that is comprised of eleven to seventeen members, including the chairperson, deputy chairperson, and secretary. Committee members are elected by the regional executive committee and approved by the regional council. The committees are responsible for coordinating and directing various institutions and departments in the zone. Zones do not have councils, except the minority ethnic groups of Himara, Awi, and Oromo in the region (Articles 69 to 75).

Below the zonal administration is the *woreda* administration. A *woreda* has a council directly elected by the local population (for a term of two years). The executive committee of the *woreda* (consisting of nine to fifteen members) is elected by the *woreda* council and has a chairperson, deputy chairperson, and secretary. The organs of the *woreda* include the office of the judiciary and attorney, security and police force, and social development. The executive committee ensures the implementation of laws and directives that come from above. It is accountable to the *woreda* constituencies as well as to the regional executive committee, via the zonal administration. The *woreda* council approves social programs and development plans, mobilizes the population for development work, levies and collects taxes, administers primary schools and junior health centers, and can issue its own internal regulations and directives.

At the bottom of the hierarchy is the *kebele* administration (KA). A KA too has its own council, directly elected by the local population. It has the following organs: executive committee, social court, and socioeconomic and security bodies. The executive committee is accountable to the *woreda* executive committee and KA council. The duties of the KA committee include outlining plans of action and mobilizing the population for development work, protection of natural resources, and approving the appointment of judges (Articles 86 to 92).

The details of these two constitutional documents show that there are opportunities to promote regional autonomy and local self-government. The constitution has created structures that allow regions and lower levels of the state hierarchy to make certain decisions. But the question is to what extent such a legal-political framework will be put into practice. The new constitution came into effect four years ago and it is hard to tell what is and what is not actually working. Here, we can only make some general observations.

The national question will probably continue to generate controversy. The critical question is: Has the EPRDF government met the demands of regional autonomy by creating new ethnically defined regions, or will this new federal state structure threaten the unity of Ethiopia? This question demands an answer from political scientists and historians. Suffice it here to say that the national question has its own history in Ethiopian development. For instance, Sorenson[25] and Adhana[26] have argued that the history of Ethiopia is constructed around the church, the monarchy, and the Amhara ethnic group. Domination and exploitation have long characterized the relationship between the central Ethiopian state and many nationalities in the country. This was what had driven the radical political forces of the 1970s to rally under the slogan of self-determination. In the mid-1980s, at the formation of the Democratic Republic of Ethiopia, the military-socialist government created new administrative areas that considered, among other things, the character of the population (language, culture, and economic activity) and its proximity to administrative centers. However, the revolutionary government sought to impose "a centralized state and party structure as a solution to the problem of national unity, almost regardless of regional diversities which demand, at the very least, substantial opportunities for local autonomy."[27] And when the EPRDF came to power, it "chose to construct a political system that reflects on-going realities."[28]

However, one must question the extent to which this arrangement contains centrifugal forces and leads to the development of a stable national economic, social, and political order. Moreover, in the absence of a strong civil society to control the behavior of local elites, abuses of power and corruption will become a growing phenomenon. Indeed, the government's own media is full of such stories in every region. For instance, in 1997, hundreds of high-ranking *woreda* officials in the Oromo region were dismissed for corruption, nepotism, and inappropriate behavior. Even worse—those whom Ethiopians like to label as *del melese* officials (postvictory officials or those who rose to power after EPRDF's takeover of the state) have become the most notorious bureaucrats who impede public participation and have become experts in laundering project money. Our point here is that a strong federal government will be needed to facilitate processes of negotiation and accommodation between the regions and between regional states and society. Moreover, the federal government must also ensure the equal distribution of opportunities among different social groups in society. If the government turns its attention away from such issues, political decentralization only disempowers the already disadvantaged communities and groups in Ethiopian society. And this will create a fertile soil for the growth of new centrifugal forces that may gradually galvanize the forces of disintegration.

In addition, there may not be an adequate organizational capacity to carry out many functions previously performed by the central state. Zonal and *woreda* offices often lack the resources, manpower, and the organizational infrastructure of planning and administration. To make matters worse, the country is faced with an erosion of stable organizational resources following the EPRDF's dismantling of many institutions in its desire to control the bureaucratic apparatus. This means that the departments at the lower levels of hierarchy remain heavily dependent on the regional and federal agencies for guidance and technical support to formulate and execute local development initiatives. Finally, regional states have largely inherited the old state apparatus, even though attempts were made in 1996/97 to create *adis mewaker* (new structures). Yet the ethnic mix of the bureaucracy has remained largely unchanged. In fact, many professionals are being assigned to work in such peripheral regions as Afar, Somali, Benshangul-Gumus, and Gambela. Therefore, politicians focus only on ethnicity issues while bureaucrats are concerned mainly with technical questions and management efficiency. Possible discriminatory practices to promote natives to senior positions will lead others to be less committed to the regional state. In fact, as competition for state resources intensifies, frustrated elites are very likely to use ethnicity as a source of bargaining power to secure opportunities (employment through ethnic identification, not competition, for example). The lack of collective vision (and trust) between politicians who make decisions and technocrats who execute programs and projects may hamper the success of development initiatives.

DECENTRALIZATION AND LOCAL AUTONOMY IN GONDAR

The Gondar region was divided into south and north by the military-socialist government in the 1980s, when its new boundaries were created to reorganize the administrative structure of the central state. The EPRDF did not change this administrative boundary, but it incorporated the fertile lands in the west of Gondar into the Tigray region, and part of Quara Woreda (West Gondar) into the Benshangul-Gumus region. Under the new federal structure, North Gondar is thus one of eleven administrative zones in the Amhara National Regional State. The NGZ has sixteen *woredas* and a population of more than two million, of whom 77 percent live in rural areas. It covers 53,168 square kilometers, most of which is at *dega* (high) and *woynadega* (middle) altitudes. The great majority of the population is concentrated in these areas, where the land has been cultivated for centuries. Agriculture remains the main source of income for the great majority of the rural population.

The NGZ has its own zonal administration that guides and coordinates five sectoral departments: agriculture; health; education; water, minerals, and energy; and road construction. The administration, as a sector, heads the security forces and courts (see Figure 8.2). Agriculture has thirteen projects, health twenty-six, education thirty-five, water, mineral, and energy twenty-six, and road construction six projects, including the administration's own three office construction projects (see Table 8.1). Community participation is seen as important and it is accounted for as a share of the project budget: 17 percent for agriculture, 4 percent for water, mineral, and energy, 10 percent for education, 30.4 percent for health, and 16.9 percent for administration. These inputs take the form of material and labor contributions (for example, doing physical work and carrying material and equipment to project sites).

The EPRDF government has a planning ideology that emphasizes *zuria melese* (iterative) planning. Officials like to illustrate their vision of the planning

Table 8.1
Project Budget, Community Contributions (as Percentage of Project Budget), and Sectors' Share as Percentage of NGZ Total Budget for Year 1996/1997

Sector	Budget (in millions of *birr*)	No. of Projects	Community Contributions (percent)	Budget Share (percent)
Agriculture	8.167	13	17.0	22.70
Water, mineral, and energy	9.033	26	4.0	25.10
Education	6.354	35	10.0	17.66
Health	0.469	26	30.0	1.30
Rural road construction	10.959	6	0	30.45
Administration	1.000	3	16.88	2.78

Note: US$1 = 6.70 *birr.*

Source: NGZ Department of Planning and Economic Development (1996).

method in the following way: Program or project initiatives are identified at the KA level through participatory needs assessment exercises. The information is then taken to the *woreda* administration. The *woreda* assesses feasibility by: (a) weighing the cost of the project, for example, against available financial resources and skilled manpower; (b) determining the extent to which community or local resources can support the project; and (c) determining how much (resources) are expected from the government. The proposal is then sent back to the KA council. Upon approval by this council, the plan is presented to the Woreda Rural Development Committee (RDC), which further reviews the same and sends it to the respective zonal departments for financing and technical assistance. The various zonal departments in turn submit their plan to the zone administration, whose executive committee reviews the plans in accordance with the overall policy framework of the Amhara National Regional State. Upon approval, each department sends a *merha geber* (an action plan) to the Department of Planning and Economic Development (DPED), which is supposed to monitor and evaluate the progress of program or project activities. Agriculture, education, health, and finance are directly represented at the *woreda* level by their respective field agencies. All departments are expected to discuss their project plans and to assess work strategies in the Woreda RDC.

This is easier said than done. In reality, the *woredas'* role has been limited to implementing plans formulated by the zonal departments. Planners at the zonal offices basically decide what is to be done, and how it should be done. Nothing can be done without the prior knowledge and approval of the zonal political elites, or department bureaucrats, and the reporting relationship is often command and control. Consider the reporting system of the Ministry of Agriculture: field station workers report every two weeks to the Woreda Department of Agriculture. The *woreda* evaluates and sends the report to the zonal department every month. The zonal department again evaluates and submits a report to the Regional Bureau of Agriculture and to the DPED every three months. While all this can ensure central control of field-level activity, it will not serve as a systematic method to appraise what is and what is not working. For instance, it may not be possible to evaluate the performance of a demonstration plot, or of any other project impact within two weeks. Nor does the upward flow of information from a cluster of field agencies give a true picture of what is happening at the ground level.

Furthermore, even though any zonal department plan calls for other sectoral ministries to get involved, matters like the selection of project sites, the provision of technical support, and the issue of involvement have never been defined within a clear institutional/organizational context (i.e., who does what and how much assistance is expected from another sectoral department). Although the DPED claims to facilitate the sharing and coordination of resources among the various departments, its activities are largely limited to touring project areas in order to monitor the progress of projects. And one must question its effectiveness, given the weak organizational capacity and the inadequate professional staff of the organization. The story is the same at the *woreda* level. For instance, the Woreda Council of Lay Armachiho faced some resistance from the employees of line agencies when it tried to influence the way they were organizing their work plans. The department employees objected to the council's move on the grounds that they were only accountable to the zonal departments. The arguments made were interesting. For example, the Woreda council wanted to develop its own recruitment criteria (gender and participation in political meetings), while the line agencies favored another set of qualifications. Similarly, the council preferred that sector departments in the *woreda* submit plans consistent with its priorities, while line agencies develop plans using another set of strategies to define their own priority areas. In another example, the Woreda RDC is supposed to review and approve any plan but has no mandate to influence the direction of departmental activities. In fact, if the *woreda* director of the Department of Agriculture accepts the RDC's advice to change the plan, he/she can face criticisms by bureaucrats at the zone's Department of Agriculture. Frustrated EPRDF officials accused the Woreda department professionals of elitism and ignorance. The department personnel in turn complained that they were dealing with illiterate politicians who had no idea of how things work in the government. Such antagonistic relations can be major factors adversely affecting performance of the government's program initiatives.

Most government departments in Gondar and elsewhere in Ethiopia are accustomed to central control and coordination. In spite of EPRDF's attempt to install the *adis mewakir* (new structure) in the state system, the bureaucracy still remains the most powerful resister of change. *Woreda*-level agencies are left with the planning of only small-scale initiatives such as soil conservation, designing demonstration sites, and tree planting. Yet, government officials are often quick to say that "it takes time to make it [their planning ideology] more practical" and to some extent this is a legitimate argument. There is little planning capacity at the KA and *woreda* levels. For instance, most of the agricultural extension work is done by ill-trained extension workers at the field level, who spend most of their time walking from one place to another (the government has provided them with mules and horses but they have preferred to walk). *Woreda* agricultural officers often complain that the lack of field capacity to gather data and process the information has overburdened them with work. They say that compiling raw field data and writing reports have diverted their attention away from planning and administrative work. The government's *akem gembata* (capacity-building) program has enabled many department personnel and political authorities to attend training sessions in the regional capital, Bahir Dar, for two to three months, but it will be a long time before the *woreda* departments achieve an adequate technical capacity to deal with multiple task assignments.

Finally, the morale among government employees appears to be low. This is in part due to nepotism and political patronage but the problem also extends to the EPRDF's own performance evaluation procedure, which the party sees as an effective means to promote accountability and transparency. This is called *gemgema* in Amharic and every government department, including rural KAs, is required to conduct a *gemgema* at least twice a year. The idea is to encourage popular control (especially over corrupt officials) to build people's confidence in the process of participation and to come away with useful lessons from such exercises. The process, however, is so corrupt and so politicized that it has actually worked against the desired objective. Three hypothetical examples will serve to illustrate this problem: First, a department director warns one of his/her employees that his/her performance on the job has been poor. The employee goes around and mobilizes opposition against the director. As a result the director, during the *gemgema* meeting, faces accusations based on false and exaggerated claims. The director may be dismissed or demoted while the employee survives. Similarly, a project director may be expected to complete all of the project phases within a year but he/she later finds out that the organizational structure is not there, there is insufficient manpower, or that the budget was not released in time to execute the project. So, by the end of the project year, only half of the work has been done. As a result, he/she will be demoted or fired. Finally, an ambitious politician or bureaucrat may create a group faction in the organization in order to build up black points against the present leader. If successful, he/she topples the man or woman at the top and rises to power. It has now become common among Ethiopians to joke that the "EPRDF's power does not last for forty-eight hours," meaning that many politicians stay in power for only a few months. All this has made employees of the state and politicians hesitant to make independent decisions in order to avoid making mistakes for which they can be held accountable. Instead, they prefer to await instructions from *ye belay akal* (the top) and, as more and more people are removed from their positions, creating stable and effective organizational leadership has become difficult.

Yet, at times *gemgema* has been instrumental in diminishing the fear of authority and in building up people's confidence in speaking against government officials. In NGZ, many corrupt officials were removed from their posts including EPRDF officials, judges, and members of the police force. In one KA administration of Lay Armachiho Woreda, two KA chairmen were removed from power within a period of one year because of corruption. The problem of *gemgema* lies in the process. It fails to acknowledge inevitable errors made in the normal routine of work. It also fails to give people an opportunity to learn from their mistakes. Some of the *gemgema* points are also ridiculous. For instance, in 1997 the chairman of the NGZ was demoted through *gemgema*. One of the points against him was that he ran away when angry peasants in Belesa Woreda shot at him during the land redistribution period. The EPRDF had expected him to make a sacrifice (a reflection of a guerilla mindset among its top officials), but the chairman had spent most of his life teaching in schools and he probably had never owned a firearm. More important, the *gemgema* process only results in a change of individuals in the organization but does little to improve the functional performance of departments. Instead, *gemgema* should begin by scanning the social, economic, and political environment, proceeding to examine what is and what is not working, and then evaluate how individual roles might have contributed to the problem.

TOWARD REGIONAL PLANNING

The new Ethiopian federal constitution envisages a strong regional state at the center and autonomous *woreda* administrative organizations, with zones playing an intermediary role to facilitate planning and budgeting decisions and the flow of resources from federal and regional agencies to the *woreda*-level agencies. But as the evidence in this chapter has shown, legal/political frameworks do little to enable lower-level agencies to exercise autonomy unless there is a practical procedure to deal with the organization and methodology of planning and to define a clear area of responsibility in a way that achieves a fit between their existing capacities and the various tasks. In this section, we develop one approach that, hopefully, helps to define areas of responsibility for different functional organizations in ways that complement or supplement the activities initiated by one organization with those of the other organization(s).

To begin with, Stöhr's notion of subsidiarity is considered[29]—a situation where there is a multilevel process of action and interaction working toward a spirit of cooperation among autonomous entities, and each entity does what it can do best. This concept can be applied in Ethiopia (at federal, state, zonal, *woreda*, and KA levels) as follows:

a. Activities that can be carried out by small community-based groups. The task of organizing such activities is less complex and requires little external input. Water and soil conservation, tree planting, and facility and road construction are more compatible with community-based activities.

b. Activities that can be organized and coordinated by *woreda* and KA organizations. These agencies possess an immense potential to organize and administer short- and medium-term project activities. They can mobilize labor and material for the construction of schools, health facilities, small dams, and rural roads. They can also organize planning meetings, and experience exchange and training sessions; promote human rights education; and administer the delivery of services.

c. Activities that are planned and administered by upper-level government agencies. There are many areas of activity suitable to the role of government departments at zonal, regional, and federal levels. For example, research centers can develop appropriate agricultural technologies and facilitate widespread adoption among farmers in ways that reduce uncertainty. Government policy instruments are needed to reform the land tenure system, protect forests, provide credit, create market infrastructures, and design training programs.

We can further simplify the task of identifying different areas of responsibilities by putting the set of activities into a policy, program, and project framework (see Figure 8.3). A policy is a broad statement of goals that strives to achieve some end value in society. As such, a policy can only tell us about the vision of change and the direction of resource flows. Programs have more narrowly focused, space- and time-bound objectives (a five-year plan, for example), while projects are those program activities that are geared to accomplishing certain objectives within specific time and resource parameters. Let us consider an additional (hypothetical) example: The Ethiopian government proclaims that food security is its top policy priority. The Ministry of Agriculture then develops an extension service and management program that facilitates the widespread adoption of fertilizers and improved seeds. The minister states that crop production will be raised by x percent within the next five years. Projects would then be the activities components of this extension program. Hence, for example, the goal of achieving food security within five years (by raising production by x percent) demands: (1) input provision; (2) adequate organizational infrastructure; (3) training extension workers; (4) devising credit and loan schemes; (5) designing demonstration sites; (6) annual evaluation of results; and (7) others. Each project also has its own set of activities. For example, designing demonstration sites will involve: (1) site selection; (2) site design; (3) recruiting model farmers; (4) defining time frames for technical advice; (5) monitoring and evaluation; and (6) others.

Although it is possible to identify areas of responsibility that are consistent

Figure 8.3
Policy-Program-Project Hierarchy

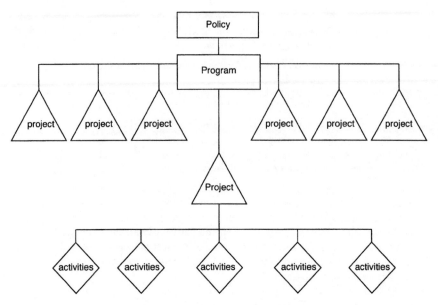

with the capacities of organizations operating at different hierarchical levels, we should not forget that this depends on the particular nature of the policy, program, or project. However, some general statements are possible. We can say that the federal and regional governments must play an important role in policy formulation where policies deal with societywide concerns. Zonal and *woreda* administration must plan and manage medium- and long-term programs and projects. But responsibilities may not be clear when we are dealing with what Rondinelli calls experimental projects, which are "generally small-scale, highly exploratory, risky ventures that do not always provide immediate or direct economic returns or yield quick and visible results."[30] Running such experimental projects should perhaps be the responsibility of both federal and regional authorities, since they often involve large expenditures and know-how. In another instance, both the federal and regional governments may be involved in some zonal or *woreda* programs to ensure that medium- or long-term objectives meet national standards. In general, we can say that the role of federal and regional governments includes providing leadership, capital investment, and management of long-term programs, while zonal and *woreda*-level agencies can be responsible for short- and medium-term programs or projects. The KA administrations and community-based organizations can play a supplementary or complementary role to support these government efforts in the local area.

Fragmented activities and too many priorities may lead to a situation where, in a quest to do everything, agencies end up doing nothing effectively. So, we

Figure 8.4
***Woreda*-Level Planning**

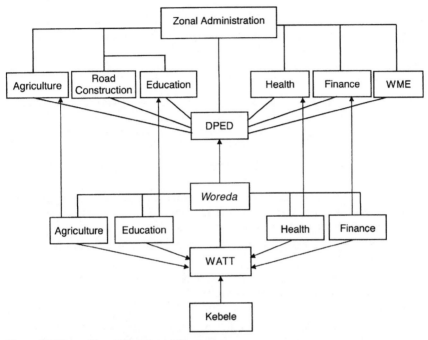

Notes: WME = Water, Mineral, and Energy
DPED = Department of Planning and Economic Development
RDC = Rural Development and Committee
WATT = Woreda Advisory and Technical Team

need a planning framework that avoids this problem. Here, we propose one approach that can better serve this purpose. We are concerned with zonal-level planning, with the *woreda* as a basic planning unit. In other words, the zone becomes a regional planning area while the *woreda* serves a regional planning function. Our choice of the *woreda* is based on the assumption that it is an area larger than the KA area and smaller than the region, so that it represents the interface between rural society and the state. With this in mind, we suggest the formation of a Woreda Advisory and Technical Team (WATT), which plays a dual role of planning, program, and project activities and mediating between the various departments (see Figure 8.4). WATT also creates a direct link with the KA-level organizations to initiate planning processes and to help to define their areas of responsibility. The central concern in this approach is creating a co-operative spirit. Cooperation means sharing ideas and experience on such issues as task and resource allocation, strategy formulation, and monitoring and evaluation. It also means increasing the knowledge of what each agency is doing in the field so that they can complement or supplement one another's activities. WATT will then do the following:

- Assist *woreda* and zonal departments to set their own priorities in a manner that integrates their plans within the *woreda* and regional planning framework and national development strategy;
- Assist community/local-level agencies to initiate exploratory studies (needs assessment, for example) and planning processes;
- Advise *woreda* and zonal departments on how to create participatory structures that bring an array of local interest groups together to develop a common perspective on the nature of problems, and to share ideas on the best ways to design effective strategies of action;
- Provide technical assistance in formulating work plans and evaluating and monitoring results;
- Assess the organizational capacities of each department and facilitate arrangements for resource sharing and temporary resource transfers (borrowing supplies, placing the technical staff of one agency with another, for example);
- Identify sources of technical and material assistance and help agencies with relevant resource networks;
- Carry out participatory monitoring and evaluation on a continuing basis, to assess the effectiveness of coordination mechanisms; and
- Undertake continuous research to help departments define issues and courses of action more accurately, thereby enabling them to adjust their strategies to changing socioeconomic and political circumstances in the local, regional, national, and global environments.

WATT can evolve out of the decentralized unit of the zone's DPED, or it can consist of representatives from the various *woreda* departments and KAs. To develop the criteria to select these individuals may be very problematic, as the interference of *woreda* politicians in the process is inevitable. As a result, government politics, rather than public participation, may shape the nature of the *woreda*'s planning agency. In order to bring an array of interest groups together in planning processes, WATT should be independent of the politicoadministrative apparatus and be concerned with planning, coordination, and monitoring issues. Moreover, WATT needs a clearly defined mandate. Although the new federal constitution has given certain decision-making powers to the *woredas*, this will be of little help in defining WATT's power. The government should, in accordance with its bottom-up planning ideology, then pass legislation that defines the role and responsibilities of a *woreda*-level planning team.

CONCLUSION

Decentralization is a process guided from above and its purpose is to devolve power, institutions, and resources to the local society. Local autonomy, on the other hand, is an organizational process from within, which works toward creating the capacity of society for self-direction and management of change. Regional planning provides a framework for the organization and methodology of planning and implementing policies, programs, and projects. In a sense, these three notions are complementary: decentralization creates the conditions of local self-reliance; local autonomy builds society's capacity to sustain institutions of economy, culture, and politics; and regional planning guides the practices of long-, medium-, and short-term planning to organize and distribute resources. Rather, what is often problematic is that, as organizational and material powers are concentrated at the center, the existence of unequal relationships at the macro-micro interface becomes an inevitable outcome. As long as this is the case, there are structural impediments for the institutionalization of local autonomy and popular participation.

Our discussion of the Ethiopian experience has attempted to draw attention to such issues. The current national leaders have been good at talking about decentralization and bottom-up planning. The new federal constitution has given regions adequate powers to govern themselves. Minority groups in the states are allowed to create their own zonal councils and to plan and administer certain types of programs. Although decentralizing the Ethiopian state to ethnically defined regions may pose a danger to the unity of the country—especially if the new federal structure fails to work toward meeting the political and material aspirations of the people—the new politicoadministrative structure provides an opportunity to the local society to have a say in the decision-making process and to manage local affairs. But, at present most of the planning and budgeting decisions are still made from the top-down and part of this can be attributed to the department's organizational culture of central control and coordination. Moreover, there is little organizational and technical capacity at the local level. In fact, Ethiopia still feels the devastating impact of a civil war that destroyed the social and economic infrastructure of the society.

The performance of decentralization policies can be improved if there is an effort to explore different options that help to determine what can and cannot be decentralized. The notions of devolution, delegation, and deconcentration tend to imply that political elites and the leaders of civil society should divide everything equally (the power, institution, and resources). Then, we find that there is inadequate local capacity to administer the function of institutions, to direct the state's resources toward productive investment, and to exercise power effectively in ways that promote local autonomy. Instead, decentralization policies can be transformed from a blueprint text to a flexible and adaptive strategy that enables both government and society to be involved in the process of learning and experience accumulation.[31] We have proposed one such framework, namely, regional planning, wherein planning and implementation involve maneuvering through a web of decision structures, task referrals, and organizational power relationships. It is possible to reduce the difficulties of planning and implementation by identifying different levels of planning functions and by defining different areas of responsibility that correspond with the capacity of each agency at different scales of activity. Hence, our approach considered the zonal administration as a planning area and the *woreda* administration as a planning function. The zone as planning area helps planners to recognize the region's distinctive social, economic, spatial, political, and cultural identity and to formulate region-specific programs or projects that strive to produce benefits consistent with the particular needs and aspirations of the local population. The *woreda* administration represents a scale larger than the KA area and smaller than the zonal administration. As a planning function the *woreda* helps to develop local needs-oriented investment criteria, to encourage participatory decision-making, and to build the local spirit to mobilize social and economic resources in the society.

NOTES

1. Goran Hyden and Michael Bratton, eds., *Governance and Politics in Africa* (London: Lynne Rienner, 1992).

2. Ibid., p. ix.

3. T. G. McGee and D. W. Edgington, "Conclusions of the Global Forum on Regional Development Policy: Redefining Regional Development in a Changing World," *UNCRD Newsletter* No. 46 (July–December 1998): 1–4.

4. Getachew Mequanent, "Capacity Building for Local Development: A Comparative Study of 'Formal' and 'Informal' Organization in Gondar, Northern Ethiopia" (Ph.D. diss., Department of Geography, Carleton University, 1998).

5. Diana Conyers, "Rural Regional Planning: Towards an Operational Theory," *Progress in Planning* 23 (1985): 1–66.

6. P. de Valk and K. H. Wekwete, eds., *Decentralizing for Participatory Planning: Comparing the Experience in Zimbabwe and Other Anglophone Countries in Eastern and Southern Africa* (London: Avebury, 1990).

7. Ibid., p. 257.

8. Dele Olowu, "Local Institutions and Development: The African Experience," *Canadian Journal of African Studies* 23 (2:1989): 219.

9. Ibid., p. 220.

10. Norman Uphoff, "Assisted Self-Reliance: Working with, Rather than for, the Poor" in Valeriana Kallab and Richard E. Feinberg, eds., *Strengthening the Poor: What Have We Learned?* (New Brunswick: Transaction Books, 1988).

11. Bishwapriya Sanyal, *Cooperative Autonomy: The Dialectic of State-NGOs Relationships in Developing Countries* (Geneva: International Labour Organization [ILO], 1994).

12. Walter B. Stöhr and D. R. Fraser Taylor, eds., *Development from Above or Below? The Dialectics of Regional Planning in Developing Countries* (New York: Wiley, 1981).

13. John Friedmann and Clyde Weaver, *Territory and Function: The Evolution of Regional Planning* (London: Edward Arnold, 1979), p. 2.

14. Stöhr and Taylor, *Development from Above or Below?*

15. Conyers, "Rural Regional Planning," p. 7.

16. Walter B. Stöhr, "Subsidiarity: A Key Concept for Regional Development Policy," in this volume.

17. D. R. Fraser Taylor and Fiona MacKenzie, *Development from Within: Survival in Rural Africa* (London: Routledge, 1992).

18. Mequanent, "Capacity Building for Local Development."

19. For a background on Ethiopian history, see, among others, Richard Greenfield, *Ethiopia: A New Political History* (London: Pall Mall Press, 1965); Richard Pankhurst, *A Social History of Ethiopia: The Northern and Central Highlands from Early Medieval Times to the Rise of Emperor Tewodros II* (Addis Ababa: Institute of Ethiopian Studies, Addis Ababa University, 1990); Bahru Zewde, *A History of Ethiopia: 1855–1974* (London: James Curry, 1991); and John Merkakis, *Ethiopia: The Anatomy of Traditional Polity* (Oxford: Clarendon, 1974).

20. Bahru Zewde, "Hayla-Sellase: From Progressive to Reactionary" in Abebe Zegeye and Siegfried Pausewang, eds., *Ethiopia in Change: Peasantry, Nationalism and Democracy* (London: British Academic Press, 1994).

21. Dessalegn Rahmato, "The Unquiet Countryside: The Collapse of 'Socialism' and Rural Agitation, 1990 and 1991" in Zegeye and Pausewang, *Ethiopia in Change*.

22. John Merkakis and Nega Ayele, *Class and Revolution in Ethiopia* (New Jersey: Red Sea Press, 1986).

23. The Eritrean People's Liberation Front (EPLF) had helped to overthrow the government. It led to Eritrea's secession from Ethiopia in 1993.

24. Edmond Keller, "Remaking the Ethiopian State" in William I. Zartman, ed., *Collapsed States: The Disintegration and Restoration of Legitimate Authority* (London: Lynne Rienner, 1995); and Terrence Lyons, "Closing the Transition: The May 1995 Elections in Ethiopia," *Journal of Modern African Studies* 34 (1:1996): 121–42.

25. John Sorenson, *Imagining Ethiopia: Struggles for History and Identity in the Horn of Africa* (New Brunswick: Rutgers University Press, 1993).

26. Adhana Haile Adhana, "Mutation of Statehood and Contemporary Politics" in Zegeye and Pausewang, *Ethiopia in Change*.

27. C. Clapham, "State and Revolution in Ethiopia," *Review of African Political Economy* (44:1989): 18.

28. Lyons, "Closing the Transition," p. 124.

29. Stöhr, "Subsidiarity."

30. Dennis Rondinelli, *Development Projects as Policy Experiments: An Adaptive Approach to Development Administration* (London: Routledge, 1993), p. 119.

31. Ibid.

9

Regional Development under Participation: Some Experiences from the Philippines

Michael von Boguslawski

THE POLICY SETTINGS: POWER TO THE PEOPLE

The basis for devolution and political decentralization in the Philippines was the Local Government Code (LGC), signed into law on 10 October 1991, at the end of Cory Aquino's presidency. The aim was "to give greater self-government and autonomy to the 76 provinces, 64 cities, 1,541 municipalities and nearly 42,000 *barangays* (villages)."[1] Devolution is understood as the transfer of responsibility, authority, powers, and resources from national to local governments, as well as from government (officials) to the citizens.

Earlier efforts—after independence in 1946—to achieve local autonomy tended to be limited to *administrative decentralization*, where the government shared functions and responsibilities mainly with regional bodies (covering several provinces) but retained oversight control. Power remained centralized and provincial governors referred to "Imperial Manila."[2]

It was only through the totally unplanned but successful EDSA Revolution[3] and "People Power" that the military regime fell within three days, and a new and more democratic avenue was opened for the Philippine people. Consequently, the new constitution of 1987 introduced the important elements of *participatory democracy* and mandated the LGC (Article 10, Sec. 3) that would transfer government planning and decision-making from the national to the local level.

Subsequent steps to more provincial autonomy were Pilot Decentralization Projects[4] and the Executive Order 319 (1988), which defined development planning from the bottom up: from the village level to the municipal (which equals small districts in other countries), to the provincial, and further to the regional and national levels. The new body created to accomplish this task was the Development Council, at each level. Consequently, some first steps toward administrative decentralization were taken (creation of nine regions). This was supported by an increase in the internal revenue allotment (IRA) to 20 percent of the general fund. In December 1990, the LGC was approved by both houses, but it took another ten months of political arguing and lobbying until then-President Aquino finally signed the same. It was considered a historic document as the Philippines introduced decentralization through legislation.

The constitution's Declaration of Policy stated the overall purpose of decentralization as follows: "the territorial and political subdivision of the State shall enjoy genuine and meaningful local autonomy to enable them to attain their fullest development as self-reliant communities and make them more effective partners in the attainment of national goals." Or, as President Aquino stated, "the new law lays down the policies that seek to institutionalize democracy at the local level. It hopes, therefore, to complete the initial process of empowering our people through direct participation in the affairs of government, by allowing them the widest possible space to decide, initiate, and innovate."

The LGC has four important aspects:

1. Basic services such as health, agriculture, social welfare, and environment and natural resources management are now under the municipality, with the central government losing its supervisory function but continuing to deliver "consultant" services to local government units (LGUs);

2. The LGC introduces a "tripartite" approach to decision-making, explicitly requesting the participation of LGUs, nongovernmental organizations (NGOs), and people's organizations (POs) as equal partners;[5]

3. The LGC shifts significant financial and revenue responsibilities to LGUs by allocating a greater share of the national revenues and allowing them to also collect their own fees and levies at the local level; and

4. Intentionally considering the introduction of the LGC as a process that might require various specific regulations, which could not be foreseen at the time of introduction.

Indeed, an outstanding setting for decentralization! But what an enormous challenge for the implementers!

- Which civil servant would be ready to go to the "sleeping" municipalities?
- How could the "technocratic know-how" reach the new decision-makers?
- Who would provide the necessary infrastructure?
- Maybe the most important: Who would participate?

THE RURAL EXPERIENCE: FROM FEUDALISM TO DEMOCRACY

Devolution was rapid, and initially, the greatest problems in devolution were linked to the Department of Health. Its staff counted for about 66 percent of all the civil servants to be devolved.[6] Enormous resentments were aired.

The most drastic change took place within the Department of Interior and Local Government (DILG). Previously, the controlling institution responsible for promotion and suspension of local government executives, DILG would have to defer to these elected community leaders. Only over time, with some amendments and substantial assistance from abroad,[7] the *administrative part* of decentralization was achieved. In fact, in the more central parts of Luzon island (the CALABARZON),[8] the cities and larger municipalities had relatively few problems in adjusting to their new function. For them, decentralization became first an administrative issue; policy-related decision-making continued more or less to remain in the domain of the traditional "leadership" in the form of the existing oligarchic structures.

The introduction of the LGC into the *rural sector* was much more difficult. Only a few kilometres away from the larger cities and towns, there were the *"forgotten barangays"* where terms such as *development, participation, self-reliance, democracy,* and *human rights* were hardly known or practiced. Instead, the rural areas were still the stronghold of the colonial experiences. Large land holdings and poorly developed social and physical infrastructure formed the harsh living conditions for the fast-growing rural masses. Although independence from Spanish, American, Japanese, and American colonialism had come in 1946, little was changed. Land was distributed to only a few, and the leading families managed to keep the growing wealth within their structures.

Consequently, opposition to the political system emerged from the few educated people not belonging to the "system." Political opposition grew steadily, supported or even spearheaded by church-related organizations such as the Federation of Free Farmers (FFF) in the 1950s, remaining freedom fighter groups (HUK movement), and later the Maoist Communist Party of the Philippines (1969) along with increasing unrest among students. Together, they effected the ruling oligarchy system to finally declare Martial Law in 1972, which lasted until the EDSA Revolution in 1986. During all these years, very little was done for the rural areas except an enormous amount of environmental destruction—large tropical forests were completely denuded, and the formerly rich fishing grounds were destroyed (by commercial coastal ground trawling). While the rich became richer, poverty among the masses grew steadily.

It was the prime objective of the LGC to break up these conditions and integrate the rural poor into the political decision-making process. This is an extremely ambitious task, which is even now at least passively opposed by the leading structure. There were basically two keys to open these regions (which comprise at least 60 percent of the total Philippine population):

1. The *"Area-Based Integrated Development Planning,"* which was meant to introduce the participatory process at the village level and—as the "summary" of *barangay* plans—at the municipal level; and

2. The "more serious" continuation of *agrarian reform,*[9] which was already started during the Marcos regime but had hardly reached the poor masses of society.

THE CASE STUDY: AREA DEVELOPMENT IN BONDOC PENINSULA

Program Background

Bondoc is part of Quezon Province;[10] its center is only about 260 km from Metro Manila. It is composed of twelve municipalities with a total of 324 *barangays* (villages) inhabited by about 420,000 people living in about 70,000 households (see Map 9.1). About 80 percent live off subsistence farming and fishing, with an average annual income of US$120 to US$150. This is reflected in the high prevalence of malnutrition: 23 percent of children in the zero-to-six-years group suffer from severe malnutrition (national average: 8.3 percent).

The peninsula has a total land area of 222,254 hectares (ha) with rather narrow coastal planes and hilly uplands. The annual precipitation is about 2,000 mm per year but depends highly on the frequency and direction of the typhoons, which cause enormous damage to agriculture. The farming system is based on coconut palms. Road infrastructure is extremely poor (almost entirely poorly maintained gravel and earth roads) and there exists no telecommunication system.

The farming system is characterized by the following issues:

• About 120,000 ha are agricultural land out of which 70,000 ha are the property of a few landlords that are only partly (25,000 ha) subjected to agrarian reform. The large landholdings are not yet covered by the agrarian reform program (two related families own about 15,000 ha).

• The agrarian reform program closely relates the potential beneficiaries with the landlords (often absentees); the tenant has to claim that his/her family has cultivated the land over one generation. If there is no claim, there is no allocation.

• Consequently, landlords can apply a large number of legal or even illegal steps to avoid land distribution. Only about 20,000 ha have been distributed over the last ten years and these were voluntarily repossessed by previous owners of 20 ha up to 50 ha holdings. Larger holdings were hardly affected.

• The cropping system is based on coconut oil production, but most of the palm stands are overage and neglected; other crops are bananas, maize, and rice.

• Tenants were traditionally harvesting only coconuts but were not allocated any land for their home production or the raising of livestock. Consequently, they have very little experience with farming techniques or farming management practices.

• Some 40,000 ha are classified as "timberlands," mostly denuded and illegally allocated to absentee landlords.

Map 9.1

Bondoc Peninsula, Quezon (Region IV, District III), Administrative Boundaries

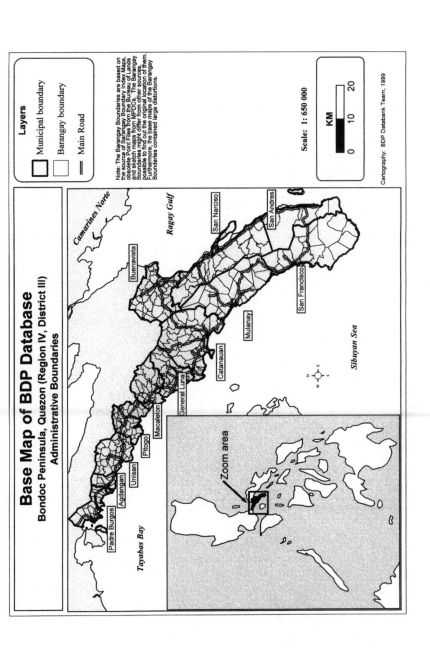

Base Map of BDP Database

Bondoc Peninsula, Quezon (Region IV, District III)
Administrative Boundaries

Layers

☐ Municipal boundary

☐ Barangay boundary

━━ Main Road

Note: The Barangay Boundaries are based on the source of Barangay Boundary Index Maps, obsolete Point Files from the Bureau of Lands and sketch maps from MPDCs. The Barangay Boundaries might differ from other sources, possible to find out the original location of them. Furthermore, the base maps of the Barangay Boundaries contained large distortions.

Scale: 1: 650 000

KM

0   10   20

Cartography: BDP Databank Team, 1999

Camarines Norte

Ragay Gulf

Buenavista

San Narciso

San Andres

San Francisco

Mulanay

Catanauan

General Luna

Sibuyan Sea

Macalelon

Pitogo

Unisan

Agdangan

Padre Burgos

Tayabas Bay

N W E S

Zoom area

- Only about 4,000 ha are rain-fed irrigated rice fields, producing only about 25 percent to 30 percent of the annual demand.
- Cash crops are bananas but the harvest is unreliable owing to weather and road conditions.
- Other crops are of only minor importance.
- Some livestock is exported (buffaloes, cattle) but this remains a domain of larger and more commercialized farms.

The fishing sector is split into a commercial section that continues to produce surplus delivered at the Manila market and an artisan fishing sector that is in very bad shape. In Bondoc, the night catch of fish is on average hardly one kilo of minor-quality fish per boat. In fact, the fast-growing coastal population is the poorest stratum of the populace.

Other income generation sources result from commerce, sale of coconut timber (often illegal), and transfer payments from local people working in Metro Manila or from contractual overseas workers.

In 1988, the Government of the Philippines requested financial assistance from the Federal Republic of Germany for the pavement of the national roads in the Bondoc Peninsula. Owing to the unstable and insurgent situation of the late 1980s, financial cooperation did not materialize[11] but technical cooperation between both governments was approved and started with effect in the mid-1990s.

Phase I: People's Mobilization

From the very beginning of the Bondoc Development Program (BDP), development was understood as a process with an economic, social, and—last but not least—political component. It was this political component that hampered the self-reliance and responsibility of the people. Consequently, it was obvious that any regional development could primarily center only around two basic efforts:

- Assistance to overcome the feudalistic background and thinking (the sociopolitical dimension of the backwardness of people); and
- Assistance with regard to access to resources (arable land and improved fishing grounds).

The project contracted NGOs for community mobilization with basically one task: to organize village people to claim their rights related to agrarian reform and to actively contribute to resource improvement.

According to the LGC, this was to be supported by LGUs but with the exception of one out of twelve mayors, there was hostility rather than support. Indeed, it was a difficult start with regard to sustainable development: even the congressman concerned opposed the program and at several stages, the program just escaped closure.

However, some eighty to ninety groups were organized and "federated" and particularly, the fisherfolk gained political influence. Slowly, the Department of Agrarian Reform (DAR) entered into a critical dialog and started at least some efforts to move agrarian reform. Some assistance was provided to cooperatives and also to some enterprises with the objective to show people-based nonagricultural income generation as livelihood. But there was still a large opposition among the *leading class*, traditional as well as modern, and several attempts to reorganize BDP succeeded as follows:

- Some of the NGOs had their own political interests; "their" POs did not develop lasting structures and continued to depend on their NGO as "spokesperson." Consequently, there was a detrimental effect from changing partners.
- Some of the line agencies (e.g., Department of Agriculture) lost interest as they were omitted from the Steering Board.[12]

Phase II: Program Decentralization—the New Start

In mid-1996, the program decided to decentralize its efforts to all twelve municipalities, even where the mayors were rather hostile. Program community organizers (COs) were located at the municipalities and maintained direct contact with the POs as well as with interested LGUs.

The BDP redefined its program purpose as follows:

"Small farmers, tenants, and fisherfolk should improve their political, social, economic, and environmental conditions with the overall goal to empower and organize small farmers, tenants, and fisherfolks plan and implement sustainable barangay development programs."

In March 1997, there were nationwide elections for *barangay* officials, the captains, and the members of councils. The BDP got involved (with the national commission (COMELEC)) in the preparation of elections, which were conducted in each of the 324 villages, allowing the candidates to present their program. This was perhaps the most important initiative of the program so far—more than 60 percent of officials were newly elected and were development-minded. Vote-buying and rigging attempts had failed in most places, the traditional leaders had lost their influence, and the door was open for development planning and implementation at the village level.

As a next step, a series of training courses for the elected officials were conducted—with half-hearted support from the DILG—in order to inform them of their roles and provisions as outlined in the LGC.

A new era of development assistance at the village level could begin. This development was closely monitored by the mayors, and some of them realized that the BDP had gained quite some influence at the base. As their election was scheduled for May 1998, the mayors changed their attitude toward the program: in many cases from disinterest or even hostility to tolerance or cooperation.

As a background, it is important to understand the different interpretations of *development*. For the traditional leaders it means some physical infrastructure investments "given to the people by the generous leader," which indicates the feudalistic tradition of the omnipotent landlord who takes and gives at his discretion.

This philosophy is very much supported or reflected in the national budget dispersal mechanisms, where the congressmen dispose of various development funds (so-called pork barrel) by virtually distributing checks (sometimes not even put in envelopes) at public meetings.[13]

The philosophy of "self-reliance, project ownership, responsibility, sustainability, accountability, self-determination, etc." is certainly the basis of the LGC but never systematically explained or virtually introduced in rural areas, even not by the NGO sector involved.

Of course, the question is: How can this philosophy be introduced in twenty-four villages where there is hardly any infrastructure and some hostility in addition?

PEOPLE'S POWER THROUGH VILLAGE PLANNING

The Settings

As in many developing countries, *planning in the Philippines* is considered important and necessary, and whoever has seen the uncoordinated industrialization in the vicinity of Metro Manila and the related resource destruction (land, water, and air) will agree. There are sector plans for the departments, and further regional, municipal, and village plans, all of which are summarized in the national plan. However, there is little coordination between plans and there is hardly any resource assessment—as plans are only indicative. The Housing and Land Use Regulation Body (HLURB) is the authority to set planning standards and recommend acceptance. Planning is standardized and the planning data required is enormous and useful only for planning of towns, cities, and industrialized areas. Related statistics for rural areas and required maps do not exist, and there is no way and need to base planning in rural areas on these.

Early in 1997, the BDP agreed with the responsible HLURB Regional Office to support planning that is virtually based on "*a limited data frame*," and this agreement was the entry point to *participatory village development planning*.

The Planning Method

In fact, one progressive municipality deployed a local consultant and spent scarce funds from the municipal budget. The result was a shopping list with only very limited participation from officials, which was consequently rejected by HLURB, mainly because there was no assessment of village potential and possible resources. Other methods were searched for.

The LGC correlates indeed well with the "four 'd's" of Robert Chambers,[14] understanding development as a continuous change: *decentralization, democracy, diversity*, and *dynamism*.

This leads to *Participatory Rural Appraisal* (PRA) as a planning basis, but would it satisfy the *hard data requirements* of government administration?

Since July 1997, the BDP has introduced Village Development Planning based on PRA. First, the twelve COs were trained by a local NGO in PRA methods. Some practical experience was gathered before teams of three COs started to conduct PRAs within the *barangays*. There were basically two criteria for choosing the villages: first, BDP gave priority to neglected villages, which were difficult to reach and politically considered "unsafe" by the administration; and second, to those villages where work had begun and where interest was expressed. During the first year, a close participatory monitoring and exchange of views and experiences took place in order to learn and adjust where necessary. In total, about forty-two village plans have been prepared by the villagers (and facilitated by BDP-COs) until late 1998.

Robert Chambers defines PRA as "a growing family of approaches and methods to enable local people to share, enhance, and analyse their knowledge of life and conditions, and to plan, act, monitor and evaluate."[15]

Originally meant only to identify and appraise the problems and potentials as well as the social, economic, and political environment, the *PRA toolbox* method is increasingly used for group and village planning in many developing countries. Major theoretical adjustments were introduced in 1996 in order to make PRA more suitable for planning (see Figure 9.1). However, we know only of a few cases where PRA was used as a basis for district or municipal planning with the express intent to form part of a higher-level plan.

The basic assumptions, learning, and issues are as follows:

- They can do it;
- Behavior change, or the new role of "leaders and experts";
- Coming together, agreeing, consenting, envisioning;
- Visualizing, documenting; and
- Presenting.

These issues differ slightly from Chambers' categories, but include lessons learned from the BDP.

The toolbox has the following features:

a. There are primary (and some secondary) data that require validation and upgrading.

b. Looking into history will lead to information on trends and processes.

c. Seasonal and/or daily calendars.

d. Venn diagrams showing institutional linkages are important.

Figure 9.1
Use of Participatory Rural Appraisal (PRA) in Planning at Bondoc

1) The depleted hilly area of southern Bondoc
2) PRA workshop—many people from the different sections of the village cooperate for 3 to 4 days during village planning
3) First convincing the neighbor of the result
4) Then follow presentation to the village assembly and
5) Finally, the plan will be presented and validated on municipality level

e. Analysis of differences, presenting the various ways of social groups (gender, youth, fisherfolk, and landless).

f. Ranking of importance, considering different views and strata.

g. Mapping: here, BDP concentrated on two different kinds of maps.
   • Mapping of the present situation considering the status and potential of resources, existing problems, etc.; and
   • Mapping of the future showing how the village will look five to ten years from the present.

h. Budgeting based on the village's own and external resources, including documentation and presentation.

PRELIMINARY EXPERIENCES

The Planning Method

From BDP's close monitoring of the planning sessions, some difficulties were experienced by facilitators regarding the planning method:

• Village preparation is very important. First, people were informed and prepared for the exercise. After a few plans were prepared, villages (through their chiefs and others) request facilitation assistance from the BDP. Still it is important to ensure that all groups from the different *sitios*,[16] gender, and tribes are informed and participation is ensured. This becomes more and more the obligation of village officials and people's representatives.

• The facilitators have to make sure that the *local leaders* and *LGU participating staff* understand their new role as resource persons. In fact, they team up in their own group and are consulted with regard to technical (and political) problems.

• At first, our staff hesitated to spend at least seven to eight days in each village. Now, there already exists a very relaxed and friendly working environment due to their interaction with the people. The villages bear all the costs for food and accommodation while the BDP provides only facilitators and materials (papers, pens, and flip charts). In fact, when the plan is drafted (after seven to ten days), documentation is done jointly and the results are then presented to the *village assembly*. The final stage is budgeting and plan compilation, which takes another week.

• In the beginning, PRA provided only the background data for planning. It was a long process for our staff to focus on the vision components of the PRA and then, to develop joint methods to translate these into a five-year development plan as requested by HLURB.

• In particular, land use planning was difficult to achieve, as the maps prepared by the people indicating potential and visions were not according to scale, and "looked un-professional" (social mapping).

During close monitoring regarding the *use of PRA data for the formulation of a plan*, BDP's CO came up with different procedures for plan formulation. From experience, some participants applied problem- or needs-oriented rather than potential-oriented methods. It took some training efforts to integrate both aspects, as problem orientation does not mobilize one's own resources but encourages the *receiver mentality* instead of starting development from one's own resources identified during PRA. And here might be the real advantage of the *participatory approach*, changing the passive into the active.

Consequently, the BDP staff developed a variable structure for the *Village Development Plan*, but all plans include the following data:

- History;
- Village profile;
- Village problems;
- Assessment of village resources;
- Vision of village in five to ten years' time;
- Five-Year Investment Program and projects and Annual Investment Programs; and
- Budget and funding sources.[17]

The results of the planning exercise, i.e., the draft plan, were then taken back to the village assembly for final approval. Here some modifications particularly with regard to priority setting were agreed upon, and the plan as well as the use of the village budget became *consensus*. Many participants suddenly realized that this new procedure was the entry point for *transparency* and *accountability* of the village officials.

First Reactions

After the compilation of the first four to five village plans, they were presented to the municipal administration. In all municipalities, there was an unexpected positive result, as for the first time since the introduction of the LGC, the villages came up with something different from the usual shopping list of the past. In particular, the villages' own contributions were indicated and a number of productive projects were mentioned (agriculture, fisheries, and environment), and not only the traditional infrastructure, which was often beyond any reasonable magnitude.

Mayors and particularly their planning officers requested spontaneously to apply the planning method at all villages (some municipalities have more than thirty!).

For the BDP field staff, this was a nice compensation for their efforts, the long walks to the villages, and other related hardships.

The next step was then to train additional facilitators for PRA-based village planning. The BDP staff identified about twenty-five interested persons from LGUs and POs, who were trained by an NGO, with more emphasis on PRA-based planning. In the future, these volunteers will assist in plan preparation, and first experiences show very good results: in one of the critical agrarian reform villages, the vice-mayor who was trained has conducted a very successful planning session. The others have just started fieldwork together with the BDP staff.

The "Translation" Process

Land-use mapping in the form of simple drawings like the samples given here were insufficient in order to convince the local and, particularly, the central government institutions. How can a zoning ordinance for land use be issued without showing proper boundaries according to scale?

As these are legal issues, exact delineation is required. Fortunately, the modern geographic information system (GIS)-supported data banking in connection with global positioning system (GPS) has opened new ways of mapping. BDP is now providing *village base maps*, which show the boundaries and some significant features of the villages such as the roads, rivers, and public buildings. With these maps, it is much easier for the *key persons* to identify land-use planning (and land tenure issues) on the ground. In fact, later checks of identified present land use are much more accurate than the only available topographical maps, which are based on 1983 aerial photos.[18] The translation of data is done through digitizing and adjusting the given land-use drawings with the digitized map of the village.

At present this translation is at an early stage. Given results can still be verified in the field through the use of GPS. Preliminary findings are encouraging. The results are acceptable to HLURB. Maps 9.2 and 9.3 show the result of the translation process for the village's resources and its five-year visions (plans).

PRELIMINARY LESSONS

1. Perhaps the most difficult lesson is to make the educated staff aware of "giving the stick away." Based on the Philippine leadership philosophy, which is also common in and even further developed by the NGO sector, the top-down approach has a very strong tradition and acceptance. "Learning to learn" is very difficult and the role of the resource person must be learned.

2. People in the villages are very keen to participate and understand PRA methods and subsequent planning methods. There is a strong drive to compromise and even consent in the group. From initial experience, there is willingness and enthusiasm for taking over responsibility and to contribute to their *own* projects with their own labor and even finances.

3. There was no serious problem with regard to the integration of different groups in the villages, specifically women and adolescent children with the rest, and coastal with upland people.

4. Some PRA tools proved important while others were introduced without much relevance to learning from the planning process. The BDP staff developed some feeling

Map 9.2
Resource Map (from PRA 1998), Barangay Olongtao Ibaba, Macalelon, Quezon

Resource Map (from Participatory Rural Appraisal, 1998)

Barangay Olongtao Ibaba, Macalelon, Quezon

Layers

Barangay boundaries from diff. sources

Main Roads

Legend

Built-up areas
Coconut
Banana
Fishpond
Rice paddy
Grassland

Legend

Farm to market road
Still to verify

Legend

Church
Telephone
Solar dryer
Health center
Barangay hall
Foot bridge
Deep well
Police post
Waiting shed
Spring
Basketball court
Elementary school
Day care center
Pump house
High school

Scale: 1:28 000
KM
0   .5   1

Cartography: BDP Database Team, Mar. 1999
Source: PRA Results, BDP-DIA, 1998

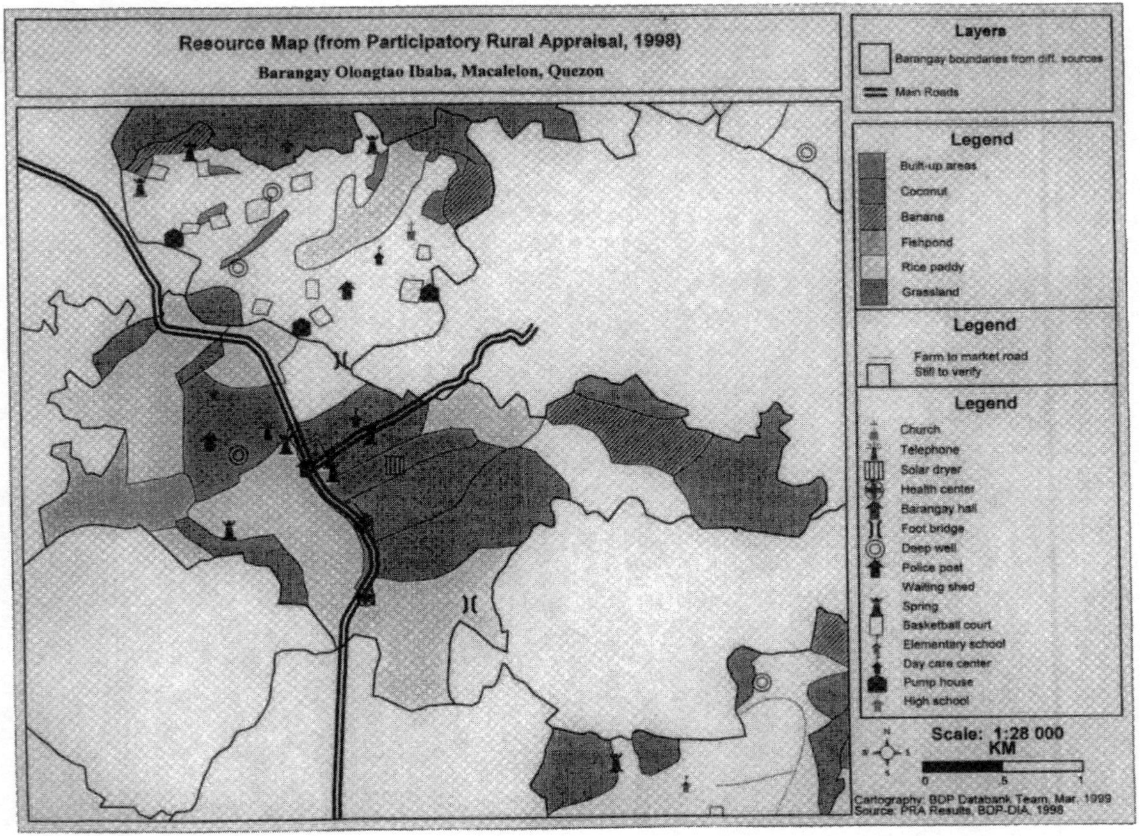

Map 9.3
Vision Map (from PRA 1998), Barangay Olongtao Ibaba, Macalelon, Quezon

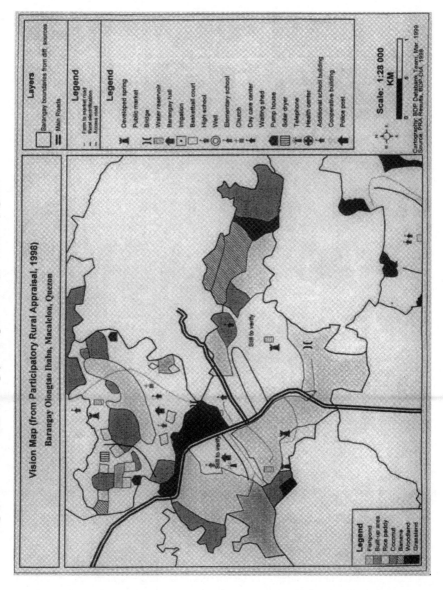

Vision Map (from Participatory Rural Appraisal, 1998)
Barangay Olongtao Ibaba, Macalelon, Quezon

for applying the most suitable tools and to vary tools where necessary. Each PRA and planning was a genuine exercise with very different results.

5. From the knowledge of the area, the proposed activities and their priorities made sense.

6. The combination of visualizing in drawings using high-tech tools for mapping is promising. The BDP will continue to develop this instrument. However, it must always be understood that these maps are based on a social mapping process.

7. The BDP is now in the process of preparing the first municipal plan based on village plans. Four municipalities have indicated an interest and are keen to organize the planning process, which will take place in two steps: (a) PRA with the town population (four to eight villages); and (b) summarizing of village plans in close coordination with the LGUs.

8. Finally, it is now time to develop new *top-down plan coordination mechanisms* at the National Economic and Development Authority (NEDA)[19] level in order to integrate national and provincial as well as sector development goals and subsequent plans without destroying the young but blooming *flower of people's empowerment and participation.*

NOTES

1. Teresa Abesamis, ed., "Technical Cooperation for the Management of Change" (Manila: NEDA, 1995).

2. The main efforts that need mention are the Barrio Charter Act (RA 2264 of 1959), which gave some fiscal powers to the villages, and the Decentralization Act (RA 5185 of 1967), which allowed LGUs to appoint some local officials.

3. This took place from 22 to 25 February 1996 on Epifanio de los Santos Avenue, which is the main north-south connection. On 25 February, President Ferdinand Marcos left for exile in Hawaii.

4. In the provinces of Tarlac, Laguna, Davao del Sur, and Negros Occidental.

5. Tom S. Villarin, "People's Empowerment: A Guide to NGO-PO Partnerships with Local Government" (Quezon City, 1996).

6. Ibid; Abesamis, "Technical Cooperation."

7. The most important may be the Local Development Assistance Program (LDAP) financed by the United States Agency for International Development (USAID).

8. The provinces of Cavite, Laguna, Batangas, Rizal, and Quezon.

9. See the Comprehensive Agrarian Reform Law (CARL) of 1986.

10. The third congressional district, but without any administrative structures.

11. The main argument of the opposition was that *agrarian reform* should come before road improvement.

12. Through an uncoordinated effort by the concerned congressman in 1995.

13. The Estrada government has stopped the system but there is no real replacement like budget transfers directly to the mayors or through line agencies.

14. Robert Chambers, *Whose Reality Counts? Putting the First Last* (London: Intermediate Technology Publications, 1997), p. 197.

15. Ibid.

16. A village has a number of different *sitios*, which can be compared to hamlets. In

Bondoc, owing to its peninsular character, most of the villages have coastal and upland *sitios*. Often, there are different views that need to be coordinated and considered.

17. See *Five-Year Barangay Development Plan of Barangay San Pablo* (Suha) (English translation).

18. Obviously taken with a relatively high cloud coverage when compared to satellite images of 1992.

19. NEDA is also the National Planning Office placed under the Office of the President. NEDA has a Central Office and Regional Offices but no further structure at the provincial or municipal levels.

10

Rhetoric and Reality: Decentralization, Planning, and Development in the Southern Mindanao Region, Philippines

Sophremiano B. Antipolo

INTRODUCTION

To what extent decentralization is an illusion, rhetoric, or reality is the overriding concern of this investigation. A number of studies in developing countries have found ample evidence that the results of decentralization have fallen short of expectations. Decentralization has been only partly effective because financial and manpower resources were not allocated in line with requirements of the reforms.[1] Must these results be attributed to a lack of commitment or ignorance of the dynamics of decentralization? Or is it precisely the outcome that the government or the state wanted—decentralization on paper without effective devolution in practice?

This chapter is organized in five sections: the overall context of the study; a brief review of the related literature; the research methodology; specific tests of hypotheses and analysis of findings; and conclusions.

BACKGROUND AND PREMISES

A major policy thrust of the current *Medium-Term Philippine Development Plan* (MTPDP) and the *Medium-Term Regional Development Plans* (MTRDPs), 1993–1998, is to actively pursue decentralization of key government functions. The chapters on development administration in the MTPDP and MTRDPs are concerned with evaluating ongoing decentralization efforts of the Government of the Philippines. While the time frame of the current plans has already passed, indications are clear that the development administration component of successive MTPDP and MTRDPs for 1999–2004 will continue the policy of decentralization.

The current MTPDP stipulated that for the twin strategy of global competitiveness and people's empowerment to work, policies must conform to the guiding principles of decentralization, democratic consultation, and reliance on nongovernmental initiatives.[2] Specifically, the MTPDP provides that "in governance, a direct outcome of the strategy of empowerment is the principle of decentralization and subsidiarity. Lower levels of government (regional and local) must be allowed to set priorities and decide matters in their own spheres of competence."[3]

The first major decentralization of government functions was authorized under Republic Act No. 5435, which created the Commission on Reorganization (hereinafter the Commission). The Commission's major accomplishment was the *Integrated Reorganization Plan* (IRP), which was adopted on 24 September 1972 by the Presidential Decree No.1 under Martial Law by then-President Ferdinand Marcos. Notwithstanding the Martial Law regime, the IRP appeared to be the first effort at regionalization—the first time ever to establish Regional Development Councils (RDCs) throughout the country. RDCs became the extensions of the National Economic and Development Authority (NEDA) Board, the central planning body of the Executive Branch of the government. The RDCs serve as planning boards at the regional level.

Indeed, decentralization through deconcentration via regionalization and some degree of devolution was pursued in the early 1970s. By the mid-1970s, attempts at giving more substance to decentralization were made through the budget process. In 1977, the Budget Reform Decree authorized regional and provincial line agencies to prepare regional budgets based on their regional and local agency plans, and coordinated by the RDCs and LDCs.

Toward the end of the 1970s up to the mid-1980s, a system of public investment planning and programming was introduced. The new system called for preparation of the Five-Year Regional Development Investment Program (RDIP) as a package of implementable projects that would link the MTRDPs and the annual budget at all levels: local, regional, and national. The RDIP categorizes programs to be funded by the national government and by the local government units (LGUs). In 1989, the NEDA Board adopted the Synchronized Planning, Programming, and Budgeting System (SPPBS) as a coordinating framework to link plans to the annual budget. This framework formalized the use of RDIP as the basis for preparation of the annual budget.

In the 1990s, two major events took place in the area of politicoadministrative development that bear relevance to decentralization:

1. The Local Government Code (LGC) was enacted in October 1991 to carry out the government's commitment to genuine local autonomy and people's empowerment. The LGC allocates a substantive portion of government funds and devolves extensive powers to the LGUs.

2. Executive Order 505 was passed in February 1992 to make RDCs more responsive to the increased needs of LGUs for technical assistance in the areas of planning, investment programming, and project development. The key features in the reorganized RDCs are the inclusion of legislators (congressmen) as regular members and the addition of some functions related to the devolution process.

More than two decades have passed since the implementation of the IRP as a mechanism for decentralization. Subsequently, many other related policies have also been issued to support the IRP. Yet, in this considerably long period of implementation, studies analyzing the decentralization process have been scanty. Moreover, few studies in the Philippines or elsewhere have focused attention on the consistency between the processes of "planning-investment programming" and "budgeting-implementation."

In decentralization, the crucial questions are what powers are actually decentralized and which areas (regions, provinces, and municipalities) actually benefit from decentralization. These are important to any discussion of the relationship between decentralization and planning since the answers will determine the extent to which regional governments and LGUs can effectively plan and implement their own development activities. Decentralization can only be really effective if it includes decentralization of the powers to make decisions, allocate resources, and implement projects. As emphasized by Conyers, the most powerful resource for plan implementation is finance.[4] Therefore, effective decentralization must include some decentralization of control over finance.

This study, therefore, addresses the issue of consistency between planning-investment programming and budgeting implementation within the broader context of two forms of decentralization, deconcentration by regionalization and devolution by implementation of the LGC.

The seemingly alluring objectives of decentralization should not blind the Philippine polity to the possibility that the actual impacts of such policy intervention might be limited or fragmented. A less impressionistic assessment might urge a less euphoric view on the gains of decentralization. The reactions of some groups to the failures of decentralization in achieving its objectives are increasing. Comments on decentralization need to be elaborated to balance some of its rhetoric with a clearer account of its socioeconomic and political impact. Cole states, "We are fearful that the current sense of disappointment in the several local authorities might develop into a wholesale disenchantment and that many of the genuinely valuable ideas and principles behind decentralization will be summarily dismissed or abandoned."[5]

It is crucial to assess rhetorical claims against actual achievements. There is a need to confront the difficulties of decentralization initiatives in order to achieve a more balanced assessment of their potential. Above all, there is a need to understand and appreciate why decentralization might have promised far more than what it can actually deliver.

This study aims to analyze decentralization in the context of the reality of

Philippine politics. Lea and Wu argue that "to be meaningful, development planning and administration must be integrated with political power, yet those who wield such power often have little knowledge of the development process."[6] Further, Lea and Courtney emphasized that an obvious difficulty in project implementation is the nature of the political reality in developing countries.[7] Often a gulf is observed between the objectives of master plan documents and real planning and development activity endorsed by political authors of the same plans.

Objectives

This study has three objectives: (1) to review the nature, substance, and extent of Philippine decentralization from the early 1970s to the 1990s; (2) to determine and examine the gulf between the rhetoric and reality of decentralization with Southern Mindanao as the case study region; and (3) to determine the effect of devolution upon the spatial equity between "high class" and "low class" municipalities in Southern Mindanao (Region XI).

The study is built around three sets of questions:

a. What has been the nature, substance, and extent of Philippine decentralization? Has decentralization through deconcentration or regionalization succeeded in rectifying interregional disparities? What are the key determinants of regional economic and social development that should be considered when pursuing decentralization?

b. What has been the reality of Philippine decentralization in Southern Mindanao? In areas where deconcentration was undertaken, were the projects provided with adequate budgets to ensure their implementation, as proposed in the RDIP? In areas where devolution took place, did LGUs receive significant levels of internal revenue allotments (IRAs) as promised by the 1991 LGC?

c. Does devolution promote spatial equity or does it aggravate existing income gaps between high-class and low-class municipalities.

Hypotheses

The central proposition of this study is that there is a gulf between the rhetoric of decentralization policy and the reality of government investment decisions. The related hypotheses are:

a. The mismatch between rhetorical claims and actual achievements of decentralization is a consequence of inadequate transfer of financial resources and powers to allocate funds;

b. The lack of decentralization in Southern Mindanao is a reflection of political realities; and

c. Devolution tends to aggravate existing spatial inequities as low-class municipalities are less able to take advantage of their taxation powers than high-class municipalities.

High-class municipalities, with generally more resources, are likely to gain more from the opportunities offered by decentralization.

METHOD

Definitions

The following definitions are used in the study:

Forms of Decentralization. The current investigation is limited to two forms of decentralization, deconcentration and devolution. Deconcentration refers to the transfer of power, authority, or responsibility or the discretion to plan, decide, and manage from a central point or local level but within the central or national government itself. The nature of the transfer is administrative and the approach is sectoral. Devolution refers to the transfer of power and authority from the national government to LGUs as the territorial and political subdivisions of the state. The nature of power transfer is political and the approach is spatial.

Sectoral Focus and Areas of Concern. To study the results of deconcentration, the gulf between decentralization policy rhetoric and the reality using the case of public works and transportation sectors is determined. These sectors are chosen as there is a debate concerning dispersal of industries and the concomitant decentralization of public works investments. To study the impact of devolution, the focus is on the financial aspects of decentralization and the appraisal of implementation of the 1991 LGC over the period 1992–97.

Research Design

This study was undertaken using a case study approach that offers the following advantages:

1. Explains causal links and describes real-life context of phenomena that are too complex for experimental research strategies;
2. Illuminates the working of the social system in a way that a series of morphological statements cannot achieve; and
3. Enables the researcher to use quantitative and qualitative methods.[8]

Field investigation was carried out in the Southern Mindanao Region of the Philippines (see Map 10.1).

To study deconcentration, the entire Philippines is studied for a macrointerregional analysis and to test the hypothesis that interregional disparities have widened. This is followed by the case study in Southern Mindanao using two infrastructure sectors, public works and transportation and communication.

To study devolution, Southern Mindanao is the study region. The devolution component of this research specifically defines the eleven Provincial Agri-

Map 10.1
Map of the Philippines Showing Southern Mindanao (Region XI)

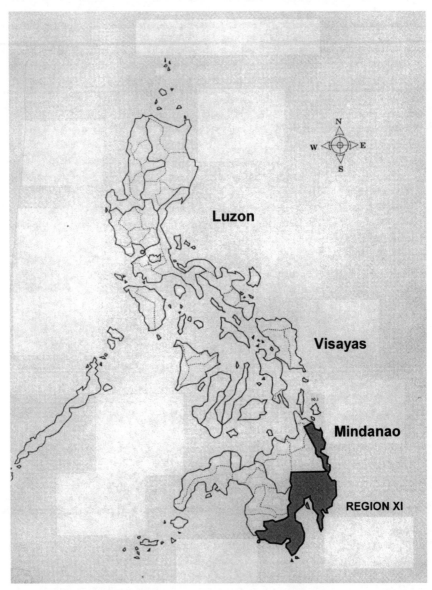

Source: Centre for Research and Communication, *Philippine Agribusiness Factbook and Directory 1991–1992* (Manila, 1992).

Industrial Centers (PAICs) as its spatial coverage (see Map 10.2). The rationale for this coverage is that the RDC of Region XI has adopted the PAICs as strategic centers for decentralizing socioeconomic activities. Further, the eleven PAICs aim to support two major agroindustrial centers, Davao City and General Santos City, which constitute the "bipolar strategy" for Region XI (see Map 10.2). The bipolar strategy is designed to support the entire Mindanao area's East ASEAN Growth strategy. The PAIC system is promoted in order to attract investments to other parts of Region XI; thus, contributing to the socioeconomic uplift of the rural areas.[9]

Two sets of sample units are studied: the eleven PAIC municipalities to determine the statistical difference between the IRAs before and after the enactment of the LGC; and the eleven contrasting low-class versus high-class municipalities to determine spatial inequities arising from decentralization.

REGIONAL PLANNING: A RESPONSE TO THE CLAMOR FOR DECENTRALIZATION

The pressure for governmental action at the regional level may come from a variety of sources. In the sixties, regional planning was a response to certain functional problems:

1. Those experienced in urban regions arising from rapid population growth, increasing urbanization, higher standards of living, and personal mobility.
2. Those of depressed industrial regions and rural regions.[10] Overall national planning considers the interregional allocation of resources.

Intraregional and interregional planning impact decentralization. The objectives of both are based on national development objectives of economic growth, full employment, and social equity. Economic growth involves the efficient utilization of resources to achieve a higher rate of output. Yet, some regions continue to have high levels of unemployment and underutilized capital assets. Thus, the injection of investment into such regions in the form of new infrastructure or industry may provide the necessary catalyst for regional economic growth, thereby aiding national economic growth. In the Philippines, Lawas argued that "regional development is a goal and instrument for national development."[11] The Philippine guru of decentralization, Raul P. de Guzman, said that "as a strategy towards democratizing the political system and accelerating the attainment of the development goals, decentralization has become an enduring issue in the landscape of public administration in the Philippines."[12]

Balanced Growth and Regional Balance

Prominent in the quest for decentralized forms of governance are "balanced growth" and "regional balance." The achievement of a regional balance between

Map 10.2
Map of Region XI Showing the Provincial Agri-industrial Centers (PAICs) and the Bipolar Strategy

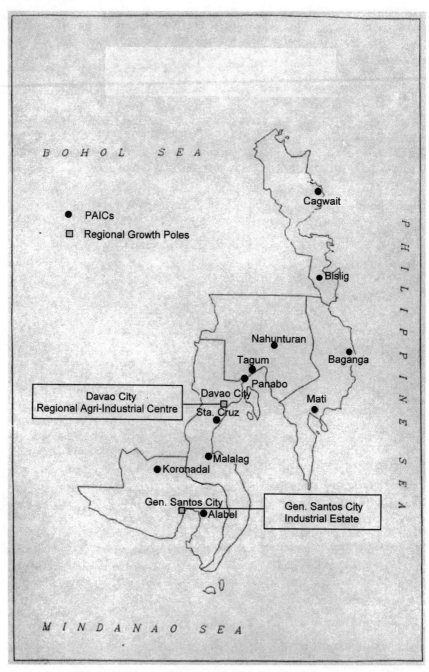

Source: National Statistics Office (NSO), *Census Facts and Figures* (Manila, 1993), p. 215.

people, jobs, and environment is fine rhetoric, but the term "balance" is somewhat confusing and has been given a variety of meanings. It could mean that poorer regions should grow faster than the rich ones so that their income levels tend to equalize—in this context, balance means convergence. Another interpretation could be that the rate of growth in poor regions should keep pace with that in prosperous regions. In this case, the nation and the constituent regions would grow at the same rate but as a consequence there would be a widening of absolute income differentials between rich and poor regions.

To operationalize the terms "balanced growth" and "regional balance," Friedmann suggests that balance does not mean a rigid mathematical balance but rather implies systematic interrelations between regions and rural and urban areas such that their differences in levels of living and opportunity will become progressively less pronounced.[13]

Rhetoric and Reality in Decentralization, Planning, and Development

Lea and Courtney found that governments are often aware that plan objectives commonly place high priority on providing housing and urban services for the very poor, but more affluent communities derive many of these benefits.[14] However, a succession of planning conferences sponsored by multilateral agencies produced technical recommendations that are unrelated to sociopolitical realities.[15] A common element underlying most conflicts in developing countries is the apparent mismatch between scale or complexity of a particular problem and resources or commitment available to resolve it.[16]

DEVOLUTION IN THE PHILIPPINES: EXPERIENCES IN THE IMPLEMENTATION OF THE 1991 LOCAL GOVERNMENT CODE

The Aquino government was interested in devolution as a centerpiece of public administration for a number of political as well as economic reasons, as follows:[17]

1. *Greater share of resources.* The fair distribution of fiscal resources among regions, provinces, cities, and municipalities. There were arguments that for devolution to be successful, more resources should be channeled to the less financially stable LGUs and away from Metro Manila, the National Capital Region (NCR).

2. *Revenue mobilization.* Executive Branch proposals indicated that the objective of decentralization was to increase revenues generated by the LGUs and revenue sharing between the central and local governments provided incentives for local tax effort.

3. *Local participation for improved services.* The government supported decentralization as an effective means to improve basic services through local participation. If people

were given the decision-making authority over the package of local services, they would be more likely to pay for services in the form of taxes and user charges.

The 1991 LGC is a detailed legal instrument for local autonomy. Its immediate impact was the creation of an enabling environment through which LGUs could be self-governing. In the words of then-President Corazon C. Aquino, the enactment of the LGC was[18] "a high point in our efforts as a people to strengthen democracy and attain a sustainable development. The new law lays down the policies and seeks to institutionalize democracy at the local level. It hopes, therefore, to complete the initial process of empowering our people through direct participation in the affairs of government, by allowing them the widest space to decide, initiate and innovate."

The LGC required devolution of many personnel from national agencies and their corresponding authorities to LGUs. This also involved stripping national agencies of their oversight and control roles. However, national agencies retained the duty to assist LGUs in technical and procedural matters until such time that LGUs could become self-sufficient.

By unleashing energies and initiatives at the front lines, local autonomy is expected to bring about greater productivity and broaden access to resources and opportunities. The following summary highlights issues from seven rapid field appraisals (RFAs):[19]

- The First RFA of July 1992 saw local government officials adopting a wait-and-see attitude.

- The Second RFA of January 1993 found local government officials beginning to move forward on LGC implementation, with national government agencies responding.

- The Third RFA of September 1993 had problems in the devolution of personnel and the IRA system, which was beginning to function.

- The Fourth RFA of June 1994 demonstrated increased momentum on the part of the LGUs as they reaped fruits of experimentation.

- The Fifth RFA of June 1995 found increased local resource mobilization and improved service delivery. However, national government agencies (NGAs) had not proactively filled new roles after devolution was accomplished.

- The Sixth RFA of May 1996 demonstrated incredible diversity. Within this diversity, the decentralization process was diffused and deepened. LGU management was more proactive and developmental, and local governments and communities were insisting on greater local autonomy.

- The Seventh RFA of August 1997 revealed innovation, quality, and relevance at the local level. Governance in the Philippines is being redefined at the local level. The LGC provides an enabling environment that allows experimentation, participation, and differentiated service delivery throughout the country. Despite the transition difficulties encountered at the beginning of the LGC implementation, the redefinition of governance has allowed LGUs to better serve their communities. A new participatory style

Table 10.1
Standard Deviation and ANOVA PCGRDP

	1975	1980	1985	1988	1990	1995
Standard Deviation	58.17	54.50	47.98	50.22	48.63	45.25
	Sum of squares	Degree of freedom		Mean square		F-ratio
Analysis of variance	164547.15	5		32909.43		
	187117.83	12		15593.15		2.110
	351664.98	17				

of leadership is emerging. Decentralization through devolution under the 1991 LGC has been an overall success.[20]

FINDINGS

Hypothesis 1: On Macro-Interregional Disparities

Since decentralization through deconcentration or regionalization was to correct interregional disparities, the questions that arise are:

1. How have the regions fared in the mid-1990s?
2. Was the economic dominance of the NCR reduced in favor of other less prosperous regions?
3. Are the other regions catching up?

The test of hypothesis here is essentially an extension of an earlier study by Lamberte et al. that ran an analysis of variance (ANOVA) covering the period 1975–88.[21] The current investigation covered seven more years up to 1995.

Ho1.1: Decentralization by deconcentration or regionalization did not rectify interregional imbalances even over a longer period (1975–95)—alternatively, there is no difference in the observed changes in the variance of per capita gross regional domestic product (PCGRDP) during the period 1975–95.

To determine whether the disparities across regions have significantly changed over time, the standard deviation of PCGRDP for each year of the six-year period was calculated. Also, a one-way ANOVA test was used to determine whether the changes were statistically significant or not.

A lower standard deviation indicates that the disparities have narrowed down during the period 1975–85 (see Table 10.1). A higher standard deviation indicates that interregional disparities have worsened between 1985 and 1988. A lower variance reflects that the interregional disparities have narrowed down again in 1995. Overall, while there was a general decrease in standard deviation over time, indicative of a narrowing down of interregional inequities, the critical

Table 10.2
Correlation Matrix of Economic Development Indicators and Infrastructure Development Indicators

Indicator	PCGRDP	AFAMI	RDENS	%HHEN	%HHWS
PCGRDP	1.000				
AFAMI	0.643*	1.000			
RDENS	0.887**	0.465	1.000		
%HHEN	0.681*	0.810**	0.696**	1.000	
%HHWS	0.459	0.234	0.082	0.090	1.000

*Significant at 0.05 level.
**Significant at 0.01 level.
PCGRDP = Per capita gross regional domestic product.
AFAMI   = Average family income.
RDENS   = Road density.
%HHEN   = Percent of households energized.
%HHWS = Percent of households with level III water supply.

question is whether the variance across regions over time is significant in order to reject the null hypothesis.

The computed F-value of 2.110 obtained from the ANOVA is lower than the tabular F-value (at df $= 17$) of 3.110. Therefore, the null hypothesis is accepted that there is no statistical difference in the observed changes in the variance of PCGRDP during the six periods. It is therefore concluded that the changes in disparity across regions are not significant. This implies that the policies and programs to promote decentralization, by deconcentration or regionalization, have not yet been effective or have yet to take effect or a combination of both.

Ho1.2: An increased government budget on economic infrastructure did not have a significant impact on regional economic growth and development.

Regional allocation of infrastructure projects and the provision of public services are often considered important determinants of the region's economic and social development.

Government spending for infrastructure had a positive effect on regional incomes. The PCGRDP was highly and significantly correlated with road density (RDENS) and percent household energized (HHEN) (see Table 10.2). Further, average family income (AFAMI) was found significantly correlated with percent HHEN. On the basis of the correlation test, the null hypothesis is rejected and it is concluded that economic infrastructure plays a significant role in regional economic growth and development.

Ho1.3: An increased government budget on social infrastructure did not have a significant impact on regional social development.

A significant positive relationship between average life expectancy (ALIFEX) and infant mortality rate (IMR) and between percent household provided with level III water supply (%HWS) and hospital bed-to-population ratio (HBPR) is observed (see Table 10.3). The correlation test does not yield enough statistical

Table 10.3
**Correlation Matrix of Social Development Indicators and Social Infrastructure/
Facilities and Services, 1995**

	ALIFEX	IMR	%HWS	HBPR	RHUPR	MMPR	BHPR
ALIFEX	1.000						
IMR	-0.990**	1.000					
%HWS	0.417	-0.414	1.000				
HBPR	-0.177	0.168	-0.680*	1.000			
RHUPR	-0.179	0.182	0.098	-0.015	1.000		
MMPR	-0.181	0.171	0.229	-0.242	0.441	1.000	
BHPR	-0.504	0.521	-0.047	0.056	0.373	-0.610	1.000

*Significant at 0.05 level.
**Significant at 0.01 level.
ALIFEX = Average life expectancy.
IMR   = Infant mortality rate.
%HWS   = Percent households with level III water supply.
HBPR   = Hospital bed-to-population ratio.
RHUPR   = Rural health unit-to-population ratio.
MMPR   = Medical manpower-to-population ratio.
BHPR   = Barangay health station-to-population ratio.

evidence to show a significant relationship between social infrastructure indicators and social development indicators. Therefore, the null hypothesis is accepted.

Economic infrastructure plays a more critical role than social infrastructure in regional growth and development.

Hypotheses Set 2: On the Rhetoric and Reality of Deconcentration

The testing of Hypotheses Set 2 aims to respond to the second set of questions: What has been the rhetoric and reality of Philippine decentralization in the Southern Mindanao Region? Were the programs and projects provided with adequate budgets to ensure their implementation?

The study seeks to verify the following main hypothesis (Ho2): The mismatch between the rhetoric and reality of Philippine decentralization—via deconcentration or regionalization—is an indication of the nature of the *realpolitik* that expresses itself as a gap that may exist between the rhetorical objectives described in the RDIP produced by the RDC and the real budget approved by the politicians.

To lend firmer statistical bases, the study formulated two null hypotheses (Ho2.1 and Ho2.2), which were tested one at a time using two sectors, public works and transportation.

Ho2.1: No significant gap persists between the RDIP requirement proposed by the RDC and the budget approved by Congress.

Table 10.4
Chi-Square Test, Public Works Sector RDIP Requirement vs. Approved Budget, Marcos Regime, 1980–1985

Year	RDIP-budget gap ('000 pesos)		Chi-square*
1980	64,710		19.68
1981	90,150		33.27
1982	121,040		48.41
1983	108,425		36.88
1984	167,600		68.80
1985	79,246		14.63
Computed chi-square			221.67

Tabular chi-square (at 0.05 percent and df = 5), 11.07.
*Chi-square formulation:

$$\text{Chi-square} = \text{sum} \frac{(Oi - Ei)^2}{Ei}$$

where: Oi = observed values = approved budget
Ei = expected values = RDIP requirement

Table 10.5
Chi-Square Test, Public Works Sector RDIP Requirement vs. Approved Budget, Aquino Regime, 1986–1991

Year	RDIP-budget gap ('000 pesos)		Chi-square*
1986	184,380		75.93
1987	8,900		00.17
1988	166,080		50.82
1989	138,380		33.71
1990	143,070		26.20
1991	-11,900		00.14
Computed chi-square			186.97

Tabular chi-square (at 0.05 percent and df = 5), 11.07.
*Refer to Table 10.4 footnotes for chi-square formulation.

Case 1: Public Works

To verify whether or not the RDIP requirement and the approved budget are significantly different, a chi-square statistical test was undertaken for each of the three political regimes. A final set of chi-square tests was also carried out for all three regimes spanning the period 1980–97.

The results reveal that the gap between the RDIP requirements endorsed by the RDC and the actual budget approved by Congress is significant as indicated by the computed chi-square values, which are greater than the tabular chi-square values at 0.05 percent level of significance and corresponding degrees of freedom. The tests revealed consistent results for all three regimes (see Tables 10.4–10.7). Therefore, the null hypothesis (Ho2.1) is rejected and it is concluded that a gulf exists between the plans and programs prepared by the RDC and the

Table 10.6
Chi-Square Test, Public Works Sector RDIP Requirement vs. Approved Budget,
Ramos Regime, 1992–1997

Year	RDIP-budget gap ('000 pesos)	Chi-square*
1992	517,060	271.63
1993	666,400	469.43
1994	407,960	258.26
1995	66,190	005.42
1996	-82,419	007.80
1997	631,916	250.41
Computed chi-square		1,262.95

Tabular chi-square value (at 0.05 percent and df = 5), 11.07.
*Refer to Table 10.4 footnotes for chi-square formulation.

Table 10.7
Chi-Square Test, Public Works Sector, All Regimes, 1980–1997

Year	RDIP-budget gap ('000 pesos)	Chi-square*
Marcos regime		
1980	64,710	19.68
1981	90,150	33.27
1982	121,040	48.41
1983	108,425	36.88
1984	167,600	68.80
1985	79,246	14.63
Aquino regime		
1986	184,380	75.93
1987	8,900	00.17
1988	166,080	50.82
1989	138,380	33.71
1990	143,070	26.20
1991	-11,900	00.14
Ramos regime		
1992	517,060	271.63
1993	666,400	469.43
1994	407,960	258.26
1995	66,190	005.42
1996	-82,419	007.80
1997	631,916	250.41
Computed chi-square		1,671.59

Tabular chi-square (at 0.05 percent and df = 17), 27.58.
*Refer to Table 10.4 footnotes for chi-square formulation.

Table 10.8

Chi-Square Test, Transportation Sector RDIP Requirement vs. Approved Budget, Marcos Regime, 1980–1985

Year	RDIP-budget gap ('000 pesos)	Chi-square*
1980	22,498	9.18
1981	23,094	9.08
1982	13,359	2.92
1983	16,670	3.49
1984	23,444	9.17
1985	13,112	2.74
Computed chi-square		36.58

Tabular chi-square value (at 0.05 percent and df = 5), 11.07.
*Refer to Table 10.4 footnotes for chi-square formulation.

actual budget as approved by the politicians through the Legislative Committee on Appropriations.

Case 2: Transportation and Communications

The transportation sector appears to be similar to that of the public works sector. Throughout the period 1980–97, the RDIP requirements recommended by the RDC for funding by the national government remains greater than the approved budget. That is, the actual appropriation for program/project implementation continued to fall short of the regional development investment requirement as proposed in the Regional Development Plan for Southern Mindanao.

To quantitatively verify the null hypothesis (Ho2.1) in the case of the transportation and communication sector, a similar round of chi-square tests was carried out.

The chi-square tests for each of the three regimes revealed that the approved budget by Congress consistently fell short of the RDIP requirements (see Tables 10.8–10.10). The computed chi-square values were consistently greater than the chi-square tabular value at 0.05 percent level of significance and corresponding degrees of freedom. Therefore, the null hypothesis that there is no significant difference between the expected RDIP values and the observed (approved) budgetary value is rejected.

A separate statistical test for the whole longitudinal period 1980–97 revealed the same results (see Table 10.11). The computed chi-square value is greater than the tabular chi-square value at 0.05 percent level of significance.

Ho2.2: There is no significant gap between the RDC-endorsed budget proposal and the Congress-approved budget.

To verify the second null hypothesis (Ho2.2), the same chi-square test was conducted.

The evidence drawn from a comparison between the RDC-endorsed budget proposal and the Congress-approved budget yielded the same results. The com-

Table 10.9
Chi-Square Test, Transportation Sector RDIP Requirement vs. Approved Budget, Aquino Regime, 1986–1991

Year	RDIP-budget gap ('000 pesos)	Chi-square*
1986	26,670	09.00
1987	36,137	15.50
1988	16,622	03.16
1989	28,899	10.53
1990	13,800	02.15
1991	3,720	00.13
Computed chi-square		40.47

Tabular chi-square value (at 0.05 percent and df = 5), 11.07.
*Refer to Table 10.4 footnotes for chi-square formulation.

Table 10.10
Chi-Square Test, Transportation Sector RDIP Requirement vs. Approved Budget, Ramos Regime, 1992–1997

Year	RDIP-budget gap ('000 pesos)	Chi-square*
1992	15,550	02.35
1993	40,470	20.79
1994	38,622	21.94
1995	25,700	11.15
1996	65,823	43.91
1997	28,634	08.59
Computed chi-square		108.73

Tabular chi-square value (at 0.05 percent and df = 5), 11.07.
*Refer to Table 10.4 footnotes for chi-square formulation.

puted chi-square values are greater than the tabular chi-square values at 0.05 percent level of significance (see Tables 10.12–10.14). Thus, the second null hypothesis (Ho2.2) is rejected, suggesting that there is, indeed, a significant difference between the RDC-endorsed budget proposal and the Congress-approved budget. Consistent findings were obtained when a longitudinal period, 1980–97, covering all the three political regimes was tested (see Table 10.15).

Hypotheses Set 3: On the Rhetoric and Reality of Devolution

Rule XXXII of the Implementing Rules and Regulations (IRR) of the 1991 LGC provides for the shares of LGUs in the proceeds of national taxes. One of these shares is the IRAs. Article 378 (Allotment of Internal Revenue Taxes) stipulates that:

The total annual IRAs due to the LGUs shall be determined on the basis of collections from national internal revenue taxes actually realized as certified by the Bureau of Internal Revenue during the third fiscal year preceding the current fiscal year as follows:

Table 10.11
Chi-Square Test, Transportation Sector RDIP Requirement vs. Approved Budget, All Regimes, 1980–1997

Year	RDIP-budget gap ('000 pesos)	Chi-square*
Marcos regime		
1980	22,498	9.18
1981	23,094	9.08
1982	13,359	2.92
1983	16,670	3.49
1984	23,444	9.17
1985	13,112	2.74
Aquino regime		
1986	26,670	09.00
1987	36,137	15.50
1988	16,622	3.16
1989	28,899	10.53
1990	13,800	2.15
1991	3,720	0.13
Ramos regime		
1992	15,550	2.35
1993	40,470	20.79
1994	38,622	21.94
1995	25,700	11.15
1996	65,823	43.91
1997	28,634	8.59
Computed chi-square		185.78

Tabular chi-square value (at 5 percent level and df = 17), 27.5.
*Refer to Table 10.4 footnotes for chi-square formulation.

Table 10.12
Chi-Square Test, RDC-Endorsed Budget vs. Congress-Approved Budget, Public Works and Transportation Sectors Combined, Marcos Regime, 1980–1985

Year	RDIP-budget gap ('000 pesos)	Chi-square*
1980	24,680	2.96
1981	25,837	3.08
1982	90,080	25.59
1983	80,837	18.50
1984	102,220	27.55
1985	4,128	0.04
Computed chi-square		77.72

Tabular chi-square value (at 0.05 percent and df = 5), 11.07.
*Refer to Table 10.4 footnotes for chi-square formulation.

Table 10.13
Chi-Square Test, Public Works and Transportation Sectors Combined
RDC-Endorsed Budget Proposal vs. Congress-Approved Budget, Aquino Regime,
1986–1991

Year	RDIP-budget gap ('000 pesos)	Chi-square*
1986	103,020	25.30
1987	-41,150	3.35
1988	105,120	20.37
1989	75,639	10.29
1990	22,370	17.21
1991	-128,985	16.97
Computed chi-square		93.49

Tabular chi-square value (at 0.05 percent and df = 5), 11.07.
*Refer to Table 10.4 footnotes for chi-square formulation.

Table 10.14
Chi-Square Test, Public Works and Transportation Sectors Combined
RDC-Endorsed Budget Proposal vs. Congress-Approved Budget, Ramos Regime,
1992–1997

Year	RDIP-budget gap ('000 pesos)	Chi-square*
1992	250,728	77.73
1993	442,550	257.51
1994	217,202	98.10
1995	-166,322	45.39
1996	-161,284	31.45
1997	142,780	17.26
Computed chi-square		527.44

Tabular chi-square value (at 0.05 percent and df = 5), 11.07.
*Refer to Table 10.4 footnotes for chi-square formulation.

(a) for the first year of effectivity of the Code (1992), thirty percent; (b) for the second year (1993), thirty-five percent; and (c) for the third year (1994), and thereafter, forty percent.

Under Hypotheses Set 3, the study tested two specific groups of null hypotheses: (1) The first group is concerned with the question whether or not the increases in the IRA over time were significant after the enactment of the LGC; and (2) the second group is concerned with the effect of devolution (1991 LGC) upon spatial equity/inequity.

Ho3.1: The IRAs of the study PAIC municipalities are not significantly different before and after the enactment of the 1991 LGC (see Tables 10.16–10.17).

Let X1 and X2 be the mean IRA of the study PAIC municipalities before and after the enactment of the LGC, respectively. We proceed by the six-step rule for hypothesistesting, as follows:

Table 10.15
Chi-Square Test, Public Works and Transportation Sectors Combined
RDC-Endorsed Budget Proposal vs. Congress-Approved Budget, All Regimes,
1980–1997

Year	RDIP-budget gap ('000 pesos)	Chi-square*
Marcos regime		
1980	24,680	2.96
1981	25,837	3.08
1982	90,080	25.59
1983	80,837	18.50
1984	102,220	27.55
1985	4,128	0.04
Aquino regime		
1986	103,020	25.30
1987	-41,150	3.35
1988	105,120	20.37
1989	75,639	10.29
1990	22,370	17.21
1991	-128,985	16.97
Ramos regime		
1992	250,728	77.73
1993	442,550	257.51
1994	217,202	98.10
1995	-166,322	45.39
1996	-161,284	31.45
1997	142,780	17.26
Computed chi-square		698.65

Tabular chi-square (at 0.05 percent and df = 17), 27.58.
*Refer to Table 10.4 footnotes for chi-square formulation.

1. Ho: X1 = X2
2. H1: X1 < X2
3. Level of significance: 0.05
4. Critical region: $t < -2.920$ at df = 2
5. Computations

Average deviation (AD) = $-30,498/3$ = $-10,166$

Standard deviation $(S^2) = \dfrac{3\ (344,664,030) - (-30,498)^2}{(3)\ (2)} = 17,310,681$

Variance (S) = square root of standard deviation = 4,161

t-test: $t = \dfrac{(AD)}{S/\text{square root of } n} = \dfrac{-10,166}{4,161/1.732} = -4.230 < t(0.05)$
$= -2.920$

Table 10.16
IRA before and after the Enactment of the Code, PAIC Municipalities,
Southern Mindanao Region 1989–1991 vs. 1992–1994
(in Thousand Pesos)

PAIC municipalities	1989	1990	1991	1992	1993	1994
Tagum	3,508	5,462	8,691	11,765	21,917	27,974
Panabo	2,566	3,871	6,856	9,975	18,853	23,883
Nabunturan	1,534	2,406	4,323	6,210	11,569	14,857
Sta Cruz	2,364	3,438	4,723	6,675	12,434	16,347
Malalag	2,436	3,611	3,591	5,476	10,200	13,212
Mati	4,296	6,163	8,233	12,309	22,931	29,522
Baganga	3,892	5,036	6,436	10,709	19,927	22,368
Koronadal	3,532	5,189	7,572	10,410	19,393	26,009
Bislig	3,673	5,374	7,473	10,326	19,237	24,733
Cagwait	792	1,401	2,041	3,540	6,594	8,441
Alabel	1,326	2,444	3,784	9,211	11,336	14,564
Mean	2,720	4,036	5,793	8,782	14,091	20,174

Sources of basic data: Local Treasury Offices, Region XI; Bureau of Local Government Finance,
Region XI; Department of Budget and Management, Region XI.

Table 10.17
Computations

Year	Mean IRA before the LGC (X1)	Mean IRA after the LGC (X2)	Deviation (D)	Deviation squared
1	2,720	8,782	-6,062	36,747,844
2	4,036	14,091	-10,055	101,103,025
3	5,793	20,174	-14,381	206,813,161
Sum			-30,498	344,664,030

Average deviation (AD) = -30,498 / 3 = -10,166

Standard deviation (S^2) = $\dfrac{3\,(344,664,030) - (-30,498)^2}{(3)\,(2)}$ = 17,310,681

Variance (S) = square root of standard deviation = 4,161

t-test:

$t = \dfrac{(AD)}{S/\sqrt{n}} = \dfrac{-10,166}{4,161 / 1.732} = -4.230 < t\,(0.05) = -2.920$

6. Conclusion: Reject Ho and conclude that the IRA after the enactment of the LGC is significantly higher than the IRA before the enactment of the LGC.

A similar test contrasting 1989–91 (before the LGC) and 1995–97 (after the LGC) yielded consistent results. To exhaust drawing alternative sets of evidence, other tests were conducted using the following indicators: (1) total municipal income; and (2) IRA contribution to municipal income. The test results sustained earlier findings—IRAs of the study PAIC municipalities are significantly higher after the enactment of the LGC. All these findings suggest that decentralization through devolution made good its rhetoric (as promised) in the 1991 LGC concerning the IRAs.

The last hypothesis tested in the area of devolution is based on the following proposition: Devolution tends to aggravate existing spatial inequities as low-class municipalities in the rural areas are less able to take advantage of (or optimize) their taxation powers than the high-class municipalities in the urban areas. Urban LGUs—with generally more resources—are likely to gain more from the opportunities offered by devolution (i.e, implementation of the 1991 LGC). The specific null hypothesis that was tested in this study is:

Ho3.2: There is no significant difference in the growth rate of local income between the low-class and high-class municipalities after the enactment of the 1991 LGC (see Tables 10.18–10.19).

To test this null hypothesis, the study compared the growth and development (measured by the growth rate of the municipal income) of the two groups of municipalities: high-class versus low-class municipalities after the enactment of the 1991 LGC. Let X1 and X2 represent the growth rate of mean income of low-class and high-class municipalities, respectively. We proceed by following the six-step rule in hypothesis-testing:

1. Ho: X1 = X2
2. H1: X1 < X2
3. Level of significance = 0.05
4. Critical region: $t < -6.314$
5. Computations
   Average deviation (AD) = 12.50
   Standard deviation (S^2) = 0.50
   Variance (S) = 0.7071
   Computed t-value = 25.000 < t0.05 = −6.314
6. Conclusion: Accept Ho3.2 and conclude that the income growth rates of low-class and high-class municipalities are not significantly different "after" the enactment of the LGC (1992–1994).

Consistent results were obtained when another round of tests was conducted using the income growth rate during the LGC implementation period, 1995–97. On the bases of the previous two sets of evidence, it can be concluded that devolution did not aggravate spatial inequities.

Table 10.18
Level and Growth Rate of Income of Low-Class vs. High-Class Municipalities after the Enactment of the Code, 1992–1994

Municipalities	Low-class municipalities		
	1992	1993	1994
Babak	5,138	7,865	10,849
Carmen	9,117	14,644	19,772
Bansalan	8,065	12,991	16,884
Hagonoy	8,254	12,648	15,771
San Isidro	5,751	8,901	13,134
Tarragona	4,279	7,047	10,782
Tampakan	6,658	10,929	12,189
Tantangan	4,131	6,996	10,671
Tago	3,431	7,671	11,845
Bayabas	3,415	3,789	6,222
Kiamba	2,248	14,809	19,085
Mean	5,499	9,845	13,382
Growth rate (%)		79.00*/	36.00**/
Municipalities	High-class municipalities		
	1992	1993	1994
Kapalong	24,719	39,709	36,100
Monkayo	14,322	20,658	29,561
Digos	22,379	34,601	40,829
Malita	16,798	38,649	39,808
Lupon	8,650	14,812	26,513
Banaybanay	7,034	11,817	15,173
Surallah	13,239	20,482	25,456
Polomolok	19,373	30,509	37,285
Tandag	8,246	13,289	18,422
Marihatag	5,648	7,646	16,690
Glan	10,467	18,372	25,454
Mean	13,716	22,777	28,299
Growth rate (%)		66.00*/	24.00**/

*Growth rate for 1992–1993.
**Growth rate for 1993–1994.

Table 10.19
Computations

Year	Growth rate of mean income, low-class municipalities	Growth rate of mean income, high-class municipalities	Deviation (D)	Deviation squared
1992–1993	79.00	66.00	13	169
1993–1994	36.00	24.00	12	144
Sum			25	313

Average deviation (AD) = 12.50
Standard deviation (S^2) = 0.50
Variance (S) = 0.7071
Computed t-value = $25.000 > t\ (0.05) = -6.314$

SUMMARY AND CONCLUSIONS

This study sought to answer three central sets of questions:

1. Has decentralization through deconcentration or regionalization succeeded in rectifying interregional disparities during the last twenty-five years?

2. In the area of deconcentration or regionalization, were the projects, especially infrastructure as proposed in the RDIP, provided with adequate budget to ensure their implementation? In the area of devolution, did the 1991 LGC make good its promise to allocate significant levels of IRAs to the LGUs?

3. Does devolution promote spatial equity or does it aggravate inequities?

In the area of devolution, the reality confirms that the 1991 LGC made good its promise for the national government to allocate the mandated share from the national taxes to the LGUs as provided in Article 378 of the LGC implementing rules and regulations. Specifically, the study concludes that:

1. The IRAs are significantly higher after the enactment of the LGC; and

2. The level and rate of growth of income differentials between the low-class and high-class municipalities were not statistically significant. The latter suggests that devolution did not aggravate spatial inequities.

The following recommendations are made:

1. Refocusing of macroeconomic policies toward more vigorous implementation of programs and projects to minimize interregional imbalances; the results of the study indicated the need for increased but rational investments in economic infrastructure in regions outside the NCR;

2. Strengthening regional institutions to support deconcentration and devolution;

3. Sustaining the gains of devolution through a more vigorous implementation of the 1991 LGC; and

4. Continuous monitoring of the spatial effects of devolution toward promoting equity among the different classes of LGUs.

NOTES

1. See D. A. Rondinelli, J. R. Nellis, and G. S. Cheema, "Decentralization in Developing Countries: A Review of Experience" (World Bank Staff Working Paper No. 581) (Washington, DC: World Bank, 1983); G. S. Cheema and D. Rondinelli, *Decentralization and Development Policy Implementation in Developing Countries* (Beverly Hills: Sage Publications, 1984); Brian Smith, "Measuring Decentralization" in George Jones, ed., *New Approaches to the Study of Central-Local Government Relationships* (London: Gower Publishing, 1985); Diana Conyers, "Decentralization and Development Planning: A Comparative Perspective" in Peter de Valk and K. H. Wekwete (eds.), *Decentralizing for Participatory Planning: Comparing the Experience in Zimbabwe and Other Anglophone Countries in Eastern and Southern Africa* (London: Avebury Publishing, 1990); and Peter de Valk "State, Decentralization, and Participation" in de Valk and Wekwete, *Decentralizing for Participatory Planning.*

2. NEDA, *Medium-Term Philippine Development Plan, 1993–1998* (Manila, 1992).

3. Ibid.

4. Conyers, "Decentralization and Development Planning."

5. Richard Cole, *Urban Politics and Decentralization: The Case of General Revenue Sharing* (Purdue, IL: Purdue University Press, 1974).

6. John Lea and Chung Tu Wu, "Decentralization and Devolution: A Review of the United Nations Conference on Human Settlements, Nairobi, 1978," *Journal of Modern African Studies* (1980).

7. John Lea and J. Courtney, *Cities in Conflict: Studies in the Planning and Management of Asian Cities* (Washington, DC: World Bank, 1985).

8. Robert Yin, *Case Study Research: Design and Methods* (London: Sage Publications, 1984)

9. NEDA Region XI, 1992.

10. John Glasson, *Introduction to Regional Planning: Concepts and Application* (London: Hutchinson, 1978).

11. Jose Lawas, *Regional Development: A Goal and Instrument for National Development* (Manila: NEDA, 1975).

12. Raul P. de Guzman, *Government and Politics in the Philippines* (Singapore: Oxford University Press, 1989).

13. John Friedmann, *Regional Policy: Readings in Theory and Application* (Cambridge, MA: MIT Press, 1978).

14. Lea and Courtney, *Cities in Conflict.*

15. Lea and Wu, "Decentralization and Devolution."

16. Lea and Courtney, *Cities in Conflict.*

17. Local Development Assistance Program (LDAP), *LDAP Policy Paper on Decentralization* (Manila: NEDA, 1990).

18. Corazon C. Aquino, "Presidential Message" in Congress of the Philippines, *Local Government Code of 1991: A Primer* (Manila, 1991).

19. Associates in Rural Development, Inc. (ARD), "Synopsis of Findings" in *Report from First to Seventh Rapid Field Appraisals* (Makati City, 1997).

20. Ibid.

21. Mario Lamberte et al., *Decentralization and Prospects for Regional Growth* (Makati City: Philippine Institute for Development Studies, 1993).

11

Development of Grass-Roots Institutions: Experience of LIFE in Pakistan (1993–98)

Fayyaz Baqir

INTRODUCTION

The Local Initiative Facility for Urban Environment (LIFE) was launched in Pakistan in August 1993. During the past few years, LIFE has designed, tested, and developed various tools for building grass-roots institutions to establish service delivery systems for low-income urban communities in Pakistan. The basic vision behind LIFE has been the development of low-cost urban services on a self-help basis by mobilizing human, financial, and social capital at the local level. This has meant providing technical guidance, strengthening inter-action between various partners, and building a local body of knowledge in addition to grant assistance to community-based organizations (CBOs) and non-governmental organizations (NGOs).

This chapter describes the successes and failures of this experience over the past five years. This process is not yet complete. However, it is a first glance back at the program development pattern to have a sense of direction for its further development. The chapter describes the conceptual framework, opera-tional parameters, perceptions, and analyses of the various partners to assess the success of the program in the development of its core component, "grass-roots institutions."

Table 11.1
Solid Waste Collection Capacity of Select Municipalities (per day)

City	Total solid waste generated	Municipal lifting capacity
Karachi	7,000 tons	3,000 tons
Faisalabad	1,000 tons	Less than 500 tons
Rawalpindi	700 tons	280 tons

Sources: UNCHS (Habitat), *An Urbanizing World: Global Report on Human Settlements 1996*; Solid Waste Management and Environment Enhancement Programme; and Urban Resource Centre, *Newsletter* (February 1996).

CONTEXT AND CONCEPTUAL FRAMEWORK FOR SUPPORTING GRASS-ROOTS INSTITUTIONS

Urbanization

An interesting pattern of urbanization has emerged during the past fifty years. The urban population in Pakistan is increasing rapidly—while there was enormous rural-urban migration in the first four decades after independence, the past decade has simultaneously witnessed large-scale urban-urban migration. In the earlier decades, rural-urban migration was rapid. According to a study conducted by the Asian Development Bank (ADB), 90 percent of the population of forty-two market towns in the densely populated province of Punjab migrated from rural areas in a short time span of ten years.[1] During the past ten years owing to urban-urban migration, 50 percent of the urban population in Punjab, for example, is now concentrated in five cities (Lahore, Faisalabad, Multan, Gujranwala, and Rawalpindi, each having a population above 1 million). About 30 percent of the country's urban population lives in cities with populations above 100,000.[2] The rapid movement of population to big urban centers and the large concentration of population in these areas has led to a situation characterized by inadequate service delivery systems. The existing service delivery either did not expand fast enough to serve the migrating population or collapsed owing to heavy pressure. According to one survey, 200 urban settlements in Punjab do not have any solid or liquid waste management system.[3] Other provinces in Pakistan also share the pattern of urbanization and service delivery emerging in Punjab. The solid waste management capacity of big urban centers is very limited (see Table 11.1). Moreover, no sanitary landfill sites are available in these cities. The municipal capacity to lift domestic waste from these cities has not improved much during the past two decades. This is one of the impacts of increased urbanization in Pakistan.

Availability of Resources

The usual explanations for this situation are the lack of resources and poor capacity in local government. A closer look at the situation, however, reveals that most urban centers have invested sufficient resources in infrastructure and equipment components of urban service delivery systems. However, they are weak in the operation and maintenance (O&M) of these systems. Their coverage is limited because of the high cost of establishing these systems and their O&M is weak owing to low collection of service delivery fees. These dimensions of urban service delivery come under the domain of governance and more precisely under the donor-government-citizen dimension.

Management of Resources

Conventional service delivery programs focusing on the construction of physical infrastructure and provision of expensive equipment as well as foreign training programs are attractive to government officials because of their hidden payoffs, but they do not solve the service delivery problem and divert the attention of local government officials from regular O&M. Emphasis on development of capital works results in high costs and unsustainable delivery of services with poor O&M of delivery systems. Government officials have a tendency to propose the replacement of existing physical infrastructure by new physical infrastructure to improve service delivery. Development is associated with mega-projects and creates a mental barrier in the government professionals against effective solutions to urban problems. The high cost of providing services also necessitates recovery of service costs by shifting the burden of payment to the most vulnerable sections of society, leading eventually to social conflict, economic polarization, and violence.

Solutions for increased coverage and acceptable urban services can be found by moving away from the domain of technical and professional to managerial- and governance-related issues. A case in point is the problem of contaminated drinking water in Dera Ismail Khan (DIK). The LIFE Coordinator in Pakistan accompanied by a group of professionals visited DIK on the request of the local Member of the National Assembly (MNA) to examine the condition of water supply and find a solution to integrate contamination of drinking water. The field team was accompanied by the MNA, Municipal Accounts Officer, Members of *Khidmat* (Service) Committee, President of the Local Bar Association, and some other Municipal Corporation (MC) employees. Commenting on the visit, the National Coordinator remarked:

We visited eleven tube wells and discovered that only four were functioning. These tube wells were owned by the District Development Authority (DDA) and were to be handed over to the MC in the near future. Three tube wells owned by the MC were locked and pumps and transformers installed for them were missing. Waterlines throughout the city crossed open drains before entering the houses. Joints on waterlines were found to be leaking and sucking in sewage in several cases. Open drains carrying the city's liquid waste were drained directly into the river. There were three overhead tanks for storing drinking water. All these tanks were leaking and were not cleaned regularly. Operators and field staff were not found on duty. A hospital visited on the way had clogged septic tanks and the fabulous Town Hall building was in ruins.

A series of meetings were held after this visit with the municipal officials and community members, and courtesy calls were made to Sana Ullah, Minister for Health, and Feteh Ullah, the local Member of Provincial Assembly (MPA). Discussions with various participants and the budget review revealed that the *octroi* collection over the past few years had decreased; property tax was not being collected by the MC anymore; use of electricity by the MC was over-charged; and there was enormous leakage in the budget. The MC spends Rs. 1.6 million on water supply, while it collects only Rs. 700,000 annually.

The basic causes of water contamination and poor service delivery were found to be the lack of sanitation facilities, poor maintenance of overhead reservoirs and waterlines, unsealed joints, poor financial management of the MC, incomplete information on illegal water connections, leakage of financial resources due to weak monitoring arrangements, and lack of community participation in solving service delivery problems. However, it is interesting to note that municipal officials believed that the problem could be solved by building a new physical infrastructure for the whole water supply system with millions of rupees as aid or grants from donor agencies. They completely overlooked the potential of solving the problem by improving the municipal management of the services.[4]

After a series of discussions with various partners, a final meeting was held with the MNA and his team to finalize the findings. It was agreed that the water contamination problem could be solved by developing a sanitation system and ensuring proper upkeep and maintenance of the water supply system. Working on both these problems using the Orangi Pilot Project's (OPP) Internal-External Development concept, where the community takes responsibility for the "internal development" at the household and lane levels and the government takes responsibility for building and maintaining infrastructure beyond the lane level, could provide a low-cost and sustainable solution.

Sources of National Wealth

Moving from micro- to macrolevel development, studies on development and poverty provide evidence of the crucial role played by community participation in national development. A study by the World Bank on sources of national wealth in contemporary global economies revealed some very interesting patterns of development that present alternative paths to countries faced with acute scarcity of resources for providing quality services in urban areas. Considering physical, natural, and social capital as the main sources of national wealth, the World Bank's calculations showed the following contributions to Japan's national wealth: 1 percent natural capital, 14 percent physical capital, and 85 percent human and social capital. The trend was almost reversed in the case of developing countries. Calculation of average contribution by various sources in 192 countries showed 16 percent contribution made by physical capital, 20 percent by natural capital, and 64 percent by human and social capital. This calculation further indicates the link between perceived lack of resources and underutilization of human and social capital. Emphasis on employing and mobilizing human and social capital has therefore been the cornerstone of the LIFE implementation strategy in Pakistan.

While the history of economic growth and resource endowment in Japan may explain major differences in the patterns of growth between the economy of that country and other developing countries, some tested models for community development in urban areas show that visions of development and managerial capacity have direct implications on sustaining these patterns of development. The service delivery system established by OPP in a squatter settlement covering a population of 1 million is a case in point. During the course of its work, OPP mobilized people to lay sewerage lines in 5,000 lanes on a self-help basis. OPP has a revolving credit of Rs. 25 million benefiting home-based enterprises in the area. People in this settlement have established 540 nongovernmental schools providing quality education to children of low-income families where most government schools are in shambles. A survey of 37 percent of the squatter settlements in Karachi also demonstrated the same active role played by low-income communities in setting up urban service delivery systems. In low-income communities in the squatter settlements surveyed by OPP, sewerage and water supply services were undertaken by the beneficiaries for 53 percent and 44 percent of households, respectively (see Table 11.2). The government provided services to only 16 percent of the households in the same area.

Internal-External Development

Taking into consideration the differences in resource endowment between community and government agencies, OPP promoted community-government collaboration in service delivery. In this model, the community contributes human and social capital and the government focuses on large outlays of physical capital. OPP's service delivery system is established on the concept of internal-external development. Internal development means development of service delivery components at the home and lane levels. In the case of sanitation, it includes constructing pour-flush latrines and laying sewerage lines in the lanes; in the case of education, it is the establishment of a one-room, one-teacher school; and in the case of income generation, the creation of home-based enterprises. OPP believes that internal development is a community's own

Table 11.2
Provision of Water and Sewerage Facilities: Comparison of Government and Community Contribution

	Lane	House	Per cent	Cost (Rs)
Self sewerage	1,324	12,798	53	15,357,600
Self water	1,100	10,309	44	13,401,700
Govt. sewerage	387	3,908	16	5,080,400
Govt. water	400	3,956	16	5,142,800

Source: Orangi Pilot Project Research and Training Institute (OPP-RTI), Karachi, 1994.

responsibility. In rapidly expanding cities with an acute resource crunch, even low-cost services at the internal level cannot be provided on a large scale sustainably by the government or donor agencies. Community members have to be "mobilized" to contribute to internal development. However, even in a very low-income community, suffering from nonavailability of basic urban services, the first psychological barrier that comes in the way of community action is the common belief that service delivery is exclusively the government's responsibility. In the case of elected local government representatives, community initiative to establish urban services is defeated by the nonfulfillment of the representatives' promises to deliver services needed by the community.

Overcoming this challenge is the first major test of any self-help program. Lack of understanding of the ways to overcome this hurdle often leads to the mistaken belief that full or partial subsidy for internal development by the government is the answer. However, proper interaction with the community members—who in most cases are the poorest of the poor—can help overcome this barrier and lay the foundation for building partnerships with government agencies. Government in this case undertakes external development.[5]

External development relates to intercommunity or city-level development activities. In the case of sanitation, for example, laying of trunk sewers or installing wastewater treatment plants comes under external development. In the process of establishing the internal development component, community-level professionals gain sound technical training. In many cases, they also update maps and area profiles and gather in-depth socioeconomic information, which is not available in government departments. The work on internal development, therefore, not only leads to the establishment of service infrastructure and delivery systems at the internal level but also helps the beneficiary communities in two important ways. First, sound technical information enables communities to negotiate with government agencies on stronger terms owing to improved technical skills; and second, it builds their trust with the government departments that are ready to take them seriously in view of their performance and strong social organization. Working on the internal-external development model, numerous communities outside Orangi have been able to establish service delivery systems for sanitation, solid waste management, health, education, and income generation. While the internal-external development model offers a solution for the provision of services at the microcommunity level, it also provides conceptual tools to find a solution at the macropolicy level.

Decentralization, Governance, and Service Delivery

Three basic concepts provide the components for developing large-scale service delivery systems in urban areas as well as the basis for introducing policy changes conducive to the provision of services at the national level. These are decentralization of development work and delegation of powers to local governments for local development; development of low-cost solutions for the provision of services based on upgradation of existing service delivery systems by low-income communities; and human resource development at the community level. These three concepts can be put together in the statement, "local development, local resources, and local professionals."

In the constitution of Pakistan, there is a federal list of subjects defining the areas where central government can exercise fiscal and administrative powers and a concurrent list describing areas under the jurisdiction of provincial/state and central government. No such list exists for local government bodies to generate revenues for local service delivery. Similarly, rigid government specifications for the use of material for providing urban services and dependence on contractors for establishing delivery systems leave little flexibility for low-cost and a reasonable quality of services, which are in line with the level of sophistication and affordability of areas receiving services.

Affordability and sustainability of services at the local level are linked with availability of community-level professionals. Many communities receive basic urban services through paraprofessionals working in the informal sector. Informal enterprises are characterized by low starting and overhead costs, incremental development, and use of locally available material and expertise. Delivery systems designed and operated by informal sector entrepreneurs can be used by local governments and the formal sector in service upgradation and quality improvement without increasing the costs significantly.

INSTRUMENTS OF PROGRAM SUPPORT: CAPACITY DEVELOPMENT

Vision of a Support System

The LIFE strategy in Pakistan was guided by OPP's approach in identifying and overcoming the barriers experienced by the community in initiating action for community development. These four barriers have been described by Akhtar Hamid Khan as: (1) *psychological barrier*, where the community believes that development work is the exclusive responsibility of the government; (2) *economic barrier*, which arises because service delivery systems developed in formal sectors are expensive and unaffordable to the community; (3) *social barrier*, which arises because people do not cooperate with one another in solving their problems; and (4) *technical barrier*, which means that the community's technical solutions need to be refined and upgraded.[6] LIFE aimed at designing processes and developing instruments that will help CBOs and NGOs overcome these barriers and provide urban basic services to low-income communities.[7]

In the very beginning, it was decided that a National Selection Committee (NSC) would be formed to lead the process of providing guidance and grant assistance to CBOs in the provision of clean drinking water and solid and liquid waste management in urban settlements. During the next five years, two successive NSCs provided guidance to the program; laid down criteria for selection of partner CBOs/NGOs; reviewed and approved project proposals; proposed and designed components of a support system to enhance the capacity of organizations seeking grant assistance; and provided guidelines for working with various stakeholders. The successes and weaknesses of LIFE in Pakistan and lessons drawn from the experience of working at the grass-roots level are described in the following sections.

Process and Mechanisms of Grant Assistance to NGOs

At the inception of LIFE in Pakistan, an NSC was formed at a national consultation meeting with various stakeholders. Members of the NSC represented diverse experiences, age groups, professional expertise, and geographic regions in Pakistan. CBOs, NGOs, government agencies, donors, women, and urban professionals with distinguished standing in community development work served on the NSC. However, representation of women was weak and involvement of the government was unpredictable owing to the high turnover of government officials in municipal government. NSC approved the project selection criteria and offered guidelines for identifying credible organizations and monitoring and evaluation of the grantee organizations' work. Discussions during the proposal assessment process were recorded and formed a body of knowledge for reviewing and processing grant assistance requests. A second NSC was formed at the end of two years, which continued the work initiated by the first NSC. However, representation of women and midlevel professionals increased significantly in the second NSC and helped in increasing the participation of NSC in further developing the program.

Project Selection Criteria

Project proposals were selected on the basis of their degree of conformity to the project selection criteria. The criteria consisted of eleven points including a review of: LIFE mandate; conceptual clarity; tangible outputs; clear sequence of activity; technical feasibility; community involvement; cost sharing by the community; realistic budget; conflict of interests; inbuilt training; and monitoring mechanisms. These criteria were developed to ensure community participation, development of effective technical solutions, and sound planning for local initiatives.

However, the eleven points did not cover all the concerns to be addressed by the NSC. The minutes of each meeting recorded gray areas and proposed solutions for dealing with them. Additional guidelines emerging from the NSC meetings included the following points:

Support Criteria. An NGO applying for a grant should have already initiated some work in the community where the project is going to be implemented. It should collaborate with the municipal government and hold public hearings, to which all NSC members should be invited. (This requirement was waived after the field test, as public hearings created undue pressure on CBOs to deliver quick results and created unrealistic expectations in the community about external financial assistance.)

Grant Assistance. Grant assistance should be provided for: (a) strengthening NGOs' capacity for providing social and technical guidance to beneficiary communities; (b) supporting action research on developing and implementing low-cost solutions; (c) staff training; and (d) providing the salary of core workers. These components of solid waste management projects, which fall under the responsibility of municipal government, should not be funded. No financial support should be given for infrastructure. The objective of grant assistance should be to support institutions and not projects alone. Program activities should be self-sufficient. Beneficiaries should pay the cost of direct benefits received. Credit rather than grants should be provided to help beneficiaries.

Research Projects. The main points are as follows:

a. Only action-based research should be supported;
b. Each research proposal should clearly spell out the before and after linkages of the research work with community-level activity; and
c. In any program area where action research is already available, it must not be duplicated.

Technical Assistance/Training. Technical assistance for implementation and monitoring support should be provided by the LIFE office.

Project Review Criteria. Community involvement should include the following:

a. Clearly defined strategies for approaching beneficiaries;
b. Communities should undertake the responsibility for O&M of the program after it has been completed, and NGOs should collect at least three months' contribution for O&M from the beneficiaries before the funds are released; and

Table 11.3
Pak Social Welfare Society, Hyderabad

No. of houses covered	1,000
No. of lanes covered	15
Beneficiary families	2,356
Project duration	3 years
Project budget	$6,396

Source: Project proposal by the Pak Social Welfare Society.

c. Involvement of the informal sector should be encouraged for supporting low-cost, sustainable delivery of services at the community level.

Monitoring and Evaluation

Field visits for identifying credible CBOs and NGOs, assessing the capacity of different organizations, and monitoring the progress of the projects offered the most important means for linking with people. The NSC had directed the national coordinator at the very beginning to assess the capacity and credibility of CBOs' work, intuitively rather than using complex criteria. Similarly, monitoring of the project was to be carried out with the purpose of listening to the people, observing and recording project progress and the difficulties encountered, and providing backup support to local activities and beneficiaries. Regular field visits, accessibility to CBOs and NGOs, and openness were the hallmarks of the program from the very beginning. During the past five years, the program was visited and contacted by hundreds of CBOs and NGOs.

Geographic Focus

Although the upper limit for grant assistance was set by LIFE at US$50,000, the average size of grants to Pakistan hardly exceeded US$5,000, and the number of households covered in the projects varied from 200 to 1,000. Table 11.3 gives a summary of a typical project for solid waste management in Hyderabad city.

These projects were scattered in a very wide area in different parts of the country. The geographic spread and small size of individual projects neither made the program visible to important stakeholders nor did it inspire the confidence of public opinion leaders. At the same time, it spread the energy of the national coordinator too thinly to properly guide and support the CBOs and NGOs receiving LIFE support.

It was, therefore, decided to introduce a geographic focus in the program; gradually phasing out from far-flung areas and increasing the number of projects in a fewer cities. This insight was discussed with small grant programs of other donors who also followed this approach in building their project portfolio. The LIFE program eventually focused on Rawalpindi city in making grants for the improvement of urban areas. With the induction of two new provincial coordinators, the program's geographic focus may now be spread over the four cities of Peshawar, Rawalpindi, Lahore, and Quetta.

Training and Technical Guidance

During the past five years, many NGOs and CBOs working for the development of low-income settlements expressed interest in receiving training in participatory approaches for implementing self-help programs. These NGOs/CBOs were sent for training to the OPP-Research and Training Institute (RTI). This training is the first step toward the process of development of the NGOs/CBOs as independent support organizations, which is the key to the development of low-income settlements in Pakistan. OPP's experience of working with NGOs/CBOs has been very encouraging. Some successful graduates from OPP formed the Anjuman Samaji Behbood in Faisalabad and the Organization for Participatory Development (OPD) in Gujranwala. Twelve groups were trained by OPP in one year. Each group consisted of six persons and the duration of training was six days. The focus of training was OPP's model programs: (a) low-cost sanitation; (b) low-cost housing; (c) health education and family planning; (d) social forestry; (e) microenterprise credit; and (f) education. Training included on-site visits in Orangi and meetings with community organizations/activists, government officials, and the OPP team. After training, some potential NGOs/CBOs were identified by OPP-RTI to be visited on site to ascertain further support.

Grantee NGO Workshops

LIFE-Pakistan holds grantee NGO workshops each year to share experiences. Along with training, grantee NGO workshops also make significant contributions to institutional development at the grass-roots level.

CASE STUDIES AND LESSONS LEARNED FROM THE FIELD

While intensive field activity strengthened the program's interaction with community activists and organizations, geographic focus enhanced interaction between grantee NGOs who formed a network called "SHIRAKAT" in Rawalpindi to meet and exchange experiences regularly and help members in building their capacities. Moving one step further with the participatory approach, a participatory evaluation of nine LIFE projects was carried out in May–June 1997 to assess the strengths of the projects and challenges faced by the CBOs/NGOs and LIFE in the implementation of their planned activities. Participatory evaluation of the program highlighted the following important points:

The Organization for Participatory Development (OPD)

OPD is a development-oriented NGO working in poorly serviced areas of Gujranwala City since 1990. In 1991, it formally introduced its first development package to areas inhabited by low-income families. Initially, OPD started its activities in three different and distant localities of Gujranwala City simultaneously. The initial experience, however, taught the OPD members that it was unmanageable with meager resources. OPD, therefore, wound up its activities in two areas and concentrated on the suburban localities of Naushehra Road where community response was positive and most enthusiastic. Unplanned housing, illiteracy, open drains, unavailability of proper medical services, scarcity of potable water, and a high birth rate are some conspicuous features of the area. The OPD development package consists of the following projects: home school education project; health education project; family enterprises credit program; low-cost sanitation project; and environmental conservation and urban forestry program.

Community Participation. According to OPD staff:

a. The most frequently asked questions during the initial process of community organization are: (i) Why are you doing this work? (ii) How will you benefit from it? (iii) Where are you getting the money from? All these questions express the communities' lack of trust in the NGO. This trust is built over time, when people start seeing results of the NGO interventions.

b. Poverty is the major element hindering community involvement in the development process. Other factors are the lack of awareness of community development and interference by the local government. At the same time, poor sanitation conditions directly affect the health of the people and negligence by the government agencies has further deteriorated the living environment in the project localities.[8]

Participation of Other Stakeholders

a. The organization tried to involve the MC to undertake the external development of the sanitation problem in the area. However, the OPD could not get any positive response from the agency. At the end of the project, when the organization was expecting collaboration from the agency, the concerned officer was transferred.

b. A total of 1,290 persons from 204 households along 16 streets are the beneficiaries of the low-cost sanitation project; however, the project has not created much interest in the surrounding communities for replication of project activity.

Building Trust with the Community. Through the project process, OPD learned many lessons. These are as follows:

a. Provide up-to-date information about the project to the community until the approval of grant assistance;
b. Gain community confidence before starting the project;
c. Employ trained organizers to mobilize the community;
d. Involve community at each step of the implementation phase; and
e. Share the results of every step with the community.

One-year funding to accomplish such a difficult task is too short. More funding is needed for a longer period to bring about behavioral change in the community. The point is not to establish sewer lines in certain streets but to bring about a change in the attitudes of the people where they can solve their own problems collectively on a self-help basis, without any outside intervention.

Another observation was that LIFE's trust in the OPD helped in developing its social capital.

The Aurat Association (AA)

AA was established in 1994 and is registered under the Voluntary Organizations Act. It started operating in 1996 after receiving a project on solid waste management from UNDP. Prior to this, it was a charity organization working with Catholic Relief Services (CRS) in the Afghan Camps of Mansehra. Its overall goal is "social, political, and economic empowerment of women in rural areas." In order to achieve this goal, it introduced a credit and saving program patterned on the Grameen Bank in Bangladesh. It is also trying to introduce sanitation, income generation, and human resource development programs with the assistance of donor agencies. At present, it has 430 saving members of whom 99 percent are women. Literacy rate among women is very low (approximately 6 percent), which makes the task quite difficult. Four out of six staff are women. Ten volunteer men and women also work for the association.[9]

Impacts of LIFE Assistance. The activities of AA not only helped it stand on its own feet but also provided an opportunity to introduce the organization in the area. During the project period, various other donors were introduced to the association and small-scale projects received approval for implementation. The association's efforts in initiating rural development were appreciated by the community.

Community Mobilization. AA encountered many difficulties in mobilizing the local community, such as: (a) lack of cooperation and distrust from the community; (b) difficulty in mobilizing female members of the community (due to resistance from the male members, who distrusted their abilities); (c) low attendance at monthly community meetings; (d) noncooperation from the municipal corporation; (e) lack of cooperation from the community in contributing workers' salaries; and (f) political interference in local elections.

Building Trust with the Community. These problems were solved through the constant efforts of the AA's staff. Household visits and meetings by two social organizers brought positive results. The association learned that community mobilization is a gradual process requiring much time and effort.

The Credit and Welfare Association (CAWA)

CAWA was registered with the Social Welfare Department on 24 June 1996. Its primary objective was to start a family credit program on the same pattern as the credit scheme of OPP. It began work in two localities of Rawalpindi City, but now operates in eleven localities including two adjoining rural areas. CAWA's work is not limited to credit, but involves other development activities as well. These activities include advocacy within the community and local government departments for infrastructure improvement, solid waste management, and pollution control, focused on the Nullah (Lai) flowing near some of the target localities, besides other community-related issues. It also lobbies with some local government departments to help solve the problems of the area.

CAWA basically operates through volunteers and part-time staff members, except for two full-time personnel. They have been funded by Trust for Voluntary Organization (TVO), United Nations Development Programme (UNDP)-LIFE, First Women's Bank, and the OPP.

The CAWA credit scheme is performing fairly well and its rate of defaulters is quite low. It extended loans to more than eighty families for establishing small businesses. Another scheme, the collective payment of utility bills, has also received good response from the community.

Problems of Working with the Government. LIFE's funding was provided primarily for institutional strengthening and helping CAWA in providing staff salaries for one year. CAWA collaborated with the Rawalpindi Municipal Corporation (RMC) in improving the sanitation conditions in one of the project's localities. The project started quite smoothly but could not be completed because of ad-hocism in the government. In the OPP, TVO, and First Women's Bank, funding has been utilized for the credit scheme.[10]

Foundation of Government-NGO Partnership. The community uses its own sources and the cost is one-seventh of the money being spent by government agencies in terms of labor and materials. Since the government's outreach in the services sector is limited and cannot reach 40 percent of the total populace, NGOs bridge the gap by mobilizing communities. But this does not mean that the community can solve all problems at all levels by itself. It can deliver services at the microlevel but not at the macrolevel. It can lay sewer lines but cannot install treatment plants or disposal stations. Development in environment or microenterprise sanitation or water supply is an interaction between the community and NGOs. Individual actors have a role to play. The community has both capacity and resources but what it requires most are organization and guidance.[11]

PARTICIPATORY EVALUATION OF LIFE

Participatory evaluation of nine LIFE projects was completed in May–June 1997. Evaluation methodology included presentation of the program by CBOs, evaluation team meetings with various stakeholders, open discussion between NGOs and community members, and site visits. The evaluation team consisted of two consultants and local participants from academe, NGOs, donors, and local governments, in each project area.[12]

APPNA SEHAT, an NGO engaged in primary health care, was approached by LIFE to conduct a participatory evaluation of nine LIFE projects that had completed either their project cycle or project period. The early months of 1997 were devoted to the preparation of project proposals and end-of-project reports, development of instruments, and formation of evaluation teams. The latter part was devoted to field visits and discussions with NGOs. This was followed by analysis of findings by APPNA SEHAT. In total, forty-five individuals with diverse backgrounds took part in the evaluation.

Lessons Drawn from the Participatory Evaluation

The observations of the participatory evaluation teams are summarized below:

NGO Capacity

- Six of the nine projects were able to achieve results as per the project proposal. These achievements pertain more to improvements in the physical environment than substantive changes in the community. Attitudinal changes in the community and their sustainability are hard to observe at this point of time.
- Some NGOs fell short of achieving objectives due to the following reasons: (a) lack of organizational capacity; (b) procedural rigidity; and (c) less than acceptable honesty of purpose in project implementation.
- Most of the projects could not actively involve all the communities. Although they contributed financially to the projects, most of the work was carried out by the NGOs. Only one NGO (Taraqee, Quetta) was able to delegate most of its activities to the community.

Participatory Approach

- The environmental issues addressed by LIFE were the dominant problems of the project areas.

- LIFE aimed to involve communities in carrying out needs assessment. This did not occur to the desired extent.
- Collaboration with relevant line departments varied. Generally, projects with good line department collaboration were better able to distinguish themselves.
- There were some problems in the maintenance of accounts by the grantee organizations.

Support System

- There was insufficient success in building the capacities of grantee NGOs. There was no mechanism to ensure continuous and systematic development of these organizations.
- The duration of the projects was too short to realize the objectives of community mobilization or bring about an attitudinal change.
- Funds received from LIFE by the grantee NGOs were considered inadequate by four organizations. Cash flow was identified as a problem by most NGOs.
- Six organizations received funds from other donors for the same activity to supplement the UNDP fund.

Recommendations

Based on the findings, the recommendations of the evaluation mission are summarized below:

- LIFE may consider projects of longer duration with the gradual phasing out of UNDP's input during the later period of the project;
- Forums are required to enable grantee NGOs to network and share their experiences for increased cooperation;
- NSC's involvement may be extended and members may be involved in supporting, monitoring, and supervising activities carried out by grantee NGOs. Funds may be allocated to ensure NSC's role; and
- LIFE may keep itself open to address other issues that could eventually ensure community acceptance and sustainability.

SCALING-UP OF THE LIFE EXPERIENCE AND INSTITUTIONAL DEVELOPMENT

Besides providing grant assistance, LIFE has also provided support to its partner organizations by holding consultation meetings for needs assessment, arranging training and technical guidance, conducting workshops for grantee NGOs for experience sharing, and making regular monitoring visits to the project areas. One important concern of these activities has been to encourage and uphold participation and collaboration between different partners building upon their strengths and resources. However, the institutional development of CBOs has two dimensions. First, it requires long-term financial support for the core expenses of CBOs to: (a) ensure continuity of their work and give them an opportunity to develop expertise and build trust with beneficiaries; (b) help them expand the scale of their work and enable them to generate revenues on a large scale; (c) build a firm beneficiary and revenue base for self-sustenance; and (d) help them become an effective receiving mechanism. Second, institutional development at the community level has meant moving: (a) from volunteerism to professionalism; (b) from CBOs to NGOs and government; (c) from projects to programs; (d) from short-term to long-term assistance; and (e) from implementation activities to the role of training resource center (see Map 11.1).

Therefore, LIFE has focused on providing long-term support to selected CBOs on the one hand, and designed long-term, large-scale initiatives with multiple partners on the other hand, to build small-scale and large-scale grass-roots institutions simultaneously. Expanding the scale of activity with other important stakeholders has assumed two different forms—designing large-scale projects and working with large-scale NGO networks. A description of two types of intervention is given below.

Scaling-up and Mainstreaming

During the scaling-up phase, LIFE has been collaborating with key actors such as MNAs, MPAs, local elected representatives, donors, and the private sector for networking, training, and mobilizing resources.

In the latter months of 1997, a meeting was held in Lahore to present LIFE's community-based methodology on solid waste management to an MNA, members of the NSC, the political secretary to the Prime Minister, members of LIFE, and community activists. The meeting concluded with a decision to initiate pilot projects in four municipal wards for possible replication in other wards after assessing the achievements. This meeting represented a breakthrough in mainstreaming LIFE methodology and provided an opportunity to build a linkage among the government, elected officials, and grass-roots activists.

Synergistic momentum is increasing as partnerships between CBOs, elected representatives, government officials, and donors emerge to address concerns in the areas of community development, gender participation, and governance. In addition, two large-scale urban projects have been initiated by the Country Office. These include: the Programme for Improvement of Livelihoods in Urban Settlement (PLUS) and the Solid Waste Management and Environment Enhancement Project (SWEEP).

PLUS

The Preparatory Assistance (PA) document PLUS was signed by the UNDP Administrator in September 1997 during his field visit to Pakistan. PLUS is a

Map 11.1
Location of Life Grantee NGOs

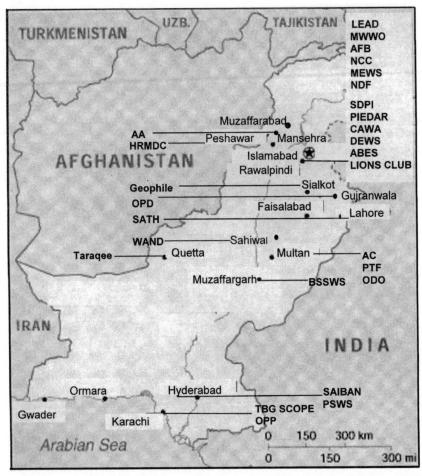

Source: Base map from http://www.lib.utexas.edu/Libs/PCL/Map-collection/cia99/Pakistan-sm99. jpg.

community-based initiative that offers an alternative approach to urban problems in low-income communities through social mobilization and self-help initiatives. PLUS addresses sustainable human development concerns by promoting employment through income generation and microcredit, basic education, urban agriculture, and improving the delivery of basic urban services. During the PA phase, the program will focus on four cities.

PLUS aims to address the problem of urban poverty in low-income settlements by: (a) strengthening the capacity of local government bodies to manage urban affairs; (b) encouraging and building the institutional capacity of community organizations; (c) bringing together stakeholders; and (d) creating an enabling environment for local-local dialog toward the strengthening of linkages between local government bodies and CBOs. PLUS will facilitate integrated urban development in selected wards of four pilot cites—Multan, Gujranwala, Faisalabad, and Rawalpindi. The budget for this program is US$540,000 over the next three years.

SWEEP

The SWEEP program was launched in October 1997 by UNDP, in collaboration with the Japanese Human Resource Development Fund. It aims to develop human resources and social capital of both RMC and CBOs to ensure the efficient and integrated management of solid waste in the city. The program builds on a donation by the Government of Japan of heavy waste collection equipment to the RMC. SWEEP's objectives are to train and build awareness among RMC staff; create and strengthen community organization; effectively clean lanes, streets, waterways, and commercial centers; and impact positively on community health.

Under SWEEP, RMC will build its relationship with communities and community organizations, scavengers and informal sector entrepreneurs, and private sector individuals and organizations. In collaboration with these actors, RMC will ensure the proper collection and disposal of solid waste.

Working with Large-Scale Networks

For mainstreaming LIFE methodology, in addition to the creation of large-scale programs, dialog for partnership has been initiated with large-scale networks. These networks include Pakistan Ex-Servicemen Society (PESS), Sindh Graduates Association (SGA), and Noble Deeds Foundation (NDF).

(a) PESS. PESS has 100,000 members in 110 chapters throughout Pakistan. PESS aims to uplift residents of rural areas through the involvement of ex-servicemen in social development. Program areas include the provision of educational facilities in rural areas (particularly for girls), health centers, shelter, and the promotion of cottage industries in rural areas. Each village elects councilors from its membership to represent the chapter at the *tahsil*, district, and national levels.

(b) SGA. Founded in 1972, the SGA has sixty-five working branches with approximately 8,000 members. SGA aims to create awareness of social issues by encouraging ownership among educated people of their villages. It focuses on developing and strengthening village-level institutions in the areas of health and education, centering on women's literacy.

(c) NDF. Founded in 1997 by members of the scientific and academic community in Rawalpindi, the foundation has 183 members, 60 of whom have Ph.D. degrees. There are 21 branch offices located throughout Rawalpindi, which facilitate volunteer activities in the wards. This NGO aims to assist in educating children from poor families, offer free medical treatment, fight against environmental degradation, and work toward improved agricultural productivity through the transfer of appropriate technology. Recently, Noble Deeds Foundation was granted funding by UNDP for a project dealing with the proper disposal of dead animals in Rawalpindi.

Resource Mobilization

Resource mobilization includes more than just funding from donors. Under LIFE, a variety of resources are being accessed in an effort to enhance the program and build capacities. While LIFE provides technical and social guidance, other sources such as the community represent an untapped entity for the mobilization of resources. Resource mobilization is not about selling goods. Rather, it is about selling benefits. By matching the interests of various groups, LIFE has been extremely successful in this respect. The various sources for mobilization are listed below.

UNDP Country Office

The UNDP Country Office has provided funding to support LIFE methodology. For instance, it provided US$100,000 in LIFE grants, US$440,000 during the Preparatory Assistance Phase of PLUS (US$2 million total), US$150,000 for SWEEP, and agreed to provide access to professionals through TOKTEN agreement and establish a trust fund for mobilizing resources for grass-roots initiatives.

Government of Japan

A major initiative under LIFE came from the Government of Japan, which contributed US$6.5 million in equipment for secondary collection. While such equipment was essential, the "software" aspects of collection also needed to be developed. By matching the needs of the program and the donor's interests, LIFE was able to mobilize another US$200,000 from the Government of Japan to meet this need. In this effort, LIFE provided a primary collection model and facilitated the linkages between these groups.

Small and New Donors

LIFE has provided professional expertise in the disbursement of grants and monitoring mechanisms to small and new donors. For example, the Government of France has given a one-time grant of US$10,000 to Rawalpindi, while PHB, an Australian private sector company, has agreed to donate US$40,000 on an annual basis.

CONCLUSION

Institutional development at the grass-roots level is a very interactive and participatory process but, at the same time, unpredictable. Owing to the unpredictability of this process, innovative responses are needed to further the progress of project activities. Long-term support is also needed by grass-roots institutions to draw meaningful lessons from experience, build trust with the partners, and experiment with different alternatives to meet the challenges of urban community development work. Bringing an end to subsidies, developing low-cost solutions, and increasing the scale of work are some other important factors that ensure the sustainability of institutions and their activities. Two paths are available to grass-roots initiatives on the way to ensure their sustainability: increasing the scale of work and degree of professionalism to turn into effective receiving mechanisms or continuing to function as community organizations and leaving the role of mainstreaming community-based initiatives to large-scale programs managed by experts. LIFE in Pakistan is working on both these alternatives in tandem. A review of activities over the past five years has led to identification of activities for institution building but final assessment of the most critical factors to ensure development of grass-roots initiatives will be possible after at least five to ten more years of experimentation in the field.

NOTES

1. Asian Development Bank (ADB), *Urban Sector Profile, 1994* (Manila, 1994).

2. Based on a discussion with Reza Ali, architect and town planner, 25 October 1998. He made a detailed analysis of Pakistan Census 1998.

3. Based on a presentation by M. A. Saleemi, Environment Protection Agency, Punjab, in the LIFE consultation workshop, Lahore, 18 October 1993.

4. Fayyaz Baqir, "Back to Office Report, D. I. Khan" (Internal document) (Islamabad: LIFE, 1998).

5. Akhtar Hameed Khan, *Orangi Pilot Project: Reminiscences and Reflections* (Karachi: Oxford University Press, 1996).

6. Ibid.

7. United Nations Development Programme (UNDP), "LIFE: Participatory Evaluation of Grantee NGOs" (Islamabad, 1997).

8. Ibid.

9. A. Nizamani, "A Case Study: Aurat Association" (Islamabad: LIFE, 1998).

10. Leadership for Environment and Development (LEAD), Pakistan, "A Case Study: Credit and Welfare Assocation" (Islamabad, 1998).

11. LIFE, "Grantee NGOs Membership Reports 1996" (Islamabad, 1996).

12. UNDP, "LIFE."

Comparing Parastatal and Local Government Service Delivery in Emerging Indian Metropolises

Devyani Mani

INTRODUCTION

Water supply and sanitation in emerging Indian metropolises may be delivered by municipal corporations[1] (e.g., Ahmedabad and Pune), metropolitanwide parastatals (e.g., Bangalore and Hyderabad), or state-level parastatals in collaboration with municipal corporations (e.g., Aurangabad and Mangalore).[2]

Constraints in service delivery are financial shortages and inefficient institutional arrangements, partly the result of low financial and administrative autonomy at the local level. Municipal governments in India date from the Madras Municipal Charter of 1687. Municipal institutions were established in other major cities from 1842 onward.[3] The municipal governments were the first to include locally elected Indian representatives. During the British rule, they had limited influence, as their tasks were restricted to district administration, to limit political participation at higher levels of government. After independence in 1947, there was an initial period of strong central control followed by the increasing assertion of the state governments.[4] As a result, with the exception of a few cities, municipal governments remained subservient to state-level politics and were frequently superseded by the state governments for indefinite periods.

The Constitutional (Seventy-Fourth) Amendment Act was passed in 1992 to strengthen democratic decentralization and acknowledge urban local governments as fully representative institutions at the third level in the Indian federation.[5] This legislation has significant implications on urban governance, as it clearly defines the mandates of urban local governments and ensures the following:

a. The regular conduct of elections and supercession only for a maximum period of six months;

b. Political representation and reservation of seats for weaker segments including women;

c. Devolution of functions; and

d. Greater financial autonomy through fiscal reviews, assignment of revenue authorities, and fiscal transfers.[6]

In terms of service delivery, this translates as greater access to financial resources, increased participation of the private sector, and improved responsiveness to previously neglected social groups.[7]

However, this momentous legislation does not sufficiently address the role of parastatals in urban development and their relationship to the municipal governments.[8] In cities with populations of over a million,[9] in addition to the municipal corporations, parastatals such as water supply and sewerage boards and urban development authorities are active in urban development tasks.[10] The World Bank advocated the creation of parastatals in the 1970s to serve as conduits for development assistance for major urban infrastructure projects. Parastatals were conceived as strictly administrative organizations to circumvent the ills plaguing municipal governments and to ensure maximum efficiency in their operation.[11]

The establishment and functioning of parastatals did not evolve exactly as envisaged because:

a. They were removed from urban local politics but were strongly affected by state-level politics.[12]

b. The transfer of functions from the municipal governments to the parastatals undermined the former and even created conflicts between the two types of public agencies.[13]

c. The envisioned efficiency of parastatals was not realized as they suffered from inefficiency, excessive bureaucracy, and corruption.[14]

d. The organizational structure of the parastatals prevented any opportunity for public participation and local accountability, further exacerbating unresponsive and poor service delivery.[15]

Several studies address infrastructure finance, institutional efficiency, and urban governance including responsiveness, accountability, and sustainability of service delivery.[16] Datta identifies some historical factors influencing upward and local accountability of municipal governments.[17] He finds that upward accountability depends on the relationship between the state and municipal governments. In some cases, dominance of the state is reflected in the supercession of municipal governments. In other cases, when different political parties are elected at the state and the municipal levels, conflicts are common. Mukhopadhyay offers valuable insights into the historical tensions between politics and bureaucracy in urban governance within the municipal governments that are divided into political and administrative wings, and between the parastatals and the state government to which they are accountable.[18]

In recent years, "report cards" have been used to assess accountability of public agencies in service delivery in some Indian metropolises.[19] The report cards have had significant impact in raising public awareness and pressurizing public agencies to become more accountable to the service consumer.[20] However, very few studies or efforts such as the report cards distinguish the dissimilarities in service delivery by parastatals and municipal governments and the inherent differences in the institutional, financial, and political environments that influence their capacity to increase responsiveness, accountability, and sustainability.[21]

This chapter therefore undertakes a comparison of delivery of water supply and sanitation by a local government and a metropolitanwide parastatal in the cities of Ahmedabad and Bangalore, respectively. The specific objectives are:

1. To assess the levels of responsiveness, accountability, and sustainability in the two different types of institutional arrangements in their approaches to planning and financing water supply and sanitation;

2. To identify the common factors constraining responsiveness, accountability, and sustainability, and those specific to each type of organization; and

3. To derive policy implications of the differences in the two types of organizational structures that may be useful in enhancing their responsiveness, accountability, and sustainability.

Ahmedabad[22] and Bangalore[23] are selected for study as they display patterns of growth occurring in emerging Indian metropolises and have two different types of institutional arrangements for water supply and sanitation delivery. In Ahmedabad, the main provider is the elected local government, the Ahmedabad Municipal Corporation (AMC); while in Bangalore, the provider is the metropolitanwide parastatal, the Bangalore Water Supply and Sewerage Board (BWSSB). The AMC is a strong metropolitan government that has never been superseded by higher levels of government and has recently taken innovative measures to improve service delivery.[24] Similarly, the BWSSB has also shown innovation in partnership with other agencies for financing its projects.[25]

The first section of the chapter presents the analytical framework, the second compares service delivery by the local government and parastatal, and the third includes the conclusions and policy recommendations for enhancing responsiveness, accountability, and sustainability for the two types of organizations.

FRAMEWORK AND METHOD

Organizational Mandates

The AMC is mandated to provide water supply and sanitation within its jurisdiction of 190.15 square kilometers as an obligatory function under the Bombay Provincial Municipal Corporation Act of 1949. The AMC was accorded the status of a municipal corporation in 1950 but its history dates from 1817. The municipal government in Ahmedabad has been responsible for water supply and sanitation since 1884. The AMC undertakes both physical and financial planning for water supply and sanitation, installation, and operation and maintenance within its jurisdiction. Physical planning entails the preparation of infrastructure master plans and design of infrastructure networks, and financial planning includes generating and managing resources for capital works and operation and maintenance (O&M).

In Bangalore, before 1961, the Karnataka Public Works Department (KPWD) maintained the waterworks and charged the costs to the Bangalore City Corporation (BCC), which was traditionally responsible for the provision of water supply and sanitation. In 1961, the entire water distribution system except for the head works was transferred to the BCC. The BWSSB was established as an autonomous statutory board in 1964 under an act of state legislature to provide water and sanitation to the Bangalore Metropolitan Area (BMA) covering 366 square kilometers, as stipulated by the World Bank as part of its financial assistance for the construction of the Cauvery Water Supply Scheme. Eventually, finances for this project were obtained from other sources, but the BWSSB remained as a parastatal for water supply and sewerage accountable to the state government. The functions of the BWSSB are listed as follows:[26]

a. To provide water supply and make arrangements for sewerage and disposal of sewage in the existing and developing regions of the BMA;
b. To investigate adequacy of water supply for domestic purposes in the BMA;
c. To prepare and implement plans and schemes for supply of water for domestic purposes within the BMA to the required standards;
d. To prepare and implement plans and schemes for proper sewerage and disposal of sewage of the BMA; and
e. To levy and collect water charges on a "no loss no profit" basis.

The three criteria of responsiveness, accountability, and sustainability used to assess the performance of the parastatal and the local government in service delivery are elaborated upon as follows:

Responsiveness

Services are said to be responsive when they match the consumers' needs and affordability. Projects for water supply and sanitation have been found unresponsive owing to distortions in project identification, design, and construction due to donor and host country biases toward ambitious projects and Western technology. The donor biases arise from the lack of sufficient information regarding local culture and production systems and the desire to sell technology and maximize aid flow. Host country biases are the result of the lack of participatory procedures allowing for local input, desire for prestige associated with large projects, opportunities for corruption, and the lack of accountability.[27]

An awareness of the service consumers' needs is strongly recommended for successful water and sanitation strategies. In addition to the quantity of service delivered, other concerns such as access, diversity, quality, reliability, condition, price, and environmental impacts are also considered important in the estimation of service demand.[28] The extent to which the institutional arrangements allow for consumer input and public participation is also important to increase responsiveness. This includes the participation of nongovernmental organizations (NGOs) and community-based organizations (CBOs) in determining levels and types of services.

The UK Citizen's Charter applies to public services at national and local levels, and to privatized utility companies' attempts to make services more responsive to consumers' needs through standards, open information, choice and consultation, courtesy and helpfulness, a well-publicized and easy-to-use complaints system, and efficient and economic delivery of public services.[29] In Malaysia's initiative to orient its public services to the consumers, service targets are set to include the nature of services, time frame for their delivery, costs, timeliness, reliability, accessibility, orderliness, comfort, and courtesy. It is realized that such a charter can only be effective if service consumers do not hesitate to confront the responsible public officials and demand quality services.[30]

In this chapter, responsiveness is assessed as follows (see Table 12.1):

a. Access to services. In Indian metropolises, the consumption of services is heterogeneous over the urban areas depending on the availability of public piped services, the use of substitutes and additional services, the socioeconomic status of the household, and the legal jurisdiction. Special emphasis is given to access to services by the urban poor and the residents of slums and squatter settlements, who constitute one-third or more of the total population in the urban areas.

b. Service levels in relation to services desired. Service consumption is often higher than that provided by the public agencies among high- and middle-income groups. In contrast, the services consumed by the poor are below acceptable standards. This also includes quality and reliability of services.

c. Affordability. Service charges are compared to the affordability of the households for services.

d. Participation of the private sector, NGOs, and CBOs in service installation.

e. Functioning of the systems and extent of community participation in their O&M.

Table 12.1
Analytical Framework

	PLANNING	FINANCING	INSTALLATION	OPERATION AND MAINTENANCE
RESPONSIVENESS	■ Access to various socio-economic groups at different locations in the city. ■ Access to urban poor in slums and squatter settlements. ■ Service levels in response to the levels desired.	■ Service charges in relation to affordability.	■ Quality of services. ■ Reliability of services. ■ Participation of private sector, NGOs, and CBOs.	■ Reliability of services. ■ Functioning of systems. ■ Community participation.
ACCOUNTABILITY	■ Public participation. ■ Involvement of NGOs and CBOs at community-level and citywide.	■ Response to popular opinion in fixing service charges. ■ Political manipulation of service charges. ■ Upward accountability to state governments and external financing agencies.	■ Transparency in selection of contractors. ■ Supervision of civil works. ■ Accountability to taxpayer.	■ System to address complaints. ■ Courteousness of staff. ■ Corruption. ■ Accountability within organization to higher levels of authority.
SUSTAINABILITY	■ Standards and technology in use in relation to availability of water resources.	■ Levels of cost recovery. ■ Service charges in response to resource management. ■ Regulating service consumption. ■ Internalizing negative externalities such as pollution.	■ Levels of wastage. ■ Quality of construction. ■ Quality of human resources for installation and supervision of system. ■ Quality of documentation related to the system's installation.	■ Quality of human resources for operation and maintenance, and repairs. ■ Community participation.

Accountability

Accountability in service delivery is both "input-based and output-based."[31] Public agencies are generally built to ensure accountability for the "inputs" such as the manpower and financial resources used by the organization. Accountability for the "outputs" such as service delivery is insufficiently addressed. In the Indian context, Datta distinguishes between "upward accountability" and "local accountability." The former relates to the relationship between the urban local governments and the state governments. He contends that as state governments have departments for urban development, a conflict of interests arises between these departments and the urban local governments. Local accountability refers to the extent to which municipal governments are accountable to their electorate. Datta observes constraints in local accountability due to the dominance of the administrative wing within the municipal governments. Moreover, he points out that the Constitutional (Seventy-Fourth) Amendment Act of 1992 does not address this inherent limitation of municipal management.[32]

To enhance output accountability, Kaul recommends tighter definition of tasks, measurement of performance, devolution of resource control, strengthening monitoring, and clarifying incentives.[33] In the World Bank program in Sri Lanka, initiatives to increase accountability in the local government are built around public participation in the preparation of annual statements to ratepayers of services.[34] In Porto Alegre, Brazil, a participatory budget process has succeeded in increasing own-source revenues and improving resource allocation, making service delivery more responsive and accountable to the consumers.[35]

According to Huther and Shah, judicial and bureaucratic efficiency, political transparency, a voice for all citizens, and the absence of corruption indicate the accountability of a public agency delivering services.[36] To demand greater accountability from monopolistic public service agencies in Indian cities, consumers use report cards to assess the efficiency, reliability, and adequacy of the service providers.[37]

This chapter focuses more on output and local accountability while recognizing the constraints in input and upward accountability affecting service delivery (see Table 12.1). Therefore, accountability is assessed in terms of:

a. The extent of citizen participation and the involvement of NGOs and CBOs at the community level and citywide;

b. Response to popular opinion in fixing service charges and the subsequent political manipulation;

c. Upward accountability to state governments and external financing agencies such as the World Bank that demand cost recovery;

d. Transparency in selection of contractors;

e. Supervision of civil works;

f. Systems to address complaints and related staff courteousness and corruption; and

g. Accountability within the organization to higher levels of authority.

Sustainability

Sustainability refers to the ability of the institutions to sustain their efforts in water resource management with appropriate financial and human resources.[38] Financial sustainability is becoming increasingly important with the need to generate resources locally for services.[39] The ability of the agencies to raise resources locally for capital works and the extent to which user charges are able to recover the costs of providing the resources and managing the environmental impacts of consumption are also assessed.[40] Training of public agency staff for improved management of water resources through planning, monitoring, and financing mechanisms is also important.[41]

Sustainability is assessed in terms of the following (see Table 12.1):

a. Impacts of standards and technologies used for sustainable management of the resource;

b. Levels of cost recovery achieved to ensure financial sustainability;

c. The response of service charging to resource management issues such as regulation of water consumption through pricing and the internalization of negative externalities such as water pollution through sewerage charges;

d. Levels of wastage due to defective installation and poor O&M;

e. Quality of human resources for system installation and O&M;

f. Quality of documentation related to the installation and O&M of services; and

g. Community participation in O&M to ensure sustainable management of resources.

PLANNING FOR WATER SUPPLY AND SANITATION

In Ahmedabad, water is supplied to new consumers by merely extending the networks without correspondingly increasing the amount of water produced due to financial constraints. This has resulted in a decline in per capita water supply from 201 liters per capita per day (LPCD) in 1981 to 138 LPCD in 1994.[42] These figures do not reflect the amount of water reaching the consumer. It is estimated that about 30 percent of the water produced is lost in leakages. The East Ahmedabad area annexed to the AMC in 1986 is only beginning to be covered with piped water supply and sewerage. In this area, water consumption is estimated at 70 LPCD.[43] Slum households with individual connections were limited to the pre-1976 slums in accordance with AMC policy to service only those slums with legal tenure. Recently, the AMC has been granting temporary tenure to slums under the slum networking program and extending services in these areas.[44]

In Bangalore, the per capita availability of water steadily increased from 89 LPCD to 118 LPCD but remains below the 135 LPCD standard. In 1994–95, domestic consumption constituted 50.33 percent of the total supply, nondomestic consumption was 11.14 percent, and free water supplied to the poor through the public taps constituted 38.53 percent of the total.

Until 1986, the sewerage network extended to all authorized construction within the AMC, except half of the slums. In the present day, residents of the *chawls* and slums have access to communal, pay-and-use, or individual sanitation facilities that are connected to sewerage. In the East Ahmedabad area, the wastewater drains into cesspools subsidized by the AMC. The rapidly expanding fringe areas in Ahmedabad and Bangalore that are not yet covered by sewerage use on-site sanitation. Pay-and-use as well as community toilets connected to Bangalore's sewerage or to low-cost on-site sanitation systems service the slums.

The Estate and Town Planning Department in the AMC prepares the master plans. The engineering department designs infrastructure networks in its specific sections for roads, drainage, and water supply. Plans made at the zonal level are submitted to the center, to ensure that specific needs of each zone are incorporated in the master plan for the city. The AMC provides basic services to the slums, in partnership with other agencies, through programs initiated by the central government and the United Nations Children's Fund (UNICEF).[45] The AMC has undertaken innovative programs since 1997 such as *Ahmedabad Parivartan* where it collaborates with NGOs, CBOs, and the private sector in providing services to the slums through a major slum networking exercise.[46]

In Bangalore, the BWSSB provides water supply and sanitation in the entire metropolitan area. A hierarchy of technical and administrative personnel assists engineers in undertaking their responsibilities. Feasibility of the projects and their planning are done along with external engineering consultants. Engineers from the Bangalore Development Authority (BDA) and the BCC are involved in plan preparation. The BCC buys water from the BWSSB for free distribution to public areas and the poor. This free public water provision is a contentious issue between the two organizations with the BWSSB alleging nonpayment of the charges due and the BCC claiming inadequate water supply. There is neither any provision for public participation in planning nor any direct arrangements for working with the poor.

Planning in both organizations emphasizes an engineering supply-oriented approach without considering prevailing patterns of service consumption and their impacts on the environment and resource sustainability (see Table 12.2).[47] The administrative nature of the BWSSB makes it less prone to local political manipulation in determining access to services but also less responsive and accessible to the poor. Interestingly, even though Ahmedabad has a poorer record of service provision to the slum residents,[48] the AMC has taken large strides toward becoming more responsive to the slum residents. Partnerships with NGOs and CBOs have moved from advocacy to greater participation in service delivery. Sustainability has low priority in both organizations but in Bangalore, water and sewerage are being planned for simultaneously, which ensures adequate disposal of wastewater. Water conservation and recycling are not being

Table 12.2
Planning for Water Supply and Sanitation

AHMEDABAD	BANGALORE
RESPONSIVENESS	
• It is estimated that around 65 percent of the households within AMC's jurisdiction have access to public piped water supply. Sewerage coverage is estimated at 80 percent of the AMC jurisdiction but only 60 percent of the households are connected to sewerage. • About 40 percent of the city's population residing in 1,029 slums and 1,383 *chawls* have little or no access to water and sanitation. Most slum residents share communal piped water and sanitation. In the 18 slums that are participating in the slum-networking program, individual water taps and sanitation facilities are being provided for each household. • Water supply is supplied only for 3.5 hours daily. • Quality of water is poor resulting in widespread incidence of waterborne diseases.	• BWSSB states that water supply coverage is nearly 100 percent and sewerage is 85 percent. • About 20 percent of the city's population reside in slums. Around 35 percent of the total water produced is distributed through public fountains that serve the slum residents. However, it is unclear how much of this water is lost through wastage. Low-cost shared pay-and-use facilities are provided for the poor. • Water levels are much lower than desired with water being supplied only for 2–3 hours every alternate day. • Water quality is better than in Ahmedabad with lower incidence of waterborne diseases.
ACCOUNTABILITY	
• Public participation, in general, for service delivery is low. The middle- and higher-income groups are apathetic to service planning. • Low-income groups and slums and squatter residents are involved in service planning under special programs such as urban community development and slum networking. Only the slums covered by programs are included and their participation remains at the community level. Other slums are yet to be drawn into service planning on a citywide basis. However, consciousness in the AMC is very high.	• Public participation in service delivery has traditionally been nonexistent. • NGOs and CBOs are involved in planning for services in specific slum communities with the BCC but not with the BWSSB on a citywide basis.
SUSTAINABILITY	
• Standards and technology in use do not respond to available surface and groundwater resources and sewage treatment facilities. • Planning does not consider prevailing practices of service augmentation in areas with piped water and the use of on-site water and sanitation services in the newly expanding urban fringe areas. • Water supply and sewerage are planned for separately. • Measures to conserve and recycle resources are not considered in planning.	• Standards and technology do not respond to available surface and groundwater resources and sewage treatment facilities. • Planning does not consider prevailing practices of service augmentation in areas with piped water and the use of on-site water and sanitation services in the newly expanding urban fringe areas. • Water supply and sewerage are planned for simultaneously. • Measures to conserve and recycle resources are not considered in planning.

considered by both agencies in planning nor is there an attempt to incorporate the on-site services being used in the planning strategy. Poorly planned on-site services result in environmental pollution, depletion of groundwater, and low use of piped networks when installed.[49]

FINANCING WATER SUPPLY AND SANITATION

The AMC prepares a capital budget annually for short-term tasks. Each department reviews its financial needs for ongoing projects including demands for various new services and improvement of existing services and forwards the estimates to the finance department.

The funds being limited, priorities are set and a provision is made for the sanctioned projects in the budget. The budgetary process does not relate expenditure layouts to strategic objectives, and the projections made are more reflective of departmental commitments than of priority assessments.[50] In recent years, the World Bank has introduced systematic procedures for project preparation, costing, and monitoring as well as accrual budgeting as a component of its institutional strengthening program. The AMC largely depends on its own taxes and charges for 85 percent to 90 percent of its current income. The *octroi* and property taxes are the most important sources of income. The property tax is charged in terms of a percentage of the "ratable value" of the building and land, where the ratable value is measured as the annual rental value less 10 percent of repairs.

Assessment of properties using this formula is complicated. This has given rise to large-scale litigation that seriously compromised AMC's performance in property tax collection until recently. Significant efforts by a past commissioner were successful in substantially improving the property tax collection since 1994 resulting in a revenue surplus of Rs. 594 million in 1995–96, which was transferred to the capital account of the AMC toward infrastructure improvements.[51] Water and conservancy (sanitary) taxes constitute two components of the property tax. The charges collected therefore are a fraction of the actual costs of service production. Also, the fixed nature of the tax makes it unresponsive to water consumption and wastewater disposal. In recent years, there have been several proposals to separate charging for water and conservancy from the property tax. The percentage of revenue spent on water supply and conservancy is in the range of 15 percent to 20 percent of the total expenditure and has increased slightly over the years.

The most important sources of finance for capital works have been government grants, public loans, loans from the Housing and Urban Development Corporation (HUDCO) and the Life Insurance Corporation (LIC), contributions from other parastatal agencies, and special project funds from central and state governments. Loans from the state government and the World Bank also were an important source until 1990. State government grants vary significantly each year. From 1986 onward, the AMC has financed its capital expenditure from its deposits, grants, and loans. Water and sewerage schemes constitute about half the total capital expenditure. When the contributions to the World Bank projects are included, these schemes accounted for almost 70 percent of the total in 1990–91. The AMC's capital expenditure fell from Rs. 319 million in 1986–87 to Rs. 186 million in 1990–91, indicating a high reliance on the World Bank and state government at that time.[52] With subsequent improvements in revenue generation and innovative partnerships with the private sector during 1997–98, the AMC received a first-in-Asia credit rating and issued municipal bonds worth US$10,000.[53]

For the installation of capital works in Bangalore, financial assistance is received as loans from the government, LIC, HUDCO, BDA, and BCC. Debentures have also been issued in order to raise funds for capital works. The sources of capital receipts vary each year. In general, government, HUDCO, and LIC loans form a major component of the capital receipts. The absolute amounts of debentures subscription have remained constant, but their proportion in terms of total capital receipts varies as the total amount of capital receipts has varied considerably during different years. This indicates a heavy dependence on external sources of finance. The total capital expenditure was less than the receipts from 1987 to 1993.

From 1993 to 1995, the expenditure far exceeded the receipts. Recent capital expenditure on major water and sewerage projects is being funded by the OECF as soft loans for urban infrastructure. The proportion spent on water far exceeds that spent on sewerage. During 1996–97, Rs. 359 million were spent on water supply and Rs. 62 million on sewerage, indicating a greater emphasis on water as well as the high cost of providing water from sources distant from Bangalore.

O&M of the water supply and sewerage systems is undertaken from the revenue collected from the water charges. The basis of the levy of water charges is one of "no profit no loss." These water charges are revised from time to time, the latest revision being in September 1993. The levy of water charges accounts for 81 percent to 93 percent of the total revenue, while the other miscellaneous receipts account for the remaining 7 percent to 19 percent. The expenditure is consistently higher than the income. Even though the interest liabilities on the loans taken for capital works are accounted for in the water rates, the revenue collection does not match the expenditure owing to the payment of interest on debt service, increases in power charges, and increases in establishment expenditure.

The system of charging in Bangalore is progressive, where those consuming higher volumes of water pay higher tariff rates. Four categories of consumers are identified: domestic, nondomestic, industries, and public fountains. Consumers in the first three categories are charged for water based on their level of consumption. Those in the fourth category are charged a fixed monthly amount per connection. Revenue earned in this last category is low, as it does not correspond to amount of water consumed. However, consumption patterns indicate that only 50 percent of the total water consumed can be attributed to the revenue-earning segments. The other half is distributed through public fountains or lost in leakage. The first two segments with the lowest tariff levels account for over 70 percent of the domestic consumption, which in turn accounts for 38 percent to 40 percent of the total water consumption.

Water charges collected are lower than the demand. The tariffs earned from domestic water consumption form 30 percent of the total revenue earned. The nondomestic segment that accounts for 8 percent to 10 percent of the total water produced contributes more than 50 percent of the revenue. Within this segment, those consuming more than 200,000 LPM account for nearly 80 percent of the total consumption. The industries, in particular, contribute 17 percent to 18 percent of the total revenue while consuming only 3 percent of the water consumed. While the share of domestic consumption of water has been growing steadily at 9 percent per annum, the share of the nondomestic consumers has been decreasing steadily. Explanations for this have been that due to the hike in tariffs, these consumers have reduced their consumption of public water and increased their consumption of water from private sources. Unaccounted-for water is partly attributed to unauthorized users of the piped networks. Consumption of water at the public fountains has increased annually by 18 percent accounting for 27 percent to 28 percent of the total water consumed.

Service financing in Bangalore is more responsive to consumption and affordability than in Ahmedabad (see Table 12.3). However, the consumption of public water is lower than the consumers' needs and the use of substitute on-site services is widely prevalent. In Ahmedabad, in areas where waterlines are being extended, residents do not discontinue using on-site services resulting in low consumption of public services.[54] It is easier to increase service charges in Bangalore than in Ahmedabad owing to prevailing patterns of service charging. Cost recovery is also much higher in Bangalore. However, the innovation demonstrated by the AMC in forging partnerships with the private sector has made generation of capital finance much more viable. In both cities, the service charges are not used to regulate consumption and discharge of wastes and are therefore not contributing to the sustainable use of resources.

INSTALLATION OF SERVICES

In both Ahmedabad and Bangalore, contractors are selected through a process of competitive tendering for execution of capital works. At the AMC engineering department, the sections for water supply and sewerage undertake the projects. A typical project undertaken by the BWSSB has both technical and administrative components. The BWSSB undertakes the latter while the former is completed in consultation with an external engineering firm. Installation of capital works includes different contract packages for the components of material and supply, civil works, electrical and mechanical equipment, and performance-based turnkey contracts for water and sewage plants. These contract packages are classified as international competitive bidding (ICB) or local competitive bidding

Table 12.3
Financing Water Supply and Sanitation

AHMEDABAD	BANGALORE
RESPONSIVENESS	
• Outdated property tax system is used for water and sewerage charges that do not correspond to the consumption patterns or the affordability of the service consumers. • Several industries are discharging toxic effluent into the cities sewerage system without any tax. • There is no system to charge for the use of on-site services that are rapidly depleting the acquifers as well as contributing to groundwater pollution.	• The system of charging is based on consumption and reflects the costs of providing the services. • There is no system to charge for the use of on-site services that are rapidly depleting the acquifers as well as contributing to groundwater pollution.
ACCOUNTABILITY	
• The AMC cannot change the system of property tax independent of the state government. • Political manipulation is inevitable while changing the system of service charging. • Conflicts between the state government and the AMC occur when different political parties are elected in the two levels of government. This has constrained the release of funds for infrastructure in the past. • AMC has greater autonomy after the Seventy-Fourth Constitutional Amendment Act. • The AMC has shown innovation in generating capital financing through municipal bonds.	• Regular increases are being made in the service charges. The state government politicizes the issue occasionally. There is high upward accountability between the BWSSB and the Karnataka state government. • BWSSB has conflicts with BCC regarding the payments for the water supplied through the public fountains. • The BWSSB has entered into partnership with other city agencies to raise finances for capital works that indirectly has implications on its accountability to the service consumers.
SUSTAINABILITY	
• Levels of cost recovery are low. • No regulation of service consumption and waste discharge.	• High levels of cost recovery. • Service consumption is regulated through price. But as the amount of water supplied is very low, consumers use alternatives more extensively than public supply. • There is no internalization of negative externalities such as environmental impacts in the service charges.

(LCB). The project begins with estimation of the project requirements, costs, and financial feasibility. External consultants to the project generally carry out these estimations.

Before beginning implementation of the project, clearances are required from the central and state governments, the state pollution board, and other local authorities.[55] If the water is drawn from a river that flows through two or more states, clearance is required from the Ministry of Water Resources, Government of India. The implementation of the typical project involves appointment of consultants, preparation of detailed design, prequalification of contractors, invitation and evaluation of tenders, manufacturing of equipment and materials, shipping and inland transportation, construction, installation, and commissioning of works. Both cities have very similar problems related to installation of services (see Table 12.4). However, in Ahmedabad, NGOs and CBOs are involved in the process in the slums to increase responsiveness. In both cities, the agencies are staffed with inadequately skilled and poorly motivated staff.

OPERATION AND MAINTENANCE OF SERVICES

The AMC has one central office and nine zonal offices.[56] The zones are responsible for the repair, maintenance, and small works of service infrastructure, while the central office concentrates on the major projects and policy decisions for the entire metropolitan area. There are coordination problems among zones when operating and maintaining the systems largely due to scarcity of equipment. Also, most zones with the exception of the western zone have insufficient capacity. O&M is undertaken by the BWSSB and carried out through the subdivisions and service stations at various locations. Both cities face very similar problems in tasks of O&M (see Table 12.5). The AMC is more accountable though to the consumers than the BWSSB. In Ahmedabad, NGOs focus on the poor and therefore service delivery for the poor is improving. The high- and middle-income groups show little interest in demanding improved services as compared to Bangalore. This could be because there are more services in Bangalore and the service charging system is responsive to consumption. As people pay more for services to the public agency, they demand better services.

CONCLUSIONS AND POLICY RECOMMENDATIONS

There are similarities and differences in service delivery by the local government and the parastatal. Both emphasize the monopolistic supply of services with a focus on the technical elements without considering the resource limitations and social and environmental impacts. In Bangalore, with a single entity for the entire metropolitan area, it is easier to plan the services comprehensively. However, the AMC has indicated innovation in partnerships with the private sector and NGOs as well as in generating finances for infrastructure locally. Resource generation and allocation for the BWSSB is relatively easier than for the AMC, which has to distribute resources among several different tasks. The imposition of user charges based on service consumption also results in higher cost recovery in Bangalore even though there are cases of meter malfunctioning and corruption in meter checking.

Table 12.4
Installation of Services

AHMEDABAD	BANGALORE
RESPONSIVENESS	
▪ Quality of construction of networks is inconsistent and sometimes poor. ▪ Private sector participates in installing secondary networks in the western fringes of the city. ▪ Private sector provides partial funds for slum upgradation. ▪ NGOs and CBOs are effectively involved in installation of low-cost water supply and sanitation in the slums.	▪ Quality of construction of networks is inconsistent and sometimes poor. ▪ Privatization of O&M is under discussion. ▪ NGOs and CBOs do not participate with the BWSSB but with the BCC for low-cost water supply and sanitation.
ACCOUNTABILITY	
▪ There is insufficient transparency in the selection of contractors for civil works. ▪ Supervision of civil works is unsatisfactory.	▪ There is insufficient transparency in the selection of contractors for civil works. ▪ Supervision of civil works is unsatisfactory. ▪ No local accountability.
SUSTAINABILITY	
▪ Human resources for supervision of installation are inadequately trained and lack motivation. ▪ Labor union is very strong making it difficult to fire inefficient staff or exact standards for efficiency. ▪ The documentation of the system is poor. So, when senior staff retire, there is insufficient knowledge of the system.	▪ Human resources for supervision of installation are inadequately trained and lack motivation. ▪ The documentation of the system is more complete than in Ahmedabad.

Increasing Responsiveness

Planning at the AMC is more collaborative and responsive whereas service financing at the BWSSB is more responsive. The BWSSB could adopt a collaborative approach to improve service delivery while the AMC must delink service charges from property tax and begin charging according to consumption. The collaborative approach must also lead to improvement in installation and O&M of services. Planning for service coverage in both agencies must become responsive to existing patterns of service consumption and the use of alternatives to augment the public water supply. The differing needs of the consumers in different areas of the city according to the existing service levels, the service levels desired, the patterns of service consumption, the socioeconomic status of the households, and the willingness to pay must be incorporated in the strategies

Table 12.5
Operation and Maintenance of Services

AHMEDABAD	BANGALORE
RESPONSIVENESS	
• Water supply is reliable but sewerage often breaks down in the monsoons. • Repair and maintenance of the system is poor. • Community participation is being incorporated only in the slums.	• Services are unreliable. • In the older areas of the city where the networks are old, breakdowns are frequent. • Community participation in slum areas is limited.
ACCOUNTABILITY	
• Poor response to complaints. • Staff are not always courteous. • Corruption is prevalent while responding to complaints. • Local accountability is established through politicians.	• Poor response to complaints. • Staff are not always courteous. • Corruption is prevalent while responding to complaints. • No system for accountability.
SUSTAINABILITY	
• High wastage due to poor maintenance. • Damaged distribution lines result in water contamination. • Human resources have insufficient skills and low motivation. • High- and middle-income groups are apathetic toward poor services due to the use of alternatives. • Civil society focuses on the poor. • Community participation is only in the slums.	• High wastage due to poor maintenance. • Human resources have insufficient skills and low motivation. • High- and middle-income groups are less apathetic than in Ahmedabad due to the presence of strong civil society demanding improved public services for all areas of the city in addition to focusing on the poor.

for improving services. Water supply and sanitation must be recognized as complementary systems and planned for simultaneously. Public participation must be encouraged at all stages of service delivery to create awareness of the environmental implications of the different modes of service delivery.

Ensuring Accountability

Input accountability is constrained by institutional structures that inhibit productivity and increase transaction costs in both agencies, particularly in the AMC. Output accountability that is accountability to the consumer is higher at the AMC, but constrained by political manipulation of the poor. In both cases, staff are without incentives for better performance and accountability. To improve accountability, several different actions need to be taken. Existing procedures need to be critically reviewed to identify areas of ineffectiveness and improved accordingly. Public agencies need to attract highly skilled and competent professionals and offer incentives to their staff for better performance. Accountability to the consumer can be improved by greater public participation, creation of ombudsmen committees, and evaluation of the public agencies' performance through mechanisms such as report cards.

Improving Sustainability

Sustainability of water resources needs to be given highest priority in the planning processes. This includes recognizing alternative systems of services being used in both cities and their environmental implications and the simultaneous planning for water and sanitation. This will require major changes in the way the AMC and the BWSSB have traditionally been planning for and delivering water supply and sanitation services. In Bangalore, the BWSSB can improve its sustainability by enhanced understanding of local consumption of services and the long-term implications. Impositions of new standards for piped and on-site services that respect resource sustainability will have to be given serious consideration. Financial sustainability can be improved by generating local resources, as has already been initiated in both cities. This must be supported by user charges that reflect the costs of service provision, encourage resource conservation, and minimize negative externalities caused by environmental degradation. The institutions will become capable of sustainable development of water supply and sanitation infrastructure only if their staff is involved in the process through training and incentive structures.

NOTES

1. In cities with populations of over a million, urban local government is known as municipal corporation or city corporation.

2. Dinesh Mehta and Pushpa Pathak, "Financing of Urban Services in India: A Case for Appropriate Pricing and Cost Recovery," *Habitat International* 22 (1998): 487–502.

3. K. C. Sivaramakrishnan, *Indian Urban Scene* (Simla: Indian Institute of Advanced Study, 1978).

4. The state governments are the second level in the Indian federal system, which has three levels.

5. Abhijit Datta, "The 74th Amendment and Municipal Finances," *Indian Town Planning Institute Journal* 12 (1: 1993): 15–16; and S. K. Kulshrestha, "Impact of the 74th Amendment of the Constitution of India on Spatial Planning Process and System," *Indian Town Planning Institute Journal* 12 (1: 1993): 11–13.

6. Abhijit Datta, "Institutional Aspects of Urban Governance" in Om Prakash Mathur, ed., *India: The Challenge of Urban Governance* (New Delhi: National Institute of Public Finance and Policy, 1999).

7. Om Prakash Mathur, "Governing Cities: Facing Up to the Challenges of Poverty and Globalization" in Mathur, *India*.

8. Asok Mukhopadhyay, "Politics and Bureaucracy in Urban Governance: The Indian Experience" in Mathur, *India*, pp. 109–28.

9. By the year 2000, thirty-nine cities in India were estimated to have populations of over a million people. See K. C. Sivaramakrishnan, Biplab Dasgupta, and M. N. Buch, *Urbanization in India: Basic Services and People's Participation* (New Delhi: Institute of Social Sciences, 1993).

10. K. C. Sivaramakrishnan and Leslie Green, *Metropolitan Management: The Asian Experience* (Washington, DC: World Bank, 1986).

11. See Mukhopadhyay, "Politics and Bureaucracy in Urban Governance"; Tridib Banerjee and Sanjoy Chakravorty, "Transfer of Planning Technology and Local Political Economy: A Retrospective Analysis of Calcutta's Planning," *Journal of the American Planning Association* 60 (Winter 1994): 71–82; and Bishwapriya Sanyal and Meenu Tewari, "Politics and Institutions in Urban Development: The Story of the Calcutta Metropolitan Development Authority" in Aurelio Menendez, ed., *The Urban Poor and Basic Infrastructure Services in Asia and the Pacific*. Volume 3 (Manila: Asian Development Bank [ADB] and Economic Development Institute [EDI], 1992).

12. Mukhopadhyay, "Politics and Bureaucracy in Urban Governance."

13. Sanyal and Tewari, "Politics and Institutions in Urban Development."

14. Mathur, "Governing Cities."

15. Ibid.; and Banerjee and Chakravorty, "Transfer of Planning Technology."

16. National Institute of Urban Affairs (NIUA), *Management of Urban Services* (Research Study Series No. 14) (New Delhi, 1986); NIUA, *Provision of Urban Water Supply: Institutional Options* (Research Study Series No. 33) (New Delhi, 1988); NIUA, *Upgrading Municipal Services: Norms and Financial Implications*. Volumes 1 and 2 (New Delhi, 1989); NIUA, *Impact of World Bank Credit on Urban Institutions and Policy* (Research Study Series No. 45) (New Delhi, 1990); NIUA, *Basic Services and the Urban Poor* (Research Study Series No. 46) (New Delhi, 1991); NIUA, *Pricing of Urban Services* (Research Study Series No. 48) (New Delhi, 1991); NIUA, *Urban Environmental Maps* (New Delhi, 1994); NIUA, "Guide-points for the State Finance Commissions: Reports of the Working Groups" (New Delhi, NIUA and Ministry of Urban Affairs and Employment, Government of India, 1995); NIUA, "Reforming Municipal Finances: Some Suggestions in the Context of India's Decentralization Initiative" (Discussion paper, Fourth National Workshop on State Finance Commissions) (New Delhi, 1995); NIUA, "Defining the Functional Domain of Urban Local Bodies: Some Suggestions in the Context of India's Decentralization Initiative" (Discussion paper, Fourth National Workshop on State Finance Commissions); NIUA, "Policy Change Agenda for Urban Infrastructure Finance" (FIRE (D) Working Paper Series No. 1) (New Delhi, 1995); and NIUA, "Municipal Bond Market for Urban Infrastructure" (FIRE (D) Working Paper Series No. 2) (New Delhi, 1995).

17. Abhijit Datta, "Institutional Aspects of Urban Governance" in Mathur, *India*.

18. Mukhopadhyay, "Politics and Bureaucracy in Urban Governance."

19. See Samuel Paul and Sita Sekhar, "A Report Card on Public Services," *Regional Development Dialogue (RDD)* 18 (Autumn 1997): 119–32; K. Gopakumar, "Professional Developments: Public Feedback as an Aid to Public Accountability: Reflections on an Alternate Approach," *Public Administration and Development* 17 (1997): 281–82; Samuel Paul, "Making Voice Work: The Report Card on Bangalore's Public Service" (Working Paper No. 1921) (Washington, DC: World Bank, 1997).

20. "Let's Do It More Often Dr. Paul," *The Times of India* (8 November 1999).

21. World Bank, "Decentralization and Infrastructure" (Notes on Decentralization) (http://www.worldbank.org/html/fpd/urban/decent/notes).

22. Ahmedabad, located in Gujarat state, is the seventh largest city in India, registering a population of 3.31 million in 1991.

23. Bangalore is the capital of Karnataka state in south India. In the 1991 census, the population of the city was 4,130,288, making it the sixth largest city in the country.

24. Pushpa Pathak, "Local Government and Sustainable Economic Development: A Case Study of Ahmedabad, India" in Josefa S. Edralin, ed., *Local Economic Development: A New Role for Asian Cities* (UNCRD Research Report Series No. 24) (Nagoya: UNCRD, 1997), pp. 67–86.

25. A. Ravindra, "Cauvery Water Supply Project for Bangalore: A Multi-Agency Approach to Financing" in UNCRD, *Urban Infrastructure Development* (UNCRD Proceedings Series No. 26) (Nagoya: UNCRD, 1998).

26. Bangalore Water Supply and Sewerage Board (BWSSB), *Handbook of Statistics— 1995–96 and 1996–97* (Bangalore, 1998).

27. Charles Howe and John A. Dixon, "Inefficiencies in Water Project Design and Operation in the Third World: An Economic Perspective," *Water Resources Research* 29 (July 1993): 1889–94.

28. W. F. Fox, *Strategic Options for Urban Infrastructure Management* (Urban Management Programme Policy Paper No. 17) (Washington, DC: World Bank, 1994).

29. Mohan Kaul, "The New Public Administration: Management Innovations in Government," *Public Administration and Development* 17 (1997): 13–26.

30. Ng Kam Chiu, "Service Targets and Methods of Redress: The Impact of Accountability in Malaysia," *Public Administration and Development* 17(1997): 175–80.

31. Charles Polidano and David Hulme, "No Magic Wands: Accountability and Governance in Developing Countries," *RDD* 18 (Autumn 1997): 1–16.

32. Datta, "Institutional Aspects of Urban Governance."

33. Mohan Kaul, "The New Public Administration," p. 15.

34. See Richard Slater, "Approaches to Strengthening Local Government: Lessons from Sri Lanka," *Public Administration and Development* 17(1997): 251–65.

35. Kyung-Hwan Kim, "Housing Finance and Urban Infrastructure Finance," *Urban Studies* 34 (October 1997): 1597–620.

36. Jeff Huther and Anwar Shah, "Applying a Simple Measure of Good Governance to the Debate on Fiscal Decentralization" (Working Paper No. 1894) (Washington, DC: World Bank, 1997).

37. Paul and Sekhar, "A Report Card on Public Services."

38. Ismail Serageldin, "Towards Sustainable Management of Water Resources" (Directions in Development) (Washington, DC: World Bank, 1995).

39. D. S. Brookshire and D. Whittington, "Water Resources Issues in the Developing Countries," *Water Resources Research* 29 (July 1993): 1883–88; Mark A. Ridgley, "Water, Sanitation, and Resource Mobilization: Expanding the Range of Choices" in G. Shabbir Cheema with Sandra E. Ward, eds., *Urban Management: Policies and Innovations in Developing Countries* (Westport, CT: Praeger, 1993), pp. 185–208.

40. See W. F. Fox, *Strategic Options for Urban Infrastructure*; and Christine Kessides, "Institutional Options for the Provision of Infrastructure" (World Bank Discussion Paper No. 212) (Washington, DC: World Bank, 1993).

41. Asit Biswas, "Capacity Building for Water Management: Some Personal Thoughts," *International Journal of Water Resources Development* 12 (1996): 399–405; and Asit Bis-

was, "Capacity Building for Integrated Water Management: Summary and Conclusions," *International Journal of Water Resources Development* 12 (1996): 513–14.

42. The minimum standard set by the Government of India is 135 LPCD. See Ahmedabad Municipal Corporation (AMC), *Statistical Yearbook* (Ahmedabad, 1995).

43. Richard Batley and S. Datta, "Urban Management in India, Part 2: Ahmedabad in the State of Gujarat: The Institutional Framework of Urban Government" (Case Study No. 8) (Birmingham: Development Administration Group, School of Public Policy, University of Birmingham, 1992).

44. "Slum Networking: A Holistic Approach for Improvement of Urban Infrastructure and Environment" (http://www.hsd.ait.ac.th/bestpractices/abi.htm).

45. The Urban Community Development (UCD) program provides social services in select slum pockets that include health care and environmental sanitation. Water and sanitation are provided to the slum areas under the Environmental Improvement Scheme, Scheme for the Urban Poor, and the AMC service provisions.

46. UNDP-World Bank Water and Sanitation Program-South Asia, *Ahmedabad Parivartan* (New Delhi, 1999).

47. Devyani Mani, "Implications of a Demand Orientation in Planning for Water Supply and Sanitation in Indian Million Plus Cities" (Ph.D. diss., Tokyo University, 1997).

48. For example, in one slum neighborhood in 1998, 43 families shared one piped water standpost. In another slum, 2,661 toilets served a population of 650,000.

49. Mani, "Implications of a Demand Orientation."

50. Batley and Datta, "Urban Management in India," p. 77.

51. Pathak, "Local Government and Sustainable Economic Development."

52. Ibid., p. 59.

53. UNCHS (Habitat), "Ahmedabad: Innovative Urban Partnerships," *Best Practices Database* (http://www.bestpractices.org/cgi-bin/bp98.cgi?cmd=detail&id=3541).

54. Mani, "Implications of a Demand Orientation."

55. Ravindra, "Cauvery Water Supply Project."

56. The structure of each zone is patterned on the AMC structure and is headed by a Deputy Municipal Commissioner (DMC). Each zone is divided horizontally into various departments with various sections for roads, water supply, drainage, buildings, and health, coordinated by an administrative section. The DMC heading the zonal office is also in charge of one department at the central level.

13

Public-Private Partnership
for the Renewal
of Santiago City Center

*Francisco Sabatini, Jaime Valenzuela,
and Marcelo Reyes*

This chapter analyzes the results of the Repopulation Program for the central areas of the capital city of Chile initiated in 1992 by the Corporation for the Development of Santiago (CDS), a private nonprofit entity created in 1985 by the city to foster urban renovation with the active participation of civil society and private businesses.

In the face of a systematic loss of population and environmental decline in the metropolitan core since the 1940s—when the city extended decidedly beyond the limits of the original "commune" and became an agglomeration of municipalities (thirty-four at present)—the CDS initiated an innovative Repopulation Program that adequately combined public policies with private investments. The program has resulted in a dramatic increase in residential construction since 1992, accompanied by supporting urban development projects of several kinds.

The description of the origins, development, and results of the Repopulation Program is completed with a critical analysis of its achievements, including issues that pose interesting questions for the future of the initiative. Some of the issues are related to success factors of the program—municipal leadership, the adoption of a strategic approach to planning and investment decisions, and changes in the general development context of Metropolitan Santiago. Another issue involves the urban development tensions and dilemmas that need to be addressed in order to consolidate the process. Mostly, they relate to the possible social and environmental costs that accompany the fulfillment of the residential vitalization objective.

Considering that the shortcomings identified can be avoided, in the last section

Figure 13.1
Santiago Metropolitan Region, Metropolitan Area, and Municipality

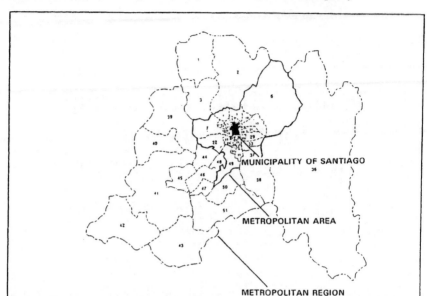

Population:
1. Chile, 13,348,937 inhabitants;
2. Santiago Metropolitan Region, 5,257,937 inhabitants;
3. Santiago City, 202,010 inhabitants.

of the chapter, some lines of inquiry are suggested as a basis for further improving the Repopulation Program.

THE REPOPULATION PROGRAM

The Loss of the Residential Function of the Metropolitan Core

The City of Santiago is located at the center of the thirty-four local governments that constitute the Santiago Metropolitan Area, an agglomeration of 4.7 million inhabitants—about one-third of the total Chilean population—and 700 km² of expanse (see Figure 13.1). The municipal territory comprised 2,239 ha and a population of 230,700 people in the last census of 1992. However, as the seat of the national capital, this small territory attracts a daily influx of 1.5 million people to work, shop, study, or engage in recreational activities in what is still the highest concentration of commercial, financial, cultural, and administrative activities in the country as well as of some important small industries.

Most of these dynamic activities concentrate in an even smaller territory, the downtown area proper, with an extension roughly equivalent to the fifty blocks that made up the original settlement founded in 1541. Starting in the 1940s, when new plans to renew the capital city were initiated, and particularly after the first line of the Santiago subway (the "Metro") entered into operation in 1975, the central business district (CBD) of Santiago has experienced a continuous renewal, which, among other consequences, has attracted more traffic congestion and air pollution to its reduced area.[1] In the same period, however, the rest of the municipal territory remained to a great extent unattended to until the late 1980s, becoming deteriorated and losing population as new residential areas developed in the metropolitan suburbs.

In this respect, Santiago is affected by a phenomenon common to large urbanized areas of the world, where the decline of the center occurs simultaneously with functional congestion and peripheral expansion of urbanized land. As residents migrate to the suburbs, in part expelled by the increased traffic congestion, pollution, and insecurity resulting from the same attractiveness that the center has for other competing uses, and in part attracted by the illusion of better living conditions there, the metropolitan core becomes specialized in nonresidential activities and, therefore, vulnerable to deterioration. This is because, generally speaking, the best keepers of the environmental quality of a place are the families living there, and when they flee to the suburbs, the quality of life rapidly begins to deteriorate. Although in theory, efficient administration could facilitate the movement of other families to the center, this is seldom done because of the high costs involved.[2]

The population living in the present territory of the City of Santiago reached a peak in 1940, with 444,306 inhabitants. Since then, a systematic loss of residents has taken place. In forty years, the population reduced by half to 232,667 inhabitants in 1980. At that point, the descent leveled off somewhat, but further decreased by another 1,600 inhabitants in the following twelve years, when the Repopulation Program started operating.

To reverse these trends, two major planning tasks were initiated in the 1980s in the city: a revision of the obsolete master plan, enforced since 1935, and a comprehensive set of studies on urban and economic development in Santiago.[3] The new zoning plan was approved in 1988, while the studies were completed in 1990. On the basis of these trends and with the leadership of the CDS, the municipality initiated a consultation process, through which the proposals of the studies were revised and modified by the community. Based on these proposals, an official document entitled "Development Proposal for the Renewal of Santiago" (1991) was prepared, which established the basis for the planning strategy and urban renewal plans of the present decade. The goal was to attain urban and economic development to enable the city to serve as a genuinely modern metropolitan center of the entire urbanized area of Santiago.

Steps had to be taken to prevent the metropolitan center from deteriorating, with emphasis on the following two sets of conditions:

a. Economic and functional vitality. The conditions that had attracted an array of activities serving the entire metropolitan area (e.g., activities that provided jobs, income, and tax revenues to the municipality) were threatened by traffic congestion, environmental degradation, and land-use conflicts. These activities were in danger of relocating to other locations in the metropolis.

b. Environmental conditions. The environmental conditions of the central area should not be allowed to deteriorate through the excessive mixture of incompatible activities, so that residential uses would not be affected by pollution, congestion, and other nuisances. Neighborhoods should be rehabilitated and provided with parks and amenities to preserve their environmental quality and anchor people to them.

This double task was extremely difficult to carry out since it required, first, the attainment of goals that were traditionally considered as being mutually exclusive; and second, the solution of complex problems created by the competition for the same location between powerful but incompatible land uses and less economically significant but environmentally healthy ones.

The Corporation for the Development of Santiago and the Repopulation Program

The CDS is an instrument to foster the economic, physical, and social development of the city. Its mandate is to address all aspects related to improving the quality of life of the citizens in the city. While the CDS is presided over by the Mayor of Santiago, it is run as a private enterprise, and in this capacity it can manage public and private resources with great flexibility for the benefit of the community.

The CDS is managed by a president, five counselors, and an executive director, plus an assembly of members, which includes three representatives of four banks, five universities, three public utility companies, three trade unions (including the powerful Chamber of Builders and Developers), the City Public Works Office, one cooperative, and seven architects. Apart from the participation of these representatives, through its work at the neighborhood level the CDS benefits from the active participation of community leaders and organizations.

To validate the studies on the urban and economic development of Santiago, the CDS created the City Participation Program. More than 16,000 neighbors and users of the commune attended a series of workshops held over a period of six months, where they revised and modified the diagnosis and proposals contained in the studies. This led to the formulation of a strategy to develop Santiago by "strengthening its neighborhoods with new residents and, at the same time, providing financial, commercial and professional services of the best quality, at the scale of a true modern metropolitan centre."[4]

The CDS has concentrated its efforts on the first component of the strategy—the Repopulation Program created by the City Council of Santiago. The program is composed of the following elements, which have evolved somewhat since their original conception:

- The *Urban Renewal Subsidy* created in 1992 by the Ministry for Housing and Urban Development at the request of the city and the CDS, which benefits families buying houses in predefined "Areas of Urban Renewal." It consists of a grant of 200 *Unidades de Fomento* (UF), or development units (US$6,600 at the time), plus a loan proportional to the cost of the house, provided that the family had already saved a minimum of UF 50 (US$1,600).[5]

- An official *List of Potential Buyers*, originally prepared by the City Housing Office, composed of families interested in living in the city territory—including the tenants of houses located therein but interested in becoming owners—and which already had the minimum savings required to qualify for the urban renewal subsidy. At present, the list is managed by the CDS.

- The *Specialized Consulting Services* provided by the Real Estate Development Unit of the CDS to private developers, including: (a) conducting land and real estate market studies to find, or to legally constitute, plots suitable for housing projects of moderate cost (2,000 m² to 3,000 m²); (b) organizing groups from the List of Potential Buyers for specific projects; (c) acting as a mediator in negotiations between developers and clients; and (d) promoting and publicizing the development projects. Since 1996, the developers have been paying a percentage of their sales to the CDS for these consulting services, which have grown in scale and complexity over the years.

- The *Joint Venture Agreements* signed between the CDS and those developers who want to have access to the List of Potential Buyers and receive the Specialized Consulting Services of the CDS. In these agreements, the terms of the negotiations concluded between the developers and clients are specified (housing size, amenities, parking spaces, and others).

Three distinct periods can be identified in the implementation of the Repopulation Program: an initial phase, 1992–94, followed by important reformulations in a second phase, 1995–96, and the present consolidation phase, from 1997 onward.

Phase I: Launching of the Repopulation Program (1992–94)

Before the initiation of the Repopulation Program, in spite of people's great interest to remain in the metropolitan center, which offered several advantages (i.e., closeness to the workplace and good and abundant services), most of the nonowner families living in the municipality could not afford to buy a house, since the price was above UF 1,200 (US$36,250). After several analyses and tests, a range of housing values was defined for the commune, from UF 500 to UF 900 (US$11,500 to US$21,000), which determined a target population earning monthly wages of US$230 to U$600 at that time. Minimum standards of construction and equipment were set for the different housing types.

Under these conditions, the first phase of the Repopulation Program was started, through the preparation of a List of Potential Buyers by the City Housing Office. From this list, groups of families with similar saving capacity and interest were identified. These applicants were monitored by the CDS in order to comply with the minimum savings requirement and to apply successfully for the subsidy and loan. They were also informed about the living conditions in city housing, which was a new experience for most of them. A total of 1,500 families that could afford houses of up to UF 900 were briefed in 1993.

The existence of these groups represented an effective and organized demand that enabled the city and the CDS to lobby for their cause at the Ministry for Housing. The ministry then decided to increase the existing minimum subsidy level from UF 150 to UF 200 for houses in the urban renewal areas of large cities in the country. The urban renewal subsidy was launched in 1993 in the Rondizzoni Condominium, the first project of the Repopulation Program, located at the southeast end of the city territory facing the large O'Higgins Metropolitan Park.

This project was the result of partnership with the Habitacoop Housing Co-operative, which had the most potential among the developers contacted in the first phase of the Repopulation Program. In effect, in spite of the urban renewal subsidy, the List of Potential Buyers, and the existence of several groups of applicants with accumulated savings, no private developers responded to the first call by the CDS. When the invitation to participate in the Repopulation Program was extended to cooperatives, only the Habitacoop responded. In January 1992, a three-party Joint Venture Agreement was signed by the city, the CDS, and Habitacoop, defining specific roles for each institution:

1. The City of Santiago was made responsible for promoting the program; identifying, capturing, and organizing the demand for Habitacoop; assisting in the definition of the housing projects with the cooperative; and monitoring the construction and acquisition of the houses.

2. The CDS was in charge of providing consultation on the land and real estate market, and identification and acquisition of the sites; and of assisting in the definition of the projects.

3. The Habitacoop Housing Cooperative was responsible for organizing applications for the urban renewal subsidy; acquiring the land; defining the architectural and construction projects; and building the houses.

Soon after the initiation of the program, the growing demand for houses led to an increase in their purchasing value, creating an important concentration of applicants who were prepared to pay from UF 1,200 to UF 1,500 (US$36,250 to US$45,312). At the end of the first phase of the program in 1995, 3,582 housing units in 12 different development projects had been built in the city territory. The annual average number of houses built during the period 1992–94 was 895 units.

As an outcome of this successful management, interest grew in the noncooperative private sector for obtaining access to the List of Potential Buyers and other services and support provided by the CDS.

Phase II: Reformulation of the Repopulation Program (1995–96)

On the basis of the experience obtained during the first three years of the Repopulation Program and in response to the interest of the private sector, some reformulations were made, especially with respect to the program's relationship with developers. These were:

- Extension of the Joint Venture Agreements with private developers, to be made primarily by the CDS, which became directly in charge of the List of Potential Buyers for houses with subsidies of up to UF 1,500;
- Development of a more aggressive strategy of publicity, promotion, and capture of housing demand;
- Formalization of the Specialized Consulting Services for market studies, acquisition of land, and application to the urban renewal subsidy; and
- Formalization of the agreements with private firms to accept rights of access to housing demand through the CDS, including collection of a fee for these services (a percentage of the sale value), which was considered savings for the firms inasmuch as these services minimized publicity costs and investment risks.

These measures have significantly improved the efficiency of the process and the actual housing sales, attracting private developers interested in building houses of higher value (above UF 1,200). These measures have also benefited the Habitacoop, which marketed units below UF 1,200 and was not required to pay for the consulting services offered by the CDS.

During this phase of the program, 2,226 housing units were built in nine development projects. The average number of units built during 1995–96 was 1,113 units per year.

Phase III: Consolidation of the Repopulation Program (1997 Onward)

The Repopulation Program has created a momentum for housing construction in the city territory, with private developers supplying housing without the direct intervention of the CDS, relying mainly on the official list of applicants. The CDS, however, still signs agreements with developers to provide consulting services for land market studies and promotion.

As of December 1997, 1,856 housing units had been built during Phase III of the Repopulation Program in six development projects.

Recapitulation of Results

The results of the Repopulation Program as of December 1997 are summarized below. These include the initial efforts of the CDS during the period 1989–92 (see Figure 13.2).

- It has been estimated that the population of the commune increased between 1992 and 1998 to more than 35,000 inhabitants (+15 percent).[6]
- Construction of more than 8,000 housing units in the municipal territory.
- Identification and assistance to more than 8,600 families in formally applying for a housing solution in the city territory, of which 75 percent had already applied.
- More than 5,400 urban renewal subsidies were granted by the Ministry of Housing and Urban Development to families buying houses in the city territory, in addition to 1,300 subsidies for surrounding municipalities.
- Since 1989, about 2 million building permits were granted by the city for residential use, of which 69 percent were granted during 1995–97.
- Some 18,200 new buildings for residential, commercial, office, and other uses were built or are under construction, of which about 40 percent were managed by the Repopulation Program.

A CRITICAL ANALYSIS OF THE REPOPULATION PROGRAM: ACHIEVEMENTS AND TENSIONS

First, it is important to discuss the factors responsible for the residential recovery in the metropolitan core of Santiago. Why are people coming to live in the city center again? How much of this achievement can be attributed to the Repopulation Program?

Second, it is necessary to know the costs involved in the fulfillment of this objective. How much was needed to pay for reversing the trend of residential abandonment of the inner city? Are the costs involved in this task inevitable? The analysis of this issue is made with the intention of arriving at conclusions that could be valid not only for Santiago but also for other cities.

Third, some lines of inquiry are suggested that need to be developed further in order to overcome the problems identified and to improve the Repopulation Program.

Success Factors

The success attained by the CDS in its Repopulation Program can be attributed to a combination of external and internal factors, the first originating from changes in the general urban context and the second from the improvement of the management capacity of the CDS. The following factors are the most significant:

Figure 13.2
Santiago Metropolitan Area and Santiago Municipality: Population Trends

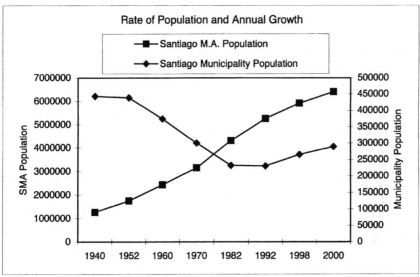

1. The opportunity offered and negotiating capacity demonstrated by the CDS, taking advantage of the dynamism of the real estate sector and public housing policies during this period. The urban renewal subsidy played a decisive role in increasing the dynamism of the housing market in the metropolitan core.

2. The leadership exercised by the mayor throughout the process and his permanent support of the work of the CDS.

3. The support that the CDS received from the technical units and experts of the City of Santiago, which evolved into a truly joint venture of the two institutions, capable of overcoming the inevitable problems and tensions between the traditional structure of the city and the executive style of the CDS.

4. The institutional and management capacity of the CDS to create several parallel programs, each working to reinforce the others (see factor no. 7 below).

5. The legitimacy obtained by the program among the citizenry, to a great extent due to the transparency with which the CDS managed and allocated the resources of the Repopulation Program.

6. The support and interest for the program demonstrated by the Chamber of Builders and Developers, a union of building entrepreneurs.

7. The prospect of progress and image change of the metropolitan core generated by the Repopulation Program attracted the attention of both people in need of housing and the developers. Several projects carried out by the city in the central core contributed to this change of image, such as the redesign of neighborhoods (e.g., Concha y Toro,

Londres, Plaza Brasil, República, Avenida Bulnes, and Puente y Estación Mapocho); the construction of the Parque de los Reyes; and the programs for the recovery of façades and heritage buildings.[7]

Other external variables may also have contributed to the success of the Repopulation Program, such as the central location of the inner city in the context of an increasingly expanded and congested metropolis, and the significant endowment of services, infrastructure, and job opportunities provided.

In effect, the congestion and infrastructure have created new competing "market niches" in the metropolitan area, where dynamic commercial subcenters have emerged. Four of the six main shopping centers of metropolitan Santiago that were developed since 1990 are located at the intersection of the main radial thoroughfares along the highway ring of Américo Vespucio.[8] Offices, public services, and high-rise housing have been added to the original commercial functions of these subcenters. At issue, however, is: Why has the inner core with its excellent accessibility and other advantages (e.g., abundant services and infrastructure) not become part of the real estate boom unlike the commercial subcenters that arose spontaneously?

On the other hand, one might ask why the residential renewal of the inner core took about ten years to take off,[9] considering that since 1985 the Chilean economy has grown steadily at an annual average rate close to 7 percent, with the real estate sector showing a similar growth. Could the delayed acceleration of the process be attributed to the late application of the urban renewal subsidy? Considering these issues, it is reasonable to assume that other factors have also intervened in the renewal of the center. We have already mentioned congestion and accessibility as forces that are redefining new market niches by themselves. In the next section, when the dilemma between competitiveness and autonomy is discussed, other factors will be analyzed.

Many international experiences indicate that the decline of the central areas in big cities such as Santiago is followed by processes of urban renewal and recovery. In effect, many of the world's cities exhibit a loss of residents and physical decline in their historic centers while suburban sprawl increases followed by central renovation efforts but in a way relatively independent of the efforts undertaken by municipal authorities.

The key question in the case of Santiago is whether the recovery of the central core would have occurred anyhow, with or without the work of the CDS and its Repopulation Program. Whatever the final answer to this question is, one can ascertain that the Repopulation Program has played at least the role of triggering the urban development process. It is likely that without the joint venture agreements made in Phase I of the program, the renewal process would have started later and developed less rapidly. Also, without these agreements, probably only small and privileged locations of Santiago would have been considered sufficiently attractive by the developers who were aiming at residential demand strata found elsewhere in the metropolitan area.

Figure 13.3
Municipality of Santiago: Location of Building Permits for Housing Projects of the Repopulation Program, 1992–98

REPOPULATION PROJECTS

BEFORE 1992
● 1985 - 1989
    1990 - 1991

NEIGHBORHOODS

1. BARRIO CENTRO
2. BARRIO BRASIL
3. BARRIO YUNGAY
4. BARRIO PARQUE DE LOS REYES
5. BARRIO LIRA
6. BARRIO ALMAGRO
7. BARRIO EJÉRCITO
8. BARRIO BOGOTÁ
9. BARRIO PARQUE O'HIGGINS
10. BARRIO PARQUE CLUB

AFTER 1992 (projects with and without agreement with the Corporation)

● 1992 without agreement   ● 1997 without agreement
● 1993 without agreement   ● 1997 with agreement
● 1993 with agreement   1998 without agreement
● 1994 without agreement   ● 1998 with agreement
● 1994 with agreement   1999 without agreement
● 1995 without agreement   1999 with agreement
● 1995 with agreement
  1996 without agreement
● 1996 with agreement

source: Corporation for
Development of Santiago

Source: IMS-CORDESAN (1998).

One can hypothesize on the role performed by the agreements in stimulating development when analyzing the spatial growth pattern of the program. Figure 13.3 shows the location of the residential projects undertaken during 1992–98. Projects built without an agreement (that is, projects developed more or less independently by private entrepreneurs) form tight clusters at two attractive and well-consolidated areas (Plaza Brazil and Avenida República), while projects built with an agreement adopt a looser pattern located at the "frontier" of these clusters and beyond. Typically, the latter were originally less consolidated and unattractive and have only now become fashionable owing to the new developments. It seems clear that the agreements under the Repopulation Program have helped to strengthen and expand the "spontaneous" urban renewal drive toward parts of the formerly depressed city territory.

Tensions and Dilemmas Associated with the Residential Renewal of the Metropolitan Core

The renewal efforts made by the CDS gave rise to tensions between the objectives sought and certain negative effects associated with them. These conflicts should be taken into account when thinking about the kind of role that is envisioned for the center of the city. They are related to the quality of life, the environment, the architectural and urban heritage, social integration, and the urban identity of the center.

It is important to analyze the tensions between competitiveness and autonomy among metropolitan municipalities, and between municipal and metropolitan development.[10] These tensions seem to have a universal character, leading to basic dilemmas that the strategic approach to urban planning must confront.

The Dilemma between Competitiveness and Autonomy among Metropolitan Municipalities

The CDS has adopted a management approach similar to what is understood as "urban strategic planning," where private real estate development projects acquire importance. Under this approach, there is a shift of emphasis from the traditional physical zoning plan to an understanding of the possibilities for triggering development processes. In dealing with these prospects for change, the key element is to create favorable conditions to attract investors and enable them to materialize their projects.

In Santiago, the municipalities that constitute the metropolitan area compete with one another to attract investments. Present policies on administrative decentralization provide them with legal and institutional tools as well as the human and financial resources necessary to undertake this task. The questions are: What must be given away or sacrificed by the municipalities in their desire to gain competitiveness? How much of their autonomy to initiate development projects for environmental, cultural, historical, and social recovery is curtailed by such compromises to make their areas more attractive to real estate developers?

The dilemma between competitiveness and autonomy seems to be intrinsic to many strategic urban planning efforts. As municipalities try to attract private investments, they become liable of losing political and economic autonomy to address environmental and social degradation. In order to attract investments, for example, a municipality must relax zoning regulations, with negative consequences for the environmental quality of the neighborhoods; or assign a considerable portion of its budget to public works, at the cost of neglecting the needs of poorer zones; or disregard the conservation of architectural and environmental heritage in the search for competitiveness. In general, environmental and social degradation can be exacerbated by real estate developments that demolish or alter valuable neighborhoods, places, or buildings, or replace poor residents with wealthier ones.

This dilemma can perhaps be better stated as a corollary to the above: The municipalities that autonomously apply standards or take protective action based on social or environmental concerns (and by doing so, go against present official policies that reject controls against private interests) usually lose competitiveness in attracting investors.

It is too early to assess the occurrence of such problems in central Santiago, but it is a danger that must be addressed if the Repopulation Program is to comply with the explicit goals of social integration and environmental preservation as part of the Corporation's mandate. One example of this danger is the increase in building height allowed after 1995 in order to gain competitiveness and attract investments. As a result, new buildings are, on the whole, taller than those constructed at the beginning of the program, when the criterion was to allow only for "medium height buildings."[11] This change is the subject of recurrent criticism of the program that disregards the preexisting building character of some areas and has created problems of parking space and service shortages due to the increased density.

Another danger is the economic pressure already felt in the central land submarkets, as the prices rise with the growing demand for sites where high-rise structures can be built. As a result, the poorer residents, the majority of whom are tenants, are threatened with expulsion. The CDS is adopting measures in some neighborhoods to protect the residents from moving, but it is not clear if the submeasures will be adequate to withstand growing pressures for the residents' eviction.

There are no easy answers to this dilemma. Perhaps the best way is to combine efforts such as increased public participation at the local level with the adoption of nationwide standards for urban renewal and development that include social, cultural, and environmental concerns, along with the development of a style of interaction between municipality and business, where the former enhances its negotiation power by adequately managing the key economic resource it controls, namely, the possibility of "creating land" through land-use standards.

Municipal versus Metropolitan Development

One of the main limitations of the CDS and its Repopulation Program is the fact that they operate in only one of the thirty-four municipalities of Metropolitan Santiago, while trying to resolve problems that, to a large degree, have their origin in forces and processes at the metropolitan level. Perhaps the most obvious of these is air pollution, which affects the whole valley of Santiago, an extension of 35 km by 80 km. The loss of population, physical deterioration, and impoverished quality of life affecting the metropolitan center are also problems connected to urban processes of a larger scale.

On the other hand, the chances that the improvements attained by the CDS in central Santiago can be extended to the metropolitan area and significantly help solve the problems of the big city are also limited by its "local" character.

A third issue associated with the relationship between the local and metropolitan levels is the zoning norms. In general, the traditional planning approach to local problems is zoning, which in the end tends to aggravate them at a wider scale. Zoning is an attempt to solve the conflicts created by mutually negative externalities produced by different land uses, by segregating them in space. But the uses that are excluded from one area end up being concentrated in other parts of the city. This has two important effects: (a) it creates a greater need for traveling, since the activities that were separated still need to be connected, contributing to traffic congestion and air contamination; and (b) as has been observed in cities all over the world, the elimination of mixed land uses usually creates functional and social spaces of marked environmental deterioration and social disintegration.

The dilemma between local and metropolitan development results, then, in the creation of "second order" externalities at the metropolitan level, caused by the spillover of externalities from the local to the metropolitan level. The effect of this phenomenon on urban poverty represents a clear example of the "perverse spiral" between local solutions and metropolitan problems.

As indicated earlier, the poor can be excluded from some areas by land use and building standards. In the long term, the evicted families locate in areas that are less attractive to the market and where zoning regulations are less strictly enforced—constituting extensive areas of poverty. These areas are also the locus of official low-income housing developments.

In these zones despair spreads, especially during times of job insecurity, and with this, the problems of social disintegration increase. Perhaps delinquency has the greatest citywide effect, harming the quality of life of every metropolitan dweller. The lack of public safety leads, in turn, to medium- and high-income families taking refuge in gated communities, thus completing the circle of social segregation.

Something similar happens with environmental externalities, since the "nuisance" activities excluded by zoning from mixed areas end up being concentrated in single-use sectors. A consequence of this transformation is that the inhabitants of the new single-use enclaves remain ignorant of the environmental problems that they "export" to other locations in the metropolitan area. Since diversity provides for a wealth of information of all kinds, the functionally homogeneous areas become, in fact, poorer in this respect.

The solution to this dilemma will require significant efforts to preserve the mixture of uses and social groups in their original locations.

FUTURE PERSPECTIVES AND RECOMMENDATIONS

As previously noted, the CDS needs to undertake further steps to revise its strategic urban development plan by clearly defining some of its objectives based on discussion and negotiation with citizens and businesses—and by translating the objectives into actual morphological images for the city territory.

The process of implementing a strategic plan guided by these objectives involves several instruments, namely: (a) zoning (the *"Plan Regulator"* or *Master Plan*); (b) development programs, such as residential renewal or the restoration of façades; and (c) negotiation procedures with citizens and businesses to attain social, environmental, and cultural objectives. The latter should be democratically specified and agreed upon, and explicitly made part of the strategic plan.

The CDS is already applying several of these elements but has not yet incorporated all of them into an integrated and strategic whole. In order to do so and improve the CDS on the basis of its experience with the Repopulation Program, it would be advisable to reinforce in a systematic manner the lines of action discussed below for a successful strategic urban planning process.

Public Participation

Public participation will allow citizens to influence the results to be obtained from development projects, counterbalancing the pressure for granting concessions to real estate developers to persuade them to invest in the city.

To be effective, public participation must be autonomous and not "instrumental" to the achievement of external objectives that are not explicitly accepted by the community. "Clientelism" is the term reserved for this common deformation of participation, a peril that increases when participation is organized by the city itself. But whether it is initiated or supported by the city or not, participation must sooner or later become independent in order to carry out the function of counterbalancing private interests in an effective way. The strengthening of local autonomy is something that the city government cannot resolve by itself. Organized citizens have an important role to play in this.

Seen from the perspective of the city, autonomous local participation can become a positive factor in the creation of a wider political space to implement its policies and programs. Moreover, the conflicts arising between real estate developers and neighbors can lead to the widening of this city "space for maneuvering." The more the forces involved in these conflicts, the more the municipalities, as natural mediators, can introduce their own interests within the solutions found to solve them.

Public participation is also an important process of obtaining acceptance at the city and national levels for the inclusion of environmental, social, and cultural requirements in new real estate investments as well as for avoiding extreme competition that may lead to the destruction of urban spaces and to new developments lacking in variety, amenity, and cultural significance. Given its importance as the seat of the national capital, Santiago City can exercise a strong influence on the central government and other municipalities to achieve increased awareness for these important concerns. Counting on an active citizenry can significantly increase this influence.

Nationally Adopted Standards for Urban Renewal and Development

The adoption of land use and building standards that include social, cultural, and environmental concerns at the national level would avoid extreme limits of competition among municipalities in order to attract private investments. When a level is reached where a firm that is faced with similar requirements cannot find another place with less demanding standards for the same project, then it could be said that these requirements are reasonable and in accordance with the values and goals adopted by society.

Negotiation of Land Use and Building Standards

Negotiation of land use and building standards between the city and the real estate developers is a key component of an urban strategic plan.

The competitiveness of an area should not be based only on the unilateral offer of advantages to attract investors, since the city has the possibility of conducting negotiations in more balanced terms. In effect, without requiring any investment, it can "create" marketable urban land just by modifying land-use standards, particularly those that affect density of use. This is the city's exclusive power that enables it to provide the "created usable space" to the real estate developers, in exchange for land for public spaces (for recreation and circulation) or financial contributions for environmental or social programs, among other possibilities.

In this way, negotiations between the city and the developers will provide options for solving the tension between municipal competitiveness and autonomy, without excessive damage to either of these two interests.

Encouragement of Mixed Land Uses

More and more urban planners and scholars defend the need to promote mixed land uses in the city, both functionally and socially. However, attainment of this goal is not in any way a simple endeavor. The existence of negative externalities in mixed-use patterns is a reality. So is the cultural resistance to them. But it is also true that there are technological developments that make the externalities less important and the functioning together of various uses more compatible.

An important issue is the extent to which the Residential Renewal Program of Santiago is adopting the traditional zoning approach that rejects mixed land uses, with the peril of being affected by the second dilemma (between local and metropolitan development). There are signs that it is to some extent adopting the traditional segregation approach, but there are also signs of a healthy departure from it.

On the one hand, the City of Santiago and the CDS have in general not adopted mixed land uses contrary to the existing practice among traditional planners and some segments of the population. In effect, the modification of the *Master Plan* in 1995 was intended to further increase the attractiveness of the Repopulation Program to private developers, through the rezoning of large areas where formerly mixed uses were allowed, into exclusively residential areas.

Clearly, this is not contributing to the solution of the problems of the city as a whole. For example, if a family wishing to set up a workshop in the basement of their home could not find a place in the city where zoning norms would allow it, a new journey to work would add to traffic congestion. Mixed uses in large sections of central areas should be considered more as an investment than as a situation of chaos that should be eradicated.

On the other hand, the Repopulation Program of the CDS is effectively contributing to a reduction in the geographic scale of the social segregation in the city. Since families with medium incomes are attracted to live in areas for predominantly middle/low- or low-income groups, a wider social integration is being achieved in the city. This is taking place in spite of the forces of expulsion of poorer residents from central Santiago noted earlier.[12]

As one can infer from the analysis made, the promotion of mixed land uses raises serious questions and problems, all of which relate to the general issue of the city as scenario for conflicts. In effect, we are facing a sort of trade-off between mixed land-use patterns, negative externalities, and local environmental conflicts, on the one hand, and zoning, second-order negative externalities, and city or metropolitanwide crisis, on the other. Traditional urban planning—which is being abandoned in academic and professional circles while still very much used in municipalities of developing countries—is gearing toward the direction of the second extreme of this polarity. In the light of the serious problems that have been accumulating in cities as a result of this approach, it seems reasonable to move decidedly in the opposite direction. To do so, we should apply a strategy combining zoning, encouragement of mixed land uses, and mediation and negotiation of conflicts—tasks in which municipalities and agencies such as the CDS have a relevant role to play.

NOTES

This chapter was prepared at the Office of the Latin American Coordinator, International Council for Local Environmental Initiatives (ICLEI) in partnership with the Corporation for the Development of Santiago (CDS). The authors would like to thank Pablo

Contrucci, Director of the Corporation, for his useful comments and information provided in the preparation of the chapter.

1. Air pollution is, by far, the most serious environmental problem of Metropolitan Santiago. Owing to a combination of man-made and geographic conditions, and in spite of the repeated efforts to abate the problem, the levels of contamination found in Santiago are commonly much higher than accepted standards for urban areas. Concentrations of carbon monoxide generated by vehicles are usually two to three times higher than accepted norms, reaching even worse levels at congested areas, such as the central business district (CBD).

2. A detailed analysis of the process of deterioration, land-use change, and residential weakening of central Santiago is presented in Jaime Valenzuela G., "Urban Decay and Local Management Strategies for the Metropolitan Centre: The Experience of the Municipality of Santiago, Chile" in UNCRD, *Latin American Regional Development in an Era of Transition* (Research Report Series No. 8) (Nagoya, 1994), pp. 65–86.

3. The *Master Plan and Zoning Ordinance of the Municipality of Santiago* was developed in two stages, 1982–94 and 1987–88, by Habitat Ltd. Consultants. The plan was again modified in 1995. The studies on urban and economic development in Santiago were commissioned by the city to the Schools of Architecture and of Economics and Administration of the Catholic University of Chile between 1988 and 1990.

4. See the "Development Proposal for the Renewal of Santiago" (1991).

5. The urban renewal subsidy is applicable only in zones predefined by Presidential Decree in the principal cities of Chile. It provides a minimum grant of UF 200 for the families buying a house, higher than the minimum for solution in other areas. The Ministry for Housing and Urban Development accepted the proposal made by the CDS in 1998 to create such a subsidy at a higher level for central areas, when it was demonstrated that housing solutions there were eleven times cheaper than in suburban locations, where all the infrastructure had to be built. There are three levels of subsidy and loans:

1. Houses costing up to UF 500 (US$16,470):

Benefit: UF 200 (US$6,590)

Minimum savings: UF 50 (US$1,650)

Maximum loan: UF 250 (US$8,230)

2. Houses costing up to UF 1,000 (US$32,935):

Benefit: UF 200 (US$6,590)

Minimum savings: UF 100 (US$3,295)

Maximum loan: UF 700 (US$23,050)

3. Houses costing up to UF 1,500 (US$49,390):

Benefit: UF 200 (US$6,590)

Minimum savings: UF 150 (US$4,940)

Maximum loan: UF 1,000 (US$32,930)

6. This figure has been calculated by the Residential Development Unit of the CDS on the basis of building permits issued for residential purposes, number of houses actually built, and number of unoccupied units in 1998. Another data source shows that the commune population increased by 53,000 people during the same period (see Habitat Ltd., *Estudios urbanos para el plan de desarrollo de Santiago*, Santiago, 1997).

7. A motto of the Residential Renewal Program was the creation of a *ciudad guerible* for prospective residents ("a city to be loved").

8. This is a highway ring encircling the totality of the Santiago Metropolitan Area, located midway between the core and the peripheral development. It has an extension of 70 kilometers and is one of the most important urban projects of Santiago. It was planned in 1960 and completed in the following thirty-five years.

9. In 1996 and 1997, many houses have been built in central Santiago compared to the first ten years of existence of the CDS.

10. These two dilemmas are discussed in Francisco Sabatini, *"Hacia una nueva plan-ificación urbana"* ("Towards a new urban planning") (Working Paper No. 24) (Santiago: Institute of Urban Studies, Catholic University of Chile, n.d.).

11. When the Repopulation Program was created, the Residential Development Unit was given the task of finding or forming sites with an area of 2,000 m^2 to 3,000 m^2, suitable for "medium height" housing projects.

12. A trend toward a reduction in the scale of social segregation connected to the transformation of the real estate sector in Santiago is postulated as a hypothesis in Francisco Sabatini, *"Liberalización de los mercados de suelo y segregación social en las ciudades latinoamericanas: el caso de Santiago, Chile"* (Blue series no. 14) (Santiago: Institute of Urban Studies, Catholic University of Chile, 1997).

Bibliography

DECENTRALIZATION

Aasen, Berit, et al. *Evaluation of Decentralization and Development: Decentralization in Developing Countries—Experiences and Lessons Learned.* Oslo: Norwegian Institute for Urban and Regional Research, 1997.

Agrawal, Arun, Charla Britt-Kapoor, and Keshav Kanel. *Decentralization in Nepal: A Comparative Analysis: A Report on the Participatory District Development Program.* Oakland, CA: Institute for Contemporary Studies, 1998.

Ayee, Joseph R. A. *An Anatomy of Public Policy Implementation: The Case of Decentralization Policies in Ghana.* London: Avebury, 1995.

Aziz, Abdul and David D. Arnold, eds. *Decentralized Governance in Asian Countries.* New Delhi: Sage Publications, 1996.

Burki, Shahid Javed, et al. *Beyond the Center: Decentralizing the State.* World Bank Latin American and Caribbean Studies. Washington, DC: World Bank, 1999.

Cohen, John M. and Stephen B. Peterson. *Administrative Decentralization: Strategies for Developing Countries.* West Hartford, CT: Kumarian Press for the United Nations, 1999.

De Souza, Celina Maria. *Constitutional Engineering in Brazil: The Politics of Federalism and Decentralization.* London: St. Martin's Press, 1997.

Dillinger, W. R. *Decentralization and Its Implications for Service Delivery.* Urban Management and Municipal Finance, 16. Washington, DC: World Bank, 1994.

Gershberg, Alex Ian. "Decentralization, Recentralization and Performance Accountability: Building an Operationally Useful Framework for Analysis," *Development Policy Review* 16 (1998): 405–31.

Inter-American Development Bank. *Economic and Social Progress in Latin America,*

1994 (Report: Special Section, "Fiscal Decentralization: The Search for Equity and Efficiency"). Washington, DC, 1994.

Jha, S. N. and P. C. Mathur. *Decentralization and Local Politics*. New Delhi: Sage Publications, 1999.

Lieten, Georges Kristoffel and Ravi Srivastava. *Unequal Partners: Power Relations, Devolution, and Development in Uttar Pradesh*. Indo-Dutch Studies on Development Alternatives, 23. New Delhi: Sage Publications, 1999.

MacKintosh, Maureen and Rathin Roy. *Economic Decentralization and Public Management Reform*. New Horizons in Public Policy Series. Northampton, MA: Edward Elgar, 1999.

Manor, James. "Democratic Decentralization in Africa and Asia," *IDS Bulletin* 26 (2: 1995): 81–88.

Murphy, Ricardo L. *Fiscal Decentralization in Latin America*. Washington, DC: Inter-American Development Bank, 1995.

Peterson, George E. *Decentralization in Latin America: Learning through Experience*. World Bank Latin American and Caribbean Studies, Viewpoints. Washington, DC: World Bank, January 1997.

Ranis, Gustav, Carlos Federico, and Diaz Alejandro. *En Route to Modern Growth: Latin America in the 1990s: Essays in Honor of Carlos Diaz-Alejandro*. Washington, DC: Inter-American Development Bank, 1995.

Uwadibie, Nwafejoku Okolie. *Decentralization and Economic Development in Nigeria: Agricultural Policies and Implementation*. Lanham, MD: University Press of America, 1999.

Vengroff, Richard and Ogwo Jombo Umeh. "A Comparative Approach to the Assessment of Decentralization Policy in Developing Countries" in Derick W. Brinkerhoff, ed. *Policy Analysis Concepts and Methods: An Institutional and Implementation Focus*. Greenwich, CT: Jai Press, 1997.

GOVERNANCE

Andersson, Å. E., et al. *Government for the Future, Unification, Fragmentation and Regionalism*. Amsterdam: North Holland, 1997.

Clague, Christopher, ed. *Institutions and Economic Development: Growth and Governance in Less-Developed and Post-Socialist Countries*. Baltimore: Johns Hopkins University Press, 1997. 390 pp.

Healey, J. and W. Tordoff. *Votes and Budgets: Comparative Studies in Accountable Governance in the South*. New York: St. Martin's Press, 1995.

Khan, M. A. *Economic Development, Poverty Alleviation and Governance: The Asian Experience*. Avebury: Ashgate Publishing Company, 1996.

Siddiqui, Kamal. *Towards Good Governance in Bangladesh: Fifty Unpleasant Essays*. Dhaka: University Press, 1996.

Taschereau, Suzanne and Jose Edgardo L. Campos, eds. *Governance Innovations: Lessons from Experience; Building Government-Citizen-Business Partnerships*. Kuala Lumpur: Institute on Governance, 1997.

LOCAL DEVELOPMENT AND PLANNING

Blakely, Edward J. *Planning Local Economic Development: Theory and Practice.* London: Sage Publications, 1994.

Brinkerhoff, Derick W. and A. Goldsmith. *Institutional Sustainability in Agriculture and Rural Development: A Global Perspective.* New York: Praeger, 1990.

Burkey, Stan. *People First: A Guide to Self-Reliant Participatory Rural Development.* London: Zed Books, 1993.

Burkhart, Patrick J. and Suzanne Reuss. *Successful Strategic Planning: A Guide for Nonprofit Agencies and Organizations.* London: Sage Publications, 1993.

Gooneratne, W. and M. Mbilinyi, eds. *Reviving Local Self-Reliance: People's Responses to the Economic Crisis in Eastern and Southern Africa.* Nagoya: United Nations Centre for Regional Development, 1992.

Haq, Khadija and Uner Kirdar. *Human Development: The Neglected Dimension.* Islamabad: North South Roundtable, 1986.

Harriss, B. "Regional Growth Linkages from Agriculture," *Journal of Development Studies* 23 (February 1987).

Kirdar, Uner and Leonard Silk, eds. *People: From Impoverishment to Empowerment.* New York: New York University Press, 1995.

Korten, David C. and Rudi Klauss, eds. *People-Centered Development: Contributions toward Theory and Planning Frameworks.* West Hartford, CT: Kumarian Press, 1984.

Lewis, Blane D. "District-Level Economic Linkages in Kenya," *World Development* 20 (June 1992): 881–97.

Mabogunje, A. L. and R. P. Misra, eds. *Regional Development Alternatives: International Perspectives.* Regional Development Series: Volume 2. Singapore: Maruzen Asia for UNCRD, 1981.

Mayfield, James B. *Go to the People: Releasing the Rural Poor through the People's School System.* West Hartford, CT: Kumarian Press, 1985.

Montgomery, John D. *Bureaucrats and People: Grassroots Participation in Third World Development.* Baltimore: Johns Hopkins University Press, 1988.

Parnes, Herbert S. *Peoplepower: Elements of Human Resource Policy.* Beverly Hills, CA: Sage, 1984.

Romeo, Leonardo. "Systems Experimentation in Support of Decentralization Reforms: Reflections on Local Development Funds," *Regional Development Dialogue* (RDD) 20 (Autumn 1999):1–17.

Smoke, Paul. "Understanding Decentralization in Asia: An Overview of Key Issues and Challenges," *Regional Development Dialogue* (RDD) 20 (Autumn 1999): 1–17.

Sundaram, K. V. *Decentralized Multilevel Planning: Principles and Practice (Asian and African Experiences).* New Delhi: Concept, 1997.

Syrett, Stephen. *Local Development: Restructuring, Locality and Economic Initiative in Portugal.* Aldershot: Avebury, 1995. 372 pp.

Index

About the Editors and Contributors

SOPHREMIANO B. ANTIPOLO is Vice President of the University of Southeastern Philippines. He previously served as regional director in Region IX of the National Economic and Development Authority, Government of the Philippines. His publications include *Decentralization: A Global and National Review*; *Environment and Sustainable Development: Policy Issues and Recommendations*; *Systems Dynamic Models for Agriculture Sector in Southern Mindanao, Philippines: Application to Policy and Planning*; *Organization Development Planning and Management: Theory, Application and Reflection*; *Strengthening Rural-Urban Linkages as an Alternative Strategy for Regional Development*; and *Education and Socio-Economic Development in the Philippines: An Intra and Interregional Analysis*.

FAYYAZ BAQIR is National Coordinator, Local Initiative Facility for Urban Environment (LIFE) Programme, United Nations Development Programme, Islamabad, Pakistan.

MICHAEL VON BOGUSLAWSKI is Project Adviser and Team Leader, German Technical Co-operation Agency (GTZ) and is currently assigned to the Bondoc Development Program, Project Management Office, Lucena City, Philippines. He is co-author of a forthcoming publication entitled, *Decentralized Regional Planning with Modern Tools* (with Olaf Haub).

JOSEFA S. EDRALIN is coordinator of the Human Security and Regional Development Project of the United Nations Centre for Regional Development

(UNCRD). She has served as coordinator of the Development Management and Governance Sub-Programme, and the Information Systems Unit of UNCRD. Her edited research publications include *Financing Metropolitan Development: Public-Private Sector Roles* (with Devyani Mani); *Metropolitan Governance and Planning in Transition: Asia-Pacific Cases*; *Local Economic Development: A New Role for Asian Cities*; and *Local Governance and Local Economic Development: Capacity-Building (Case Studies in Asia and Latin America)*.

HUGH EMRYS EVANS is adjunct professor at the School of Policy Planning and Development, University of Southern California. He is also chief technical advisor for the PARUL Programme in Indonesia. He is author of *Guidelines for a Rural-Urban Linkage Approach to Poverty Alleviation* [for UNDP and the Regional Development Planning Board (BAPPENAS), Government of Indonesia]; *The Design of Local Development Fund Programs: Learning from Experience* (for the United Nations Capital Development Fund); and co-author of "Cambodia Area Rehabilitation and Regeneration Project (SEILA/CARERE 2): Report of the Joint Evaluation Mission"; and "Rural-Urban Partnership Programme (RUPP): Report of Interim Evaluation Mission" (for UNDP and the Government of Nepal).

JOAQUIN L. GONZALEZ III is director, Executive Master of Public Administration Program, School of Professional Programs and Undergraduate Studies, Golden Gate University, San Francisco, CA. His several books include *Opting for Partnership: Governance Innovations in Southeast Asia* (with Kathleen Lauder and Brenda Melles); *Philippine Labour Migration: Critical Dimensions of Public Policy*; *Development Sustainability through Community Participation: Mixed Results from the Philippine Health Sector*; *Succeed in Business: Philippines* (with Luis Ma. Calingo); and *Governance Innovations in the Asia-Pacific Region: Trends, Cases, and Issues* (co-edited with Gambhir Bhatta).

KATHLEEN LAUDER is director of the Institute on Governance, in Petaling Jaya, Malaysia. She is co-author of *Opting for Partnership: Governance Innovations in Southeast Asia* (with Joaquin L. Gonzalez III and Brenda Melles).

DEVYANI MANI is senior researcher at UNCRD. She previously was planning consultant in Ahmedabad, India, and associate architect with the Vastu Shilpa Foundation. Her publications include articles, book chapters, and edited research publications on urban infrastructure provision, urban governance, and training of provincial planners.

GETACHEW MEQUANENT is consultant for the Multiculturalism Program, Department of Canadian Heritage, Government of Canada.

WALTER O. OYUGI is professor of government at the University of Nairobi, Kenya. His edited books include *Politics and Administration in East Africa* and *Research and Teaching of Political Science and Public Administration.*

MARCELO REYES BUSCH is Metropolitan Region Secretary, Urban Projects Coordination, Housing and Urbanism Ministry, Santiago, Chile. He has worked with the Corporation for the Development of Santiago, Municipality of Santiago, Chile.

FRANCISCO SABATINI is professor at the Institute for Urban Studies, Catholic University of Chile. He is the co-author of *Participación ciudadana para enfrentar los conflictos ambientales* (with Claudia Sepúlveda and Hernán Blanco); *Conflictos ambientales: entre a globalización y la sociedad civil* (with Claudia Sepúlveda); and *Barrio y participación.* He has published numerous articles and book chapters on local environmental conflicts.

WALTER B. STÖHR is professor emeritus at the University of Economics and Business Administration, Vienna, Austria, where he founded and directed the Institute of Urban and Regional Planning. Previously he was professor of regional planning at McMaster University, Hamilton, Canada, and senior regional planning adviser for the Ford Foundation in Santiago, Chile. He has published books and articles on: regional planning in developing countries; spatial equity and regional development; globalization, international economic restructuring, and regional development; local/regional mobilization strategies and sustainable development; and regional technology policy. His edited books include *Global Challenge and Local Response: Initiatives for Economic Regeneration in Contemporary Europe*; *International Economic Restructuring and the Regional Community* (with H. Muegge); and *Development From Above or Below? The Dialectics of Regional Planning in Developing Countries* (with D. R. Fraser Taylor).

PETRA STREMPLAT-PLATTE is senior planning adviser, German Technical Co-operation Agency (GTZ), Eschborn, Federal Republic of Germany.

D. R. FRASER TAYLOR is professor of international affairs, and geography and environmental studies in the Department of Geography, Carleton University. His edited books include *Policy Issues in Modern Geography*; *Visualization in Modern Cartography* (with Alan MacEachren); *Development From Within: Survival in Rural Africa* (with Fiona Mackenzie); and *Development From Above or Below? The Dialectics of Regional Planning in Developing Countries* (with Walter B. Stöhr). He is author of numerous articles related to cartography.

JAIME VALENZUELA G. is deputy secretary general for Latin America and the Caribbean, International Council for Local Environmental Initiatives (ICLEI). Previously he was director of the PCM Programme, Local Governments Development and Training Center, International Union of Local Authorities (IULA) in Quito, Ecuador. His published papers deal with urban planning and management.

ROBERTSON WORK, JR. is principal technical advisor for decentralized governance, Management Development and Governance Division, UNDP. Previously he coordinated the UNDP LIFE Programme and monitored the UNDP/UNCHS/World Bank Urban Management Programme. He has worked for the Institute of Cultural Affairs International, and has been a consultant to several multilateral agencies, national governments, private corporations, NGOs, and community-based organizations. His recent publications include *Decentralized Governance: A Global Matrix of Experiences; Impact of Participation on Local Governance* (a nine-volume series); and *Participatory Local Governance*.